Limits to Liberalization

A book in the series Cornell Studies in Political Economy

A list of titles in this series is available at www.cornellpress.cornell.edu.

Limits to Liberalization

Local Culture in a Global Marketplace

Patricia M. Goff

Cornell University Press
Ithaca and London

First published 2007 by Cornell University Press

Printed in the United States of America

Library of Congress Cataloging-in-Publication Data

Goff, Patricia M.
    Limits to liberalization : local culture in a global marketplace /
Patricia M. Goff.
        p. cm. — (Cornell studies in political economy)
Includes bibliographical references and index.
ISBN-13: 978-0-8014-4458-6 (cloth : alk. paper)
1. Canada. Treaties, etc. 1992 Oct. 7. 2. General Agreement on
Tariffs and Trade (Organization) 3. Cultural property—Protection
—Canada. 4. Cultural property—Protection—European Union
countries. 5. Cultural industries—Canada. 6. Cultural industries
—European Union countries. 7. Free trade—North America.
8. International trade. 9. Canada—Cultural policy. 10. European
Union countries—Cultural policy. I. Title. II. Series.
HF1746.G64 2007
382'.450705—dc22
2006032681

Cornell University Press strives to use environmentally responsible
suppliers and materials to the fullest extent possible in the publishing of its books. Such materials include vegetable-based, low-VOC
inks and acid-free papers that are recycled, totally chlorine-free, or
partly composed of nonwood fibers. For further information, visit
our website at www.cornellpress.cornell.edu.

Cloth printing   10 9 8 7 6 5 4 3 2 1

Contents

Acknowledgments   vii

Introduction   1

Chapter 1 Protectionism Reconsidered   17

Chapter 2 Canada and NAFTA   36

Chapter 3 GATT, Europe, and Audiovisual Industries   83

Chapter 4 Institutionalizing Cultural Protectionism   125

Chapter 5 Beyond Culture Industries:
            Cultures of Agriculture and Health Care   146

Conclusion   169

References   177

Index   189

Acknowledgments

There may have been a certain inevitability that I would gravitate toward this research topic. The three countries at its center are the three countries that have been most meaningful to me personally. Growing up, I made regular family visits to France. As soon as I was old enough, I found ways to spend extended periods of time there. Most of my life, though (and my citizenship), has been split between the United States and Canada, fueling my own personal case study of the complexity of identity.

In the early 1990s, I was a Canadian living in the United States with an acute case of Francophilia, reading media reports of GATT negotiations over audiovisual industries. I felt the American commentators just didn't "get it" in the same way they hadn't "gotten" the Canadian position on cultural industries during NAFTA negotiations. This didn't necessarily surprise me. However, it did surprise me to discover that there were limited scholarly resources available to illuminate the European and Canadian positions. And so a research program was born.

At Northwestern University, Michael Loriaux agreed that there was a puzzle, encouraged me to solve it, and paved the way for research in Paris. Jim Schwoch brought his vast knowledge of the political economy of media industries as well as his good humor to the project. Bruce Cumings gave encouragement, excellent advice, consistent support, and perhaps the most precious gift at critical moments—he boosted my confidence.

Many of these ideas were developed during a year as a Visiting Scholar at the Center for International Studies at the University of Southern California. Special thanks go to Laurie Brand, Hayward Alker, Ann Tickner, John Odell, Steve Lamy, and Cindy O'Hagan for creating a truly wonderful environment for discussing alternative approaches to international political economy.

Many people helped me find my way around interviews and archives in Paris, Brussels, Ottawa, and Toronto. I am especially grateful to Ezra Suleiman; Leila Vignal from the office of the EU Trade Commissioner; and Ted Kelly at the Canadian Department of Foreign Affairs and International Trade. Special thanks go also to Garry Neil, Peter Grant, Sheila Copps, and all who graciously shared their perspective in answer to my questions.

Numerous friends and colleagues asked probing questions, offered encouragement, and read portions of the book. Audie Klotz did all of this and more, cheerfully and consistently. Each conversation with Bob Wolfe pushed me to think more deeply and innovatively about my ideas. His influence permeates this book. For a variety of reasons, I am grateful to Vicki Birchfield, Aida Hozic, Ailsa Henderson, Bessma Momani, Doug Blum, Karen Engle, Andrew Thompson, Herman Schwartz, Len Seabrooke, Carol Kfouri, Paul Goff, Mary Ann and Neil Goff, and Leo and Agnes Goff. I am especially grateful to Peter Katzenstein and Roger Haydon at Cornell University Press for their guidance and enthusiasm and to two anonymous reviewers who offered invaluable suggestions.

I have an extraordinarily generous and supportive family. This book is dedicated to them, especially the "original six," with love and gratitude.

P.M.G.

Waterloo, Ontario

Limits to Liberalization

Introduction

It is by now commonplace to note the sweeping changes that have accompanied globalization. Financial transactions have increased in volume and speed. Transportation and communication links have made the movement of goods and persons easier and less costly, and the movement of information instantaneous. As a result of consistent efforts to lower barriers to trade, exports account for larger portions of the gross domestic product (GDP) of trading nations. For the most part, we view these changes in a positive light. They are tagged as "advances" and equated with "progress." States opt out of the global economy at their peril, recognizing that the quest for new and lucrative markets has superseded the traditional quest for territory.

But with these advances come threats to collective identity, favored national practices, and domestic social bargains. Economic liberalization can be a particularly potent source; when such threats arise, governments that otherwise embrace economic liberalization may seek to retain or implement domestic policies as a defense. Yet they have difficulty in doing so when the policy measures they favor appear to interfere with international trade. Policies undertaken to fulfill specific domestic sociocultural goals are often evaluated not on their ability to attain these goals, but on their contribution to the advancement of trade liberalization. If they come up lacking on the latter score, they are characterized as protectionism and targeted for dismantlement. The very policies that governments rely on to provide safeguards against liberalization are themselves viewed as barriers to greater liberalization. As a result, governments risk losing domestic policy instruments on which they rely to offset the perceived costs of liberalization.

This book focuses on one specific area where this dynamic is prominent—government efforts to implement cultural policies in the face of condemnation by trading partners who view these measures as discriminatory trade practices. To illuminate this dynamic, I focus on the treatment of culture industries in the two largest trade agreements struck in the last fifty years: the North American Free Trade Agreement (NAFTA) and the Uruguay Round of the General Agreement on Tariffs and Trade (GATT). The NAFTA case has its origins in the Canada–U.S. Free Trade Agreement (CUSFTA).[1] During CUSFTA talks, the Canadian government declared that culture industries—film, television, and radio broadcasting; periodical and book publishing; video and sound recording—were not on the negotiating table. Canadian negotiators jeopardized the entire agreement by refusing to sign CUSFTA unless this sector was excluded from the treaty.

Canada has an extensive network of institutions and government policies pertaining to culture industries. For example, the Canadian Radio-Television and Telecommunications Commission (CRTC) stipulates that the Canadian broadcasting system must be owned and controlled by Canadians and establishes minimum Canadian content requirements for Canadian radio and television stations. In insisting on exclusion of culture industries from CUSFTA, the Canadian government sought to safeguard its right to continue these and related cultural policies. Canada succeeded in negotiating a special carve-out for culture industries and, despite U.S. efforts to reopen the issue during NAFTA negotiations four years later, culture industries retained the negotiated exemption in the North American Free Trade Agreement.[2]

In the closing days of the Uruguay Round of GATT talks,[3] the United States and the European Union (EU), led by France, engaged in a bitter exchange over the regulation of trade in audiovisual industries. During negotiations, "audiovisual" was often interpreted to mean the film and television industries. But the term is ambiguous enough to encompass digital technologies and new media.[4] The EU stalled the Uruguay Round in late 1993 by insisting on the continuation

1. Talks between Canada and the United States took place from May 1986 to December 1987. The Canada–U.S. Free Trade Agreement officially took effect on January 1, 1989.

2. Negotiations between Canada, the United States, and Mexico began in June 1991. NAFTA officially went into effect on January 1, 1994.

3. The Uruguay Round of GATT negotiations spanned the seven-year period from 1986 to 1993, officially taking effect January 1, 1995.

4. The EU was able to confine its demand to audiovisual industries, mostly for linguistic reasons. Dubbing and subtitling are common practices in the audiovisual industries, making it relatively simple for foreign filmed entertainment products to enter the European market. Canada finds itself

of subsidies to the European film and television industries and quotas restricting the percentage of non-European content on European television. The French, for example, use a percentage of box office proceeds to subsidize their film industry. In addition, a 1989 European Community directive, known as Television without Frontiers, mandates that no less than 50 percent of television programming across member states be European in origin. In the final days of negotiations, the EU made the right to continue these and related practices a condition of accepting the overall GATT agreement, echoing the Canadian position in CUSFTA.[5] With a deadline looming, the Europeans and the Americans "agreed to disagree" and audiovisual industries were left out of the final treaty. They would surface again within the framework of the General Agreement on Trade in Services (GATS), but the immediate outcome of the Uruguay Round provided at least temporary support for the European position.

During these trade negotiations, Canada and the European Union faced strong opposition from the United States. American negotiators claimed that excluding culture industries from the agreements would have the effect of limiting U.S. access to the Canadian and European markets for filmed entertainment, publishing, and recording industries. In addition, the U.S. negotiators objected to actions that they claimed would contravene prevailing norms favoring the free flow of information and open trade. Nevertheless, despite the leverage that the American superpower brings to the bargaining table, its wishes did not prevail, and culture industries received special treatment in the regulations of the GATT and NAFTA agreements.

Why did the Canadians and Europeans want to shield culture industries from the provisions of the trading regime? Culture industries are not infant industries, nor are they disproportionately large providers of jobs or contributors to the balance of payments. They are not national champions in the commercial sense. They are not particularly crucial to GDP, or at least no more crucial than other sectors that have been liberalized. In other words, the key impulses that trade scholars typically identify as motivating protectionism are not in play in the cultural sector. Understanding the Canadian and European stance with regard to culture industries in the NAFTA and GATT talks requires us to acknowledge that these industries are bound up with sociocultural concerns

---

in a different position, prompting it to call for exclusion of the full range of culture industries. Geographic proximity makes it relatively easy for Canadians to capture American television signals and the common language shared by the majority of Americans and Canadians erects no natural barrier.

5. Although France was the most vocal European Union member protesting inclusion of audiovisual industries in the GATT, EU member states negotiate as a bloc. Therefore, what is often perceived in the American media to be a French stance on this issue was actually European Union policy.

about identity formation and the ongoing challenge of maintaining and pro-moting cultural diversity.

There is a pervasive sense in many countries that culture industries contribute more than just commercial gain. They do indeed produce consumption goods and lucrative tradable commodities, but they are also carriers of meaning whose value surpasses their ability to generate profit and provide entertainment. As such, cultural products have both commercial *and* sociocultural value. Their very existence is an emblem of a thriving cultural community. In addition, they can play a central role in the creation, transmission, and evaluation of the customs and beliefs that underpin collective identity. They are at once a repository of col-lective memories and a forum for dissident voices. They contribute to what makes a country distinctive and have the capacity to buttress a set of sociocultural—even ethical—commitments to a specific vision of society. But government regulation is needed in places like Canada and the EU to ensure that local industries are not merely conduits for American content. Liberalizing culture industries threatens to disturb their ability to play a sociocultural role by reconceptualizing govern-ment measures as trade impediments to be eliminated.

Yet policies designed to safeguard domestic culture industries differ in signifi-cant ways from more traditional examples of protectionism. They do not signal a return to autarchic or inward-looking trade policies. In fact, they come amidst unprecedented efforts to lower barriers to trade, championed by countries that rely on trade for their own economic well-being. Indeed, cultural policies are not new. In places like Canada and Europe, such approaches have been in place for decades. What is new is the extension of the trading regime to sectors previ-ously outside its purview. The seeming incompatibility of some cultural policies with trading regime principles does not imply the return of protectionism in a new guise. Rather, it demonstrates the urgent need for an expansion of the con-versation around trade and protectionism, which currently relies on a narrow vocabulary that forecloses discussion of the sociocultural contribution of certain goods and services, as well as the social and cultural motivations that inform trade policymaking when sectors previously reserved for domestic policy find their way onto the agenda of the trading regime.

Consonant with this expansion of the discourse must be an effort to recon-cile trade theories that originated many decades ago with new developments, including a global economy, trade in services, and a trading regime that now focuses more on harmonizing national regulatory frameworks than lowering tar-iffs. While the logic of free trade may not be outdated, the notion that policies that promote domestic industries are always an antiliberal defense against rival competitors certainly is. This view is founded on outmoded assumptions about what constitutes and motivates protection. As a result, it misses the much more complex interplay of rival objectives played out in trade policy. The fact that this is not yet widely acknowledged has the effect of constraining governments that seek to pursue sociocultural goals via specific commercial sectors.

Popular discourse in the United States during GATT and NAFTA negotiations ignored the fact that governments are willing to incur economic losses to pursue sociocultural goals. American commentators characterized Canada and the European Union as using cultural resistance to pursue an agenda of veiled economic protectionism. Invoking the notion of protectionism in this context has at least two significant consequences. First, it prompts us to evaluate measures designed to support local cultural producers not as cultural policy, but as trade policy. Second, it discourages an inquiry into *why* government officials are unwilling to expose the cultural sector to the forces of liberalization and open trade. Instead, the very label "protectionist" carries with it a set of explanations for why governments pursue such policies. These explanations, grounded in liberal economic thinking, give short shrift to many of the sociocultural considerations that motivated the European and Canadian governments and, as a result, provide an unsatisfactory account of Canada's and the EU's negotiating stance. By taking these governments' sociocultural concerns seriously, this book explains why the European Union and Canada were willing to make exclusion of culture industries a condition of successful completion of these trade negotiations.

The Cultural Costs of Liberalization

Many see liberalization of the cultural sector to be fraught with trade-offs. What is the nature of these trade-offs? In what ways do government officials and others expect liberalization to jeopardize their respective identities and cultures? At least three things have come to be associated with globalization's effects on culture that the Canadian and EU governments *do not mean* when they make an argument from culture and identity to shield their culture industries from the trading regime. First, they are not trying to exclude foreign cultural products from their markets. Second, they are not trying to protect some defined, bounded, integrated, or settled national identity. Third, they are not working under the assumption that exposure to foreign, mostly American, cultural products will automatically homogenize their societies in an uncomplicated cause-and-effect sequence.

What, then, *do* they mean? They are interested in promoting social cohesion, a sense of belonging, and cultural particularity, which are, in turn, linked to broader political efforts to consolidate relatively loose federations and to negotiate regional, cultural, linguistic, and economic heterogeneity. In Canada, regional disparities, increasingly multiethnic and unassimilated immigrant populations, combined with aboriginal peoples seeking a right to self-determination, threaten Canadian unity. Many in Canadian government and cultural circles suggest that U.S. domination of Canadian culture industries could exacerbate this problem by obstructing the process of domestic, internal communication. Canadian government efforts to protect domestic cultural producers continue a long-standing tradition of employing culture industries in the nation-building process in an effort to strengthen "Canada" as a political and cultural entity.

Similarly, the European Union encourages the development of shared meanings among citizens of the now twenty-five member states. Strengthening the "European Union" as a political and cultural entity can move European integration forward toward full political union. Many EU leaders view an enhanced sense of belonging to Europe (as opposed to—or in addition to—a sense of belonging to a specific member state) as a necessary precursor to expanding the authority and legitimacy of European Union institutions. This effort to make room for the process of identity formation is coupled with a desire to have local culture industries and cultural producers as a sign of a thriving cultural community and to secure the democratic right of members of a community to participate in the national (and global) conversation via culture industries.

Promoting social cohesion, a sense of cultural belonging, and collective particularity are not new preoccupations for governments. However, in the past, governments adopted approaches that would contravene contemporary democratic and multicultural impulses. For example, in the nineteenth century, the French army became "the school of the fatherland," teaching, among other things, "what it meant to be a French citizen" (Weber 1976, 298). The French school system also played an important socializing role. Teaching French, while prohibiting the use of regional languages, was seen as "a labor of patriotic character" (Weber 1976, 311). The state set national curriculum standards in order to cultivate a love of France, springing from the assumption that "education has a directly political intention, that of making a disparate mass of individuals into one nation . . . the persistent desire to create citizens . . . aware of the community in which they are destined to lead their lives" (Rosanvallon 1990, 108, my translation). The French state also worked to produce a nation of Frenchmen by dividing French territory into centrally administered departments, imposing a national system of weights and measures, and establishing national holidays.

Such strategies of identity formation are neither desirable nor possible in contemporary Canada or Europe. The EU faces great resistance to designating a European language, especially since this would, in all probability, be English.

In addition, the education ministers of the member states have had little success in harmonizing curriculum so as to teach "European history" or "European literature" (Theiler 2005). Canada faces similar obstacles. The country is officially bilingual and any effort to impose English on the population would surely cause Québec to secede. In fact, the federal and provincial governments have actually moved in the opposite direction, embracing both official languages and making multiculturalism the law of the land.

So we are left with a set of cultural goals and limited means for achieving them. The Canadian and EU position in the trade negotiations sprang, in part, from the assumption that culture industries can play a central role in the construction of political community by providing a forum in which a repertoire of signs, traditions, values, myths, and intersubjective understandings that make up collective identity can be transmitted and debated. This is not the only realm where such efforts are being made. For example, the European Union facilitates student exchanges between member states through its Erasmus program. Nonetheless, because of citizens' broad exposure to television, film, and music, culture industries are among the more pervasive and effective ways to (re)produce, perpetuate, and/or destabilize certain notions that may influence awareness of cultural particularity, citizenship formation, and institutional legitimacy.

Envisioning such a role for culture industries rests on recognition of the fact that "cultures do not stand still for their portraits" (Neumann 2002, 628). Critics of the Canadian and European stance have suggested that these governments aim to preserve some established notion of what it means to be Canadian or European. This is misleading. In fact, these governments endeavor to retain some autonomy in the area of cultural policy precisely because the content of these identities is indeterminate and contested, in addition to the fact that they are dynamic and always evolving in response to circumstances. Without a space for indigenous public discourse, both Canada and the European Union lose a potent means of participating in the *ongoing* work of promoting collective identity formation and social cohesiveness.

It is important to note that this is not a top-down inculcation of belief. In authoritarian societies, cultural products can be infused with certain values by privileging certain stories or themes. But democratic governments can only influence the content of texts in indirect ways. Indeed, it is not at all apparent that these governments have a clear sense of which symbols, meanings, and values they would emphasize even if they could determine content. Rather, the Canadian and European cultural policy frameworks represent an effort *to facilitate a process*. Sewell (1999) argues that culture is a dialectic of two components. The first component is culture as a system of symbols and meanings. The second is culture as practice. "The system has no existence apart from the succession of practices that instantiate, reproduce, or—most interestingly—transform it" (Sewell 1999, 47). The cultural policy measures that the Canadian and European governments seek to shelter from trade principles are more concerned with making room for the *practices* that instantiate, reproduce, or transform their respective identities than with the symbols and meanings that underpin them. As I explain in subsequent chapters, these governments then rely on their citizens to provide distinctive content.

This approach captures a desire to promote local culture industries as an emblem of a vibrant cultural community and as a source of a variety of cultural forms. It also springs from the insight that culture industries provide shared referents and sources. They are "forms of imagining," (Anderson 1991, 24) creating "unified fields of exchange and communication" (Anderson 1991, 44) that ensure that "substantial groups of people [are] in a position to think of themselves as living lives *parallel* to those of other substantial groups of people" (Anderson 1991, 188). Culture industries play an important role in the creation of community by facilitating "the process of continuous and dense communication that sustains shared assumptions" (Bateson 1990, 150; see also Maxwell 1996). Canadian and European officials perceive culture industries to be a means by which collective consciousness can be achieved and an "imagined community" created. The cultural sector is one key mechanism through which regional groups come to know each other and to debate socioeconomic and political issues. While consensus may not be forthcoming, shared meanings and understandings are likely to emerge from such a process of internal communication. Culture industries can, therefore, play a central role in (re)producing and perpetuating the *idea* of Canada and the *idea* of Europe.

Indeed, Sewell (1999, 56) reminds us that, even though states and communications media are cultural actors with considerable resources, the "typical cultural strategy of dominant actors and institutions is not so much to establish uniformity as it is to organize difference. . . . The kind of coherence produced by this process of organizing difference may be far from the tight cultural integration depicted in classic ethnographies." Instead, these actors control access; they include and exclude; they define who has priority and who does not. They do this by making resources available to local producers and by creating a space for local voices. This may or may not translate into a *certain version* of an identity. Nonetheless, officials rely on vibrant local voices to contribute to domestic identity formation in ways foreign voices simply cannot.

None of this can happen unless governments can create a zone of domestic cultural activity through regulatory policy. Yet regulatory approaches are not identical across nations. Every country has a unique historical experience that shapes the parameters of political debate and creates policy legacies and patterns. In Dobbin's (1994) formulation, "problems perceived and solutions conceived" vary across national contexts. Policymakers do not start with a clean slate; instead, they function within a normative environment in which certain approaches and goals are favored. This contention does not presume consensus among policymakers. Nor does it deny any explicit intentionality, conscious choice, or protection of interests on the part of policymakers. Nevertheless, not all policies are entertained as viable options. Certainly, some policies are ruled out because they are costly or inefficient. But some are ruled out because they contradict assumptions about "how we do things," where "we" can be a national community. (Indeed, some policies are ruled in *despite their cost* precisely because they reflect favored approaches). Norms are periodically contravened. They evolve in response to historical events, and the prevailing normative environment is one of many factors affecting policy outcomes. Still, we can identify certain normative assumptions that guide policymakers.

In his discussion of the French developmental state, Loriaux (1999) argues that state elites "pursu[e] moral goods whose definition is informed by a certain mythological construction of how the world works and what we should accomplish in it" (1999, 253). This argument implies, among other things, that comparison of policy choices across two or more countries requires much more than identification of economic interests. Even policymakers embracing the same economic assumptions may arrive at very different policy choices because these assumptions are filtered through a different set of "myths, rules, and norms that inform human action" (Loriaux 1999, 252).

Loriaux's work on policymakers who have been socialized into a certain normative framework, in which a set of historically constructed myths "generate and justify routines (secular 'rituals') that embed themselves in discursive habits and institutional procedures" (1999, 254), suggests that identity limits and structures the range of policy choices. I do not take this to mean that there is an inherently French way of doing things. Instead, such an analysis suggests that there is a range of policies and approaches that has been favored in France because of such things as its historical development, resource endowments, and institutional structures. As a result, a certain type of state involvement, for example, has come to be associated with France. This is not an inevitable or unchanging feature of French political life. But there are patterns across time and resistance to efforts to alter them.

Therefore, when Canadian or European officials object to the inclusion of culture industries in the major trade agreements because such a step compromises identity, in part they are objecting to the reconceptualization of their unique, historical approaches to cultural policymaking as trade impediments. This reconceptualization would amount to a fairly radical change in the nature and extent of the role the state could play in cultural life, which would, among other things, pose a threat to the public broadcasting system in their respective countries, for example, or to the cultivation of art house cinema, especially valued in France. If culture industries were to be incorporated into the NAFTA and GATT regimes, the range of favored cultural policies could be called into question, and not due to a natural, internal progression in policy. Resistance to these sorts of abrupt and externally imposed changes affirms that there are parameters within which economic interests are pursued within a given context. As Dobbin (1994, 11) puts it, "the idea that national economies follow different cultural patterns is at odds with the modern worldview, in which economics, like physics, is governed by a single set of laws under one general theory." Nonetheless, there is "something cultural guiding policy-making" (Dobbin 1994, 1).

That there is something cultural guiding policymaking suggests that the arguments of Canadian and European governments function on two levels. The first taps into what Sewell (1999, 41) calls the "traditional spheres of meaning production"—the culture industries—and the contribution a vibrant domestic cultural sector can make to the promotion of social cohesiveness and collective particularity. The second taps into domestic preferences for certain policy approaches and practices—the "repertoire of actions that exist for a particular type of subject in a particular type of context" (Neumann 2002, 633). This aspect gives the cultural argument resonance beyond culture industries, as I explain in chapter 5. When former Canadian Prime Minister Jean Chrétien states that a privatized health care system will mean "there is no more Canada" (Adams and Laghi 2000), and therefore it is a cultural imperative to shield that sector from liberalization, he is appealing to culture and identity as a set of social practices and as a set of policy practices. With regard to culture industries, there is a demand for autonomy to ensure that the products of that sector can reflect contemporary Canadian concerns, values, symbols, and understandings, thus contributing to identity formation. At the same time, though, with regard not only to culture industries, but to a range of sectors, there is a demand for autonomy to implement policies that themselves have meaning in a given cultural context.

Offsetting the Cultural Costs of Liberalization

Canadian and EU demands for room to offset the *cultural* costs of liberalization are new and reflect contemporary goals and circumstances. Nonetheless, in every era since free trade became accepted policy, people have expressed skepticism about the ability of the market to fulfill noneconomic objectives, and they have worried about the socioeconomic dislocations that seem inevitably to accompany market activity. There is, therefore, a continuity that extends from the early days of market openness forward to the current day, which places the Canadian and European governments in a long-standing debate about the costs societies are willing to incur in return for the commercial benefits of laissez-faire economics. Participants in this debate do not all agree on the nature of these costs, nor do they agree on the remedies (though most see a role for the state). This disagreement springs from the fact that commentators typically respond to specific circumstances in their own historical contexts (Pickel 2005).

Criticism of the liberal ideology that provides the rationale for free trade has peaked twice—once in response to nineteenth-century classical liberalism and later in response to late-twentieth-century neoliberalism (Helleiner 2003). Canadian and EU concerns about liberalization of the cultural sector belong to the later phase. Helleiner (2003) argues that, in both instances, criticism was organized around three schools of thought—Marxism, Listian economic nationalism, and embedded liberalism. These three categories remain useful in understanding resistance to liberalization of the cultural sector.

Both historical periods feature critics who reject the potential of market openness completely. In the earlier period, Marx and his followers railed against the dehumanization of the worker. Ruskin followed suit, though his was not an ideological position, but a religious one. He saw moral decay in the embrace of "economic man." He was also one of the first to express concern for the natural environment. In addition, the art critic in him worried that the ugliness he saw in industrializing England was ill-suited to the production of great art (Ruskin 1901; Ruskin 1967). As such, Marx and Ruskin are intellectual precursors to the contemporary debate over the threat that liberalization poses to culture industries. However, the revolutionary remedies they proposed to counteract the dislocations of the market align them less with the Canadian and European governments and more with contemporary, radical antiglobalization activists.

The Canadian and European governments do not question the general potential of market openness to produce prosperity. However, they maintain that the market cannot deliver the sociocultural outcomes associated with culture industries in the face of U.S. domination of this sector. As I explain in subsequent chapters, the Canadians and Europeans insist that they cannot simultaneously liberalize the cultural sector and mobilize this sector in the pursuit of cultural sovereignty, cultural particularity, and identity formation. As such, their position exhibits strains of both Listian economic nationalism and embedded liberalism. Of course, the content of their arguments and the strategies they endorse to counteract the costs of openness do not mirror these schools identically. Instead, the Canadian and EU stance on culture industries confirms that the three categories of criticism remain meaningful for understanding contemporary concerns about neoliberalism; however, each school is itself evolving in response to changing realities (Helleiner 2003).

Canadian and EU officials seek to promote a domestic industry not strictly for economic reasons, but also for sociocultural ones. Culture industry policymaking is motivated not by universal concerns over economic efficiency, but by national concerns over cultural identity and collective particularity. These concerns are, in some ways, compatible with the insights of Listian economic nationalism. Friedrich List supported free trade in principle, though he believed that it was generally beneficial under certain circumstances that did not exist for Germany in the nineteenth century. Only an industrialized Germany could benefit from free trade with an industrialized Great Britain. As a result, he supported targeted tariffs and regulations to promote German industrialization, while at the same time opposing protectionism in other sectors, like agriculture. List's overall motivation was German prosperity and security (List 1966). Indeed, he criticized liberals like Adam Smith for failing to recognize the principle of nationality. In List's account, Smith "does not make the economy of the separate nation, but the economy of society generally, i.e. of the whole human race, the object of its investigations" (List 1966, 181). Such a "cosmopolitical" approach ignores the fact that

> Between each individual and entire humanity, however, stands THE NATION, with its special language and literature, with its particular origin and history, with its special manners and customs, laws and institutions, with the claims of all these for existence, independence, perfection, and continuance for the future, and with its separate territory; a society which, united by a thousand ties of mind and of interests, combines itself into one independent whole, which recognizes the law of right for and within itself, and in its united character is still opposed to other societies of a similar kind in their national liberty, and consequently can only under the existing conditions of the world maintain self-existence and independence by its own power and resources. (List 1966, 174, emphasis in original)

List sought to strengthen German manufacturing with an eye to enhancing German power, while the Canadians and Europeans seek to strengthen their respective cultural sectors so as to promote cultural distinctiveness. Necessarily, this important difference suggests that Listian economic nationalism can only offer limited insights into culture industry policymaking. Nonetheless, List anticipates the position staked out by the Canadian and EU governments with regard to culture industries by reminding us that "a nation is a sovereign political body. Its destiny is to safeguard and to maintain its independence by its own efforts. Its duty is to preserve and to develop its prosperity, culture, nationality, language, and freedom—in short, its entire social and political position in the world" (List 1983, 31).

While Canadian and EU opposition to culture industry liberalization exhibits some aspects of Listian economic nationalism, it is most clearly aligned with the third school of thought that Helleiner (2003) identifies, embedded liberalism, based on the work of Karl Polanyi. Polanyi's analysis was universalist in tone, focusing less on national political issues, and more on society-centered concerns and broader social issues. He too saw the benefits of free trade, but he argued that the "stupendous industrial achievements of market economy had been bought at the price of great harm to the substance of society" (2001, 195). In Polanyi's account, the market should not operate independent of society. The economy should be "embedded" in society, or made subordinate to its collective purposes. This embeddedness implies, among other things, creating a buffer against the social dislocations the market causes. If the state shirks this responsibility, society will react. In this formulation, protectionism is not an ideological or an interest-group-driven action. Nor is it to be condemned. It is a natural human response to social disruption (Polanyi 2001, 151). Polanyi conceptualized this dynamic as the "double movement," which both prescribes and predicts social protection alongside economic liberalism.

Polanyi anticipated the body of literature that contends that liberalization does not necessarily imply a diminished role for the state, but rather an expanded or revised one (Rodrik 1997; Vogel 1996). He also provided the conceptual basis for the institutional arrangements that the United States and Great Britain created after World War II, dubbed the "embedded liberalism compromise" (Ruggie 1982). Ruggie (2002, 1) describes this compromise as "a grand social bargain whereby all sectors of society agreed to open markets, which in some cases had become heavily administered if not autarchic in the 1930s, but *also* to share the social adjustment costs that open markets inevitably produce." According to this arrangement, liberal openness and domestic interventionism were not incompatible.

The embedded liberalism compromise struck in the 1940s rested on international monetary and trade regimes that made allowances for a domestic network of social safety net policies. These included policies to protect against dislocations in employment and to stabilize domestic economies. At the same time that governments abolished exchange controls, they also established the International Monetary Fund to provide short-term assistance in the case of balance-of-payment shortfalls. At the same time that governments lowered tariffs and institutionalized nondiscriminatory trade rules, they also allowed the formation of regional economic areas and established escape clauses to protect domestic producers from injury in certain circumstances. This particular constellation of policy provisions was very much a reflection of the time in which it was adopted. The architects of the Bretton Woods institutions and the embedded liberalism compromise were informed by fresh memories of the economic dislocations of the interwar period and its aftermath and sought to ensure that those experiences would not be repeated. As Ruggie (1991, 203) puts it, by 1944, the "historical first principle" guiding decision makers in the advanced industrialized countries was "no liberalization without safeguards."

In recent years, the debate over embedded liberalism has focused on whether the compromise is still intact (Hart and Prakash 1997; Kirshner 1999). This debate presumes that a contemporary compromise will be largely identical to the one struck just after World War II. However, as Wolfe and Mendelsohn (2004, 262) argue, "embedded liberalism is not a fixed bargain about levels of social spending or tariff bindings but a dynamic commitment to allowing countries to be different within a multilateral framework." By this definition, Canadian and European efforts to shelter culture industries from liberalization are a contemporary manifestation of ongoing citizen demands for protection from the dislocations that accompany economic liberalization. They are a contemporary manifestation of embedded liberalism. This time, the dislocation is *cultural*, not social. But the policy position springs from a similar logic.

It should not be surprising that a contemporary embedded liberalism compromise would not be identical to that forged after World War II. Certainly, many of the concerns that were prominent in the 1940s remain central, especially those related to social welfare provisions. Yet a new context, characterized by globalized production and an expanding trade regime, is spawning new concerns. Resistance to liberalization of the cultural sector is emblematic of these new concerns wherein "anxieties about globalization appear to reflect individuals' fears not only about potential economic losses, *but also losses measured in identity and accountability*" (Ruggie 2002, 3, emphasis mine). "*The integrity of cultures* and sovereignty of states increasingly are seen to be at stake" (Ruggie 2002, 2, emphasis mine). Similarly, in their analysis of Canadian public opinion, Mendelsohn and Wolfe (2001) show that respondents' attitudes toward globalization and trade reflect concerns about their identities as citizens, as well as their core social values, as much or even more so than they reflect economic interests.

Ignoring such concerns can have practical implications, including the possibility of public backlash from those who feel their identity or security is threatened by globalization (Rodrik 1997; Ruggie 2002; Wolfe 1998). The Battle in Seattle, the antiglobalization movement, and similar occurrences have made this clear. Insomuch as we have started to recognize that the latest round of liberalization may come at some cost, we have focused on areas where human life and well-being are threatened—human rights, labor standards, and the environment. For example, Ruggie notes that there is

> a growing imbalance in global rule making. Those rules that favor global market expansion have become more robust and enforceable in the last decade or two—intellectual property rights, for example, or dispute resolution in the World Trade Organization. But rules intended to promote equally valid social objectives, be they labor standards, human rights, environmental quality or poverty reduction, lag behind and in some instances have actually become weaker. (Ruggie 2002, 2)

It is not surprising that analysts have emphasized the tension between liberalization and social protection in these areas. What is surprising, however, is that few people have recognized that efforts by the Canadian, European Union, and other governments to continue their cultural policies while simultaneously promoting a liberal trading order *also* represent components of an evolving and reconfigured compromise of embedded liberalism and not the return of protectionism in a new guise. Indeed, any current debate about how to cushion societies from the contemporary costs of liberalization is incomplete if it ignores cultural concerns.

These cultural concerns are not limited to culture industries. Furthermore, the Canadian and European governments belong to a large constituency of individuals and groups who resist incurring the costs of liberalization across a variety of realms. In fact, Canadian and European resistance to culture industry liberalization is emblematic of a much larger discomfort with the social and cultural costs of economic openness. In the past, national governments have been able to implement measures that ensure that certain sectors can continue to perform both their commercial and sociocultural functions. Yet in the evolving context of the trading regime, such policy measures are often understood as impediments to trade rather than as coequal national policy practices intended to ensure the achievement of social and cultural objectives. As such, they are targeted for dismantlement. However, any dismantlement should be preceded by vigorous public debate about how to ensure that domestic sociocultural goals and practices are not undermined by the pursuit of economic openness. Therefore, through a sustained analysis of recent trade negotiations involving culture industries, which clearly exemplify the tension between the trading regime as it is currently constituted and the achievement of valued, domestic sociocultural goals, this book demonstrates the need to reevaluate prevailing assumptions about protectionism and reignite the debate over embedded liberalism as it might be constituted in the current global economic environment.

The heightened attention that policymakers are giving to identity indicates that a new class of trade policy debates has emerged. There is no doubt that there are economic stakes in trade talks generally, and in the disagreements over culture industries specifically. But in this book I demonstrate that cultural considerations can sometimes override economic ones in determining the European and Canadian positions with regard to the cultural sector. The effort to shield culture industries demonstrates that trade negotiations are yet another contemporary forum in which identity issues are being contested, and in which cultural strategies, instruments, and objectives are increasingly central.

This book begins as an explanation of why culture industries were excluded from NAFTA and GATT and develops into an examination of the challenges of devising trade rules for commodities that have embedded in them both commercial and sociocultural value. As the reach of the trading regime expands to include a range of goods and services not previously under its purview, we see efforts to limit liberalization in some sectors. However, these limiting efforts do not spring from traditional concerns or conform to traditional expectations. Rather, the growing trend to resist liberalization of specific sectors in the name of sociocultural concerns represents an effort to confront newly emerging costs of liberalization, which necessitate a reassessment of the motives and goals of protectionism generally, and of appropriate policy responses more specifically. This book seeks to justify and initiate just such a reassessment.

In chapter 1, I explore in greater depth prevailing arguments about free trade and protectionism and expose their inapplicability to culture industries. In chapters 2 and 3, I provide case-study discussions of the Canadian perspective on culture industries in North American Free Trade and the European perspective on audiovisual industries in the Uruguay Round of the General Agreement on Tariffs and Trade. In chapter 4, I analyze the alternative avenues governments are exploring to promote national cultural particularity and global cultural diversity. In chapter 5, I take the conclusions drawn from the culture industry cases and apply them to other sectors, namely health provision services and genetically modified organisms. I reexamine the various strands of my argument and analysis in the Conclusion.

Chapter 1

Protectionism Reconsidered

Consecutive U.S. governments have worked to convince their counterparts in Canada, France, and more recently, South Korea, Malaysia, Australia, Eastern Europe, and elsewhere, that government support measures to local culture industries leave U.S. cultural producers at an unfair disadvantage. Until the 1980s, U.S. officials protested such cultural policy measures on an ad hoc basis. However, developments in the latter part of the twentieth century shifted these debates into the realm of multilateral trade negotiations.

What began as an "irritant" in Canada–U.S. bilateral relations moved onto the international trade agenda when the Canadian government stalled Canada–U.S. Free Trade (CUSFTA) talks with demands that culture industries be excluded from the trade agreement. Years later, Canada maintained its position in NAFTA, negotiating a limited exemption for culture industries. The European Union later invoked the CUSFTA/NAFTA precedent in the Uruguay Round GATT talks and, once again, the United States found itself facing a negotiating partner for whom support measures to culture industries represented a potential deal-breaker. While NAFTA gave culture industries limited protection and the GATT outcome acknowledged European demands by leaving the audiovisual sector out of the final treaty, the debate did not end. Rather, the General Agreement on Trade in Services (GATS) opened a new chapter in the debate about culture industries by enshrining a multilateral commitment to the liberalization of services, including audiovisual services. Though few countries have listed their audiovisual industries as open for liberalization, negotiations at the GATS are ongoing.

Therefore, the importance of culture industries in CUSFTA/NAFTA and Uruguay Round GATT talks, as well as the expanding reach of the trading regime to services, has given them a new salience at the international level.

The fact that the debates over culture industries emerged most recently and vociferously during multilateral trade negotiations served to define them, first and foremost, as a trade issue, highlighting the commercial value of the sector and prompting evaluation of government cultural policies against trade regime rules about market access and nondiscriminatory trade practices. Further, it set the stage for the ongoing debate to unfold as a question of free trade versus protectionism and as yet another battle between those who oppose measures to promote domestic industries—free traders—and those who support such measures—protectionists.

The culture industry debates, however, resist such easy characterization since noncommercial, sociocultural concerns—a desire to promote and preserve cultural diversity and collective identity—are so central to the sector. While a large body of theory exists to explain why governments seek protection for certain sectors, this literature offers an unsatisfactory explanation of culture industry trade policy because it fails to give adequate attention to the sociocultural motivators of cultural policy.

As a result, the concepts and assumptions that usually guide discussions of the relative merits of free trade and protection have limited applicability in the case of culture industries. The cultural sector does produce lucrative commercial products and cultural policies do often favor domestic producers. Nonetheless, the value of cultural products is not solely commercial, and cultural policies that can appear discriminatory serve unique noncommercial, sociocultural goals that generally get short shrift in most discussions of protectionism and in charged statements by actors who claim to be harmed by their trading partners' cultural policies. In addition to their commercial value, films, television programs, music and books transmit images and perspectives marked by specific worldviews. They are a powerful medium through which opinions are formed and identities defined. They provide the most visible prism through which national values and customs are refracted. They are potentially both imbued with and constitutive of the common meanings that undergird the societies of which they are a product. Therefore, government efforts to protect these industries go beyond economic concerns to a desire to uphold the distinctiveness of their respective cultures and to maintain control of what is perceived to be an instrument of power in the (re)production of political community.

Such a policy does not deny the economic value of these industries. They must be economically viable to fulfill their cultural role and making a cultural contribution does not preclude a commercial return. Nonetheless, the rationale for cultural policies—and for the exclusion of culture industries from trade agreements—is driven by concern that liberalizing the cultural sector will lead to a cultural loss. On a global level, diversity will be diminished if certain national voices can no longer be heard. On a national and regional level, states will forfeit their cultural sovereignty and opportunities for locals to influence collective particularity will be reduced if one of the key sites of identity formation is dominated by foreign voices.

Examining culture industry policy through the lens of trade and protectionism has two problematic consequences. First, it invokes a set of erroneous assumptions and explanations regarding why cultural policies are undertaken. These assumptions and explanations fail to capture the fact that support measures to filmmakers and tariffs on steel are qualitatively different policies. Second, twentieth-century history (especially the Depression era experience and Smoot Hawley) and theory (especially the rise of neoliberalism) have left us with the belief that protectionism is "an intellectual pariah" (Tanzi and Coelho 1993, 212). As a result, branding cultural policies as protectionism automatically condemns them as harmful and undesirable, foreclosing a discussion of the distinctive issues that trade in cultural products should bring to the fore.

The debate over culture industry trade—especially as it evolved during NAFTA and GATT negotiations—signals a new category of challenges to the project of trade liberalization. These challenges have surfaced first and most obviously in the cultural sector, but they will not be limited to it, necessitating a widening of the conversation over protectionism. The effort to check liberalization of the culture industries is qualitatively different from conventional protectionism because it concerns rival social goals or rival understandings of the general welfare. Traditional discussions of protectionism assume that we are weighing the economic welfare of a specific sector or industry against the aggregate economic welfare. As Krauss (1978, 6) puts it, "the conflict between the economic interests of specific groups within the community and the economic interests of the community as a whole is the essence of the free trade versus protectionism controversy. Free traders argue from the standpoint of the overall economy; protectionists argue from the standpoint of particular interest groups." In such a contest, economists persuasively argue that the aggregate economic welfare should win out and protectionist measures should be avoided. The disagreements over culture industries, however, weigh the *sociocultural* welfare of a society against its economic welfare. As a result, the traditional rationale for why governments must avoid support measures is called into question. So is the very usefulness of the term *protectionism* in the context of these debates.

In this chapter, I show that there are sociocultural gains from the cultural policies that free traders label as protectionist. I do not contest the basic assumption that trade generally improves the aggregate economic welfare while protection can be shown to harm it. I do, however, challenge whether aggregate economic welfare should be our sole criterion for evaluating (trade) policies. There are consequences for our ability to achieve sociocultural goals when certain cultural policy measures are routinely classified as protectionist. Framing the debate in terms of free trade and protectionism effectively constrains policymakers by leaving them open to accusations of harming, at a minimum, their trading partners and, at a maximum, the global economy if they introduce support measures. If we start from the assumption that the aggregate economic welfare is the highest value, any measure that diminishes it is suspect and the onus is on anyone who proposes such a measure to justify it. Cultural policymakers find themselves on the defensive, confronted by the assumption that, since protectionist policies diminish the aggregate economic welfare, all policies that may resemble protectionism are necessarily bad. This view presumes that society's highest value is the general economic welfare; however such a contention cannot be sustained—if indeed it ever could—as the trading regime expands its reach to include sectors previously reserved for domestic policy and sectors that fulfill more than just commercial purposes.

As Dymond and Hart (2000, 2) explain, there has been a "major paradigm shift" in the trade regime since the Uruguay Round. "The WTO shifted the centre of gravity of international trade rules from negative prescription to positive rule making" (2000, 2). We must now seize the "much needed opportunity to examine the object and purpose of multilateral trade policy" (2000, 2) in light of this paradigm shift. Yet much of our language and many of our assumptions remain the same despite this paradigm shift. Instead of insisting that our theories evolve to accommodate new developments, standard analyses of culture industry trade policy suggest that many are content to fit new developments into extant theories at the expense of a full understanding of the issues at stake. We continue to assume that trade liberalization is unambiguously good. However, trade liberalization means something altogether different in the current period. Tariffs have been reduced to all-time lows in most sectors, and growth in services trade is eclipsing growth in goods trade. Liberalization today has more to do with harmonizing domestic regulatory standards than lowering barriers to the movement of goods. Similarly, we continue to assume that protectionism is easily recognized and generally bad. However, many policies that are cast as protectionism are undertaken for reasons that have little to do with delivering economic benefits to local industry. In this chapter, I explore this unhappy fit between twentieth-century language and assumptions about trade and twenty-first-century developments in the real world of the trade regime.

The Benefits of Free Trade

Received wisdom among liberal economists since Adam Smith's *Wealth of Nations* (1776) is that free trade maximizes the aggregate economic welfare. Smith's belief in the efficiency of the "invisible hand" of the self-regulating market was a direct challenge to eighteenth-century mercantilist thought. The mercantilist impulse was to amass quantities of silver and gold perceived as crucial to national security and economic stability. Exporting was favored, but imports were viewed in a negative light because their purchase required depletion of precious metal resources. Smith argued that such mercantilist policies, accompanied by a high degree of government intervention, hindered economic growth. Instead, he proposed using the amassed wealth to facilitate free trade and, in so doing, improve the general economic welfare and produce a more efficient outcome.

Smith drew an analogy between nations and households. He suggested that a tailor might provide his household with clothing that he can produce efficiently. But he then turns to the shoemaker for shoes for the household. He does not make something at home that can be purchased more cheaply. Smith reasoned that the same thing would be true for nations. "If a foreign country can supply us with a commodity cheaper than we ourselves can make it, better buy it of them with some part of the produce of our own industry, employed in a way in which we have some advantage" (2000, 424). Just as individuals or households have certain strengths, so can nations identify commodities that they can produce more efficiently than other nations. Concentration on these activities, contended Smith, would contribute to the overall wealth of each nation.

David Ricardo (1911) refined Smith's argument by demonstrating that there are gains associated with trade even for countries that cannot identify an absolute advantage in the production of certain commodities. In his familiar formulation of the theory of comparative advantage, Ricardo used the examples of Portuguese wine and English cloth production to demonstrate that gains from trade ensue not only in situations of absolute advantage; gains accrue when a country specializes in the production and export of goods that it can produce *relatively* more efficiently—or relatively less inefficiently. As Gomes (2003, 54) explains, through specialization "a country can consume beyond its production-possibility frontier. The real-income effect produced is the same as if there had been an outward shift in the country's production frontier."

Modern theorists have revised and added precision to the classical argument, while maintaining the general thrust of the liberal assertion that free trade maximizes the aggregate economic welfare whereas restrictions to trade impose costs. For example, Heckscher and Ohlin demonstrated that trade patterns and comparative advantage derive from factor endowments. Not every economy is equally endowed with land, labor, or capital, the principle factors of production. Heckscher and Ohlin show that it is more efficient for countries to specialize in the production of goods that rely on their most abundant factor. Land-rich countries will export land-intensive goods; labor-rich countries will export labor-intensive goods.

While classical theory forms the basis of the argument demonstrating gains from trade, contemporary economists also point to more recent discoveries. As Irwin (2002, 21) notes, "the economic case for free trade . . . is not based on outdated theories in musty old books." In fact, Irwin (2002) argues that sustained attention to the gains identified by classical economists obscures other benefits that we are just now recognizing. Classical arguments emphasize the gains from specialization. A division of labor based on comparative advantage allows access to a greater variety of products using the same resource inputs. Producers allocate resources more efficiently and reduce their opportunity costs. Nonetheless, Irwin notes that this is just one set of benefits that trade delivers.

> Ever since Adam Smith and David Ricardo described the gains from trade in a systematic way, economists have stressed the benefits of improved resource allocation as the main advantage of trade. But economists have found mounting evidence that trade not only helps to allocate existing resources properly, but also makes those resources more productive. . . . The welfare benefits of a greater variety of products as a result of trade have also been ignored until recently, and yet preliminary evidence suggests that they are quite important. (2002, 3)

Free trade also improves overall economic performance by increasing competition in the domestic market and benefits consumers through exposure to a greater variety of goods, two gains that are overlooked in traditional analyses (Irwin 2002, 32–33).

Recent developments have prompted economists to investigate not only previously unheralded benefits of interindustry trade, but the implications for trade theory of increasingly important intraindustry trade. Economists have taken great interest in trade of similar products between similar economies because it arguably contradicts what the central idea underpinning trade theory—comparative advantage—would predict. Analysts posit that the logic and benefit of intraindustry trade lie on both the demand and supply sides of the equation. On the demand side, intraindustry trade enhances product differentiation and consumer choice. "The higher the incomes of consumers, the more consumers can seek variety in the products that they buy. Thus, affluent people vary their choices of wines, beers, automobiles, music, clothing, travel experiences, and so on. Some varieties will be imported, while the varieties produced in the country can be exported to consumers in other countries" (Pugel and Lindert 2000, 102). On the supply side, scale economies accompany this consumer demand, lowering costs and enhancing efficiency and productivity.

The corollary of the "gains-from-trade" argument is the "costs-of-protectionism" argument. As Irwin (2002, 55) puts it,

> when considering the benefits of free trade, we also have to take into account the costs of protectionist policies. Such policies include tariffs, quotas, voluntary restraint agreements, and other means of blocking imports or impeding exports. When a country imposes trade restrictions, it forgoes the gains from specialization. Specifically, when imports of a certain good are restricted, it becomes more scarce in the domestic market. Scarcity drives up the price, benefiting domestic producers of the product because consumers are forced to pay more for it. As a result, import restrictions redistribute income from domestic consumers to domestic producers. This redistribution is hard to justify.

Scholars of protectionism also lament the inefficiencies of "protectionist policies [that] distort prices and therefore economic incentives. This distortion leads to wasted resources, known as a deadweight loss. As import restrictions push the domestic price of a good above the world price, domestic firms produce more, while consumers reduce their overall purchases and suffer a real income loss as a result of higher prices" (Irwin 2002, 55). Pugel and Lindert emphasize that this redistribution of income to the producer is inefficient and results in a net loss for the world economy.

My purpose in examining conventional wisdom on the gains from trade is twofold. First, it is to show that there is a general, and in many respects unassailable, assumption among economists (and many political scientists) that there are clear and substantial gains from trade. There are exceptions to this—circumstances under which trade may not be the optimal policy, which I discuss below. Nonetheless, these are exceptions. Second, there is an assumption that these gains are primarily quantifiable gains in income. The consumer also gains from expanded product variety, but primarily, the gains are economic in nature—prices are lower, resources are allocated more efficiently, and so on.

Some analysts acknowledge that there may be political gains from trade. Early thinkers like John Stuart Mill made the case that open trade could foster peace among nations, and contemporary economists and political scientists invoke and develop this line of thinking. More recently, analysts have noted the political gains that came from U.S. efforts to enhance trade with Europe through the Marshall Plan (Bhagwati 1995, 39). Policies of constructive engagement, which presume that commercial relations with authoritarian governments might quicken their transition toward capitalist democracy, echo this perspective. Political scientists are particularly receptive to the argument that trade can lead to peace. Still, these political consequences of open trade are "additional" gains from trade that represent an added bonus beyond the primary economic benefits. Insomuch as governments undertake free trade as a policy, it is most common to assume that they are motivated primarily by the prospect of economic—and not political—gains.

Ultimately, the trade literature presumes that the key values in assessing the merits of free trade are greater economic efficiency, a desire to maximize aggregate wealth, and the importance of benefiting the consumer over the producer. Furthermore, as Gomes (2003, 38) puts it, the clear message of classical international trade theory is that "free trade, like honesty, is the best policy." This is the perspective that provides the backdrop to discussions of culture industry trade policy.

Explaining Protectionism

Needless to say, despite the obvious economic gains from trade, protectionism still occurs. Given the apparent economic losses of protectionism (and the assumption that raising the general economic welfare is always a goal of governments), the puzzle becomes, "why protect?" As Bhagwati (1995, 72) puts it, "international economists have long been frustrated by the dissonance between the elegance of their irrefutable demonstration of the advantages of free trade and the inelegance with which practical politics embraces protection."

Both economists and political scientists have offered a variety of explanations for protectionism that incorporate economic and political factors. Most prevailing explanations posit political gain from protectionism, an unsurprising conclusion given that the purely economic argument in favor of free trade predicts economic loss from protection. Nevertheless, some economists note that protection can occasionally produce an economic benefit. For example, Irwin (2002, 62) explains that "trade protection can, under certain conditions, improve welfare. Broadly speaking, trade measures can be beneficial when they are used to improve the terms of trade, to promote industries with positive externalities, or to capture rents in international markets." Nonetheless, Irwin offers this analysis guardedly. In fact, he goes on later to retract it, saying that "an improvement in the exporting country's terms of trade implies a deterioration in the importing country's terms of trade and actually leaves the world as a whole worse off (2002, 63)."

Perhaps more widely accepted, though still controversial, are strategic trade theory arguments, prompted by the Asian Tigers' success with industrial policy during the 1980s. Strategic trade policy is based on the notion that there may be sectors or industries that can make a greater contribution to the economy than others. For example, Krugman (1986) argues that governments can design strategies to help firms or industries compete in oligopolistic markets. In making this argument, he allows that some economic activities may be more important than others because of spillovers or a higher potential for productivity growth. Strategic sectors are those generating a substantial "rent"[1] or an important spillover effect (external economy).[2] For example, if a domestic semiconductor industry can be shown to quicken the pace of innovation in the related computer industry, this spillover effect might justify policy to protect the semiconductor industry. This theory is controversial because it flies in the face of the logic of cultivating a "natural" comparative advantage. Indeed, as debates have evolved, Krugman and others have voiced skepticism about the wisdom of such policies. More common among economists than arguments that posit economic benefit coming from protectionism is acknowledgment that free trade may not be the best policy in the exceptional cases of market imperfections—too few competitors to provide perfect competition, for example, or the pollution that ensues from manufacturing activity.

Political scientists have made important contributions to the debate over why governments protect certain sectors and not others. Many of these arguments explain government recourse to protection as a function of the demands made by domestic pressure groups. "Domestic groups seek protection or liberalization because such policies increase their incomes" (Milner 1999, 95). Public officials are inclined to satisfy these demands to boost their chances for reelection (Baldwin 1996, 147). Baldwin (1996, 148) echoes Milner in maintaining that "the nature of the policies sought by individuals and firms depends on the effect of the policies on their economic welfare." Interest groups can ostensibly be successful in demanding protection under certain circumstances in part because

1. Krugman (1986, 12) defines "rent" as "payment to an input higher than what that input could earn in alternative use." He goes on to say: "It could mean a higher rate of profit in an industry than is earned in other industries of equivalent riskiness, or higher wages in an industry than equally skilled workers earn in other sectors."

2. Citing Krugman (1986, 13) again, "by an 'external economy' economists mean a benefit from some activity that accrues to other individuals or firms than those engaging in the activity. The most plausible example is the diffusion of knowledge generated in one area to other firms and other sectors." Further, sectors generating spillover effects "yield high returns to society because in addition to their own earnings they provide benefits to capital and labor employed elsewhere."

those who are traditionally thought to suffer from the protectionist policy—the consumers—are dispersed and difficult to organize.

Milner goes on to explain that in recent decades

> development of the pressure group model has attempted to delineate more specifically the groups who should favor and oppose protection and the conditions under which they may be most influential. One motive for this has been the observation that the extent of protection and the demands for it vary both across industries and across countries. . . . The main divide has been between so-called factoral versus sectoral or firm-based theories of preferences. In both cases, *preferences are deduced as a result of the changes in income* that accrue to different actors when policy changes from free trade to protection or vice versa. (1999, 95, emphasis mine)

Interestingly, then, even when political scientists offer pressure group explanations associated with political gain, economic welfare is still central.

Overall, our discussions of free trade and protectionism are overwhelmingly dominated by economic rationales. The analysis of free trade and protectionism is so well-developed and appears so timeless that we rely on it still, even though new issues are coming to the fore. This is true to such a degree that when noneconomic arguments are introduced, analysts are typically so skeptical as to discount them. We often see the requisite reference to Adam Smith's acknowledgment that national defense may trump trade. But generally there is an unwillingness to accept noneconomic arguments as persuasive, and this has been particularly noteworthy in the debates over cultural policy. For example, Joel Richard Paul (2000, 3) maintains that "most international trade law scholars, for example, dismiss cultural resistance as transparent protectionism." Cable (1996, 234) concurs: "It is more than probable that these protests, couched in high-minded cultural terms, are simply a cover for interest group protection. But it is significant that arguments are constructed in these terms." Bhagwati (1999, 4) attributes this view specifically to unsophisticated business lobbyists (rather than to economists convinced of the merits of free trade), saying that "the lobbyists, who cry protectionism whenever foreign nations worry about threats to culture from free trade, work and flourish within an American culture that is unable to appreciate the cultural concerns of others and therefore encourages the presumption that these complaints must 'really' be a mask for protectionism."

Such rationales for protectionism, especially those that rely overwhelmingly on the assumption that trade and protectionist policy is motivated by economic gain, provide little insight into culture industry trade policy. Below I test the conventional explanations for protectionism against the circumstances of the culture industries in the countries at the center of the GATT and NAFTA trade disputes, France and Canada. The day has not arrived where we can talk about "European" audiovisual industries, but where it is possible to comment on them, I do so. I show that promoting economic gain takes a back seat to avoiding cultural loss as a key motivator of culture industry trade policy.

Infant Industry. The infant industry argument posits that country A may have a comparative advantage or see the potential for success in a certain economic activity, but country B has already established itself in this activity. The activity may be broadly conceived, such as the development of a manufacturing sector in a developing country, or it can pertain to efforts to enter a particular industry. Country A would be inclined to protect the activity until it can compete independently with country B. Without protection in its infancy, the sector or industry may never establish itself in the face of early cost inefficiency. Some classical economists accept the infant industry argument in part because the protectionist policy is intended to be a temporary solution. In addition, the temporary protection can be viewed as having a long-run payoff for the individual domestic economy and for the system as a whole.

The French audiovisual industries—film and television—are not infant industries. The French claim that their countrymen, the Lumière brothers, invented commercial film projection in the late 1800s and that the first spectators who paid to see a film did so in Paris in 1895 (Jeancolas 1995). While private commercial television may be new to France, the French television industry is not young. It is true that television did not arrive in the majority of French households until later than other advanced industrialized countries. In 1959, only the large urban centers received television signals, but ten years later 95 percent of French territory would have television access (Bourdon 1990, 12). By the late 1960s, two channels existed and three-quarters of their programming was produced by the French television industry (Bourdon 1990, 13). "By the end of the 1960s the ORTF [*Office de Radiodiffusion-Télévision Française*] was one of the European giants in television production, programming and transmission, ranking alongside other public service broadcasting organizations such as the BBC in Britain" (Kuhn 1995, 110).

Of the Canadian culture industries, only feature film production might be conceptualized as an infant industry. Regular radio broadcasting began in 1919, and the Canadian Broadcasting Act of 1936 inaugurated the Canadian Broadcasting Corporation. By the 1950s, both private and public radio broadcasting industries existed and thrived. The first Canadian television station went on the air in Montreal in 1952 (Audley 1983, 253), and magazine and book publishing predate all of these.

Optimal Tariff. According to the optimal tariff argument, Country A applies a tariff to an industry when it is not a price taker[3] in the industry. Instead, the country has a large enough share of the world market for the product affected by the tariff that it can unilaterally influence its market price. The tariff is not a prohibitive one, designed to keep the import out of Country A's market. Instead, Country A exploits its monopsonist[4] power and, in so doing, ensures a continued supply of the import at a lower price.

Clearly this argument is of little help in explaining European and Canadian behavior. The tariff is not one of the instruments generally used by French or European cultural policymakers. Instead, subsidies, tax incentives, and quotas are employed to support television and film in France and across the EU. Similarly, Canada has imposed tariffs on books and master tapes. However, in 1979 it removed the tariff on books and now typically favors other instruments for supporting Canadian culture industries. In addition, neither Canada nor any EU member state is a price taker in the market for culture industries.

Provider of Jobs. Irwin (2002, 3) calls the employment rationale "the most frequent argument in favor of limiting trade." This argument contends that if free trade threatens domestic jobs, governments are inclined to protect the threatened industry so as not to alienate the voting public and to ensure a high rate of employment. It is difficult to determine just how many jobs culture industries provide. Published statistics do not agree on what related industries to include. (Some include advertising agencies, concession workers in theaters, etc.) At the time of the CUSFTA and NAFTA negotiations, there were roughly 600,000 so-called cultural workers in Canada, including artists working in the visual arts, heritage, and libraries, creative endeavors not included in the Canadian trade negotiator's notion of culture industries (Statistics Canada 1995, 27). More recent data would suggest that approximately 200,000 of these workers worked in the culture industries.[5] While this is not an insubstantial number, it is comparable to—and even lower than—the numbers employed in other industries that are arguably threatened as much as culture industries by free trade, but for which the Canadian government did not demand special consideration in the trade agreements. In fact, the largest provider of manufacturing jobs in Canada is the automobile industry, yet it was the first to be opened to competitive international trade in the Auto Pact of 1965. This suggests that, contrary

3. A country is a "price taker" when its share of the world market for a specific good is not large enough that it can affect the price of the good unilaterally.

4. Where monopoly power is equated with the notion of a single seller, monopsony power is equated with the notion of a single buyer.

5. Canadian Cultural Observatory, Culturescope website, QuickFacts factsheet on "Economic Impact" (last updated June 2002), http://www.culturescope.ca, accessed July 23, 2004.

to expectations, the Canadian government has indeed encouraged free trade in some high employment industries, like automobile manufacture.

Furthermore, the rise of "Hollywood North"—U.S. television and movie production crews filming in Canada in order to benefit from the advantageous currency exchange and from the wealth of highly skilled Canadian technicians—has not led the Canadian government to scale back its support policies for local cultural producers. Instead, it has pursued what might be termed a two-track policy in this area. The Production Services Tax Credit encourages the employment of Canadians in the film and video industry by allowing Canadian *or* foreign-owned entities to deduct a percentage of wages and salaries paid to Canadians. This program has fueled so-called "runaway production" from California to Canada with the result that many in the U.S. film industry would like to see the tax credit that currently treats Canadians and Americans equally made available only to Canadians. Ironically, one of the policies that the U.S. entertainment industry has found most objectionable is arguably the only measure in the range of government policies that is *not* discriminatory. As a result, it is not under threat from liberalization of the culture industry sector in the same way that policies with cultural purposes are, suggesting that Canadian negotiators do not have to exclude culture industries from trade agreements to ensure continuation of favored job creation policies in this sector. They must, however, do so to preserve cultural policy measures that promote cultural goals.

In Europe, a similar analysis holds. The EU has not ignored the fact that audiovisual industries employ many people. Unemployment rates are much higher in Europe, so it is a strategic decision to accentuate the job creation aspects of European cultural policies. Nonetheless, the types of policies pursued are not always the most effective at job creation. Rather, they have other purposes. The EU maintains that the audiovisual industries cannot fulfill their sociocultural purposes unless they are viable economically. Once again, economic concerns line up alongside sociocultural ones.

Balance of Trade. Protectionist policies can be used as a means of correcting a balance of trade deficit or to increase a balance of trade surplus. There is no doubt that France and Canada each run substantial balance of trade deficits with the United States in most of the culture industries, with the exception of radio broadcasting. French and Canadian governments have no illusions about the limited potential for exporting their cultural products to the United States. France and Canada might be able, in the long run, to reduce the balance of trade deficit, but it would still be a deficit. This is, in large part, due to the tastes manifested by Americans over the years. Dubbed and subtitled films and television programs are typically not embraced in any general way by U.S. audiences, thus making it unlikely that foreign-language products would ever find much of an export market in the United States. Similarly, stories set in the American context fare better in the U.S. market than those set in a foreign context. European and Canadian stories often undergo an "Americanization process"—the essence of the plot is transplanted to an American context—so as to be more appealing to U.S. audiences. While export of cultural products is desirable and encouraged, the bulk of the cultural policies that Canadian and European governments are seeking to shield from liberalization are designed to increase or ensure the access of local producers to their own domestic markets.

Strategic Trade Policy. The strategic trade policy argument assumes that the payoff to protection is an economic one. In other words, a strategic industry is targeted because doing so will ultimately raise national income.[6] While culture industries have a cultural and political payoff, there is little evidence that protecting them will make a disproportionately large contribution to the European or Canadian economies. Workers in the culture industries do not earn higher wages than equally skilled workers would earn in other industries. There is little spillover of technology from radio, television, film, book publishing, or sound recording. In fact, the argument can be made that commercial television and radio were on the receiving end of technological spillover from innovations originally designed for military use.

Declining Industry. This argument assumes that the country instituting the protectionist policy was once on top in the protected industry but is now being threatened by newcomers capitalizing on low wages and other advantages of backwardness to catch up. Clearly, this characterization captures neither the Canadian or French culture industries, nor the threat posed by the United States.

Interest Groups. There is no denying that interest groups operate on the terrain of cultural policy. This argument becomes less useful, though, when we explore which groups seem to be favored by cultural policies. In the Canadian context, for example, one would predict that the large media conglomerates that operate private television stations might exercise some disproportionate influence with the Canadian government, given the financial and other resources at their disposal. However, this appears not to be the case. Measures like domestic content quotas actually impose costs on this group. On the other hand, those who benefit from many cultural policies are actually the groups that seem less likely to have much political influence. In addition, polls show that the Canadian public has consistently supported cultural policies, suggesting contrary to the logic of the interest group models of protectionism that the *consumer* is at least as supportive of support measures as the producers that benefit directly.

---

6. Krugman 1986, 14. Krugman goes on to specify that *labor and capital* receive higher benefits, in the form of higher wages or profit, than they would in other industries. See especially pages 1–22.

The European context is similar. Theiler (2005) further suggests that European audiovisual policies were driven by officials within EU institutions, noting that "using culture and education as identity forgers had few outspoken advocates, save for the relatively weak pro-European movements and some related organizations" (Theiler 2005, 149).

National Security. Traditionally, the trade literature gives the lion's share of its attention to economic arguments for free trade and protectionism. Irwin's history of free trade is a representative case: "By economic arguments, I mean those that address the economist's stringent standard of whether a particular policy will increase aggregate economic wealth, where wealth is suitably defined as, for example, real national income. Debates surrounding the economics of free trade and protection all revolve around the question of efficiency" (1996, 4). Like other trade policy scholars, Irwin acknowledges that "there are a multitude of noneconomic arguments for protection that are a perennial feature of trade policy debates. These include political arguments (e.g., protection of an industry for national defense) or others broadly geared toward achieving some vaguely national or social objective (e.g., greater self-sufficiency in certain goods)." Yet he simply excludes them from his analysis, assuming that such arguments are not part of the trade economist's project: "Such considerations may or may not be important, but they will not be considered here" (Irwin 1996, 5).

Some trade scholars will make an exception for the national security argument to justify limited and temporary protection. From this perspective, control over certain industries and products can be considered essential to national security. Traditionally this has included such items as steel, the supply of which should not be left in the hands of another country in the event of a national military emergency. More recently, the oil industry has called for import barriers for the sake of national security in response to OPEC embargoes. These categories of items are necessary in defending a nation-state against military aggression and threats to economic welfare.

It is true that many seemingly nonstrategic items can be portrayed as vital to national security so as to justify import barriers. In 1984, the president of the Footwear Industry of America appeared before the Senate Armed Services Committee and was quoted as saying the following:

> In the event of war or other national emergency, it is highly unlikely that the domestic footwear industry could provide sufficient footwear for the military and civilian population. . . . We won't be able to wait for ships to deliver shoes from Taiwan, or Korea or Brazil or Eastern Europe . . . improper footwear can lead to needless casualties and turn sure victory into possible defeat. (Chanda and Manning 1984, 70)

The same sort of rhetorical strategies have not been employed to depict culture industries as vital to national security. Perhaps in the former Soviet bloc these industries might have been construed as such due to the central role that propaganda played in sustaining support for regimes. However, in advanced industrialized Western democracies, state propaganda takes a different form. Certainly, if the European Union and Canada sought to use domestic culture industries as propaganda resources, they would attempt to influence *content* of cultural products, something neither country attempts to do.

It is interesting to note that there is a separate article in the North American Free Trade Agreement releasing the signatories from the obligations of the agreement if they interfere with national security. Article 2102 indicates that the notion of national security that the parties to the agreement subscribe to could not accommodate culture industries.

1. Subject to Articles 607 (Energy—National Security Measures) and 1018 (Government Procurement—Exceptions), nothing in this Agreement shall be construed:
>   (a) to require any Party to furnish or allow access to any information the disclosure of which it determines to be contrary to its essential security interests;
>   (b) to prevent any Party from taking any actions that it considers necessary for the protection of its essential security interests
>> (i) relating to the traffic in arms, ammunition and implements of war and to such traffic and transactions in other goods, materials, services and technology undertaken directly or indirectly for the purpose of supplying a military or other security establishment,
>> (ii) taken in time of war or other emergency in international relations, or
>> (iii) relating to the implementation of national policies or international agreements respecting the non-proliferation of nuclear weapons or other nuclear explosive devices; or
>   (c) to prevent any Party from taking action in pursuance of its obligations under the United Nations Charter for the maintenance of international peace and security. (*North American Free Trade Agreement* 1992, 21–22)

National security arguments are not particularly useful where culture industry policy is concerned. They pertain to moments when the state is threatened as a legal or a territorial entity, especially times of war. However, the stance taken by Canadian and European officials with regard to the cultural sector confronts a perceived threat to Canada and the EU as *cultural* entities. Were culture industries thrown open to liberalization, Canada and the EU would still occupy the same space on maps and they would still function as leading industrialized actors internationally. But the worry is that their respective imagined communities, represented through shared understandings, values, traditions, and practices, will be so changed as to be unrecognizable. The national security argument, therefore, offers limited opportunities for our analysis to move out of the material realm and into the less tangible realm where identity and cultural concerns reside.

The thread running through the various arguments for protection is that they are, for the most part, motivated by material gain or avoidance of economic loss. While each argument may have political implications, the emphasis is on economic issues. But, the European Union and Canada can be viewed as often *sacrificing* economic gain by following the cultural exclusion policy, at least in terms of overall national economic welfare. For example, European and Canadian television stations could be more economically profitable if they bought low-cost U.S. serials. An episode of an American program typically costs between $60,000–$100,000 while production of a local, one-hour drama program can cost up to $1 million. But policies like percentage indigenous content requirements indicate that these governments are placing other goals and values—specifically those pertaining to collective identity formation—before economic profit and efficiency.

This analysis suggests not only that cultural policies spring from different motivations than conventional protectionist policies do, but that they also have different *effects*, often imposing costs on domestic groups rather than bringing them relief. Therefore, it seems clear that the standard explanations for protectionism are of little use where culture industry trade policies are concerned and in other sectors where broader social and cultural concerns are at stake. Baldwin (1996) argues that we nonetheless continue to rely on them because "of the vast amount of economic activity that does seem to be explained satisfactorily on the basis of the self-interest simplification" (Baldwin 1996, 151). Surely, however, we can no longer ignore the growing list of activities moving onto the trade agenda that resist conventional trade policy analysis. The culture industry debate calls for a reassessment of our assumptions about protectionism, especially when more than just commercial goals are in play.

Even economists acknowledge that an overreliance on the economic arguments of classical trade theory means that rival goals fall out of the equation.

> The classical economists, if not Adam Smith, took as given the economic objective of achieving the greatest possible material wealth of a country.

However, they never argued that material wealth should be always and everywhere the solitary goal of economic policy. They recognized that economic analysis was silent about what society's preferences should be and could scarcely object if society wished to sacrifice some material wealth to achieve other objectives. (Smith's belief that defense is more important than opulence reflected this position.) But to the extent that material considerations were thought to be important (as they almost always are, at least to some extent), the classical economists strongly believed that economic analysis could greatly inform economic policy and thereby contribute to improved material circumstances. (Irwin 1996, 180)

Similarly, Jagdish Bhagwati notes that "the lobbyists who understand little of the theory of free trade, but understand how to (mis)invoke it for their own advantage, are no friends of free trade" (1999, 2). Indeed, Bhagwati provides important insights into the question of protectionism and sociocultural concerns. He is perhaps the leading theorist—and proponent—of free trade of our time. In his book, *Protectionism* (1995), he makes it clear that free trade is the best policy and protectionism is to be avoided. When trade policy presents itself as a way to achieve social objectives, Bhagwati (1995, 122) notes that one must always ask whether "there are no better, less costly policies that might achieve these objectives?" He (1995, 123) continues: "The temptation to make trade policy captive to sundry major and minor objectives, unmindful of costs and benefits and of alternatives, is surely to be rejected." He is not persuaded by those who wish to discuss "fair trade" over free trade and he suggests that workers' rights might better be protected by channels other than those associated with the trade regime, including the International Labor Organization.

Bhagwati's position, however, is complex. Despite his unequivocal desire to "keep protectionism at bay" (1995, 130), Bhagwati condemns "this turn to the bilateral 'open foreign markets aggressively' policies, based on exaggerated 'I am more open than thou' presumptions, that afflicts current U.S. policymakers" (1995, 126). Bhagwati (1995, 126–27) goes on:

Another aspect of the concern with unfair trade is the increasing tendency to object to virtually any state intervention abroad as producing a departure from fair trade among competing producers. This approach. . . is surely a wrongheaded one. Any sensible economist will point out the need to distinguish between those state interventions that correct for market failure and those that create it. . . . Therefore, international codes and national rulings that reflect the belief that all export subsidies (for example) are necessarily reprehensible and destroy fair competition are based on egregious fallacies. I would also like to see a far greater tolerance of other countries' social objectives, some of which lead to interventions in trade that the U.S. export lobbies oppose on the grounds that they are unfair. It is not surprising, for example, that Canada, Australia, and many other countries take measures to support their own arts and letters. Even the United States would be unwilling to leave cultural matters wholly to the marketplace; witness the restrictions on foreign ownership of U.S. media. And yet, in the recent negotiations on the U.S.-Canada free-trade area, the U.S. media industry's strenuous and thoughtless objections to Canada's interventions in support of Canadian cultural identity were a major source of friction.

Perspectives like Bhagwati's confirm that efforts to re-create or prolong the embedded liberalism compromise are being mistaken for protectionism. An embedded liberalism compromise is still desirable, albeit one that reflects contemporary realities. The costs to openness associated with the current period include threats to collective identity and sociocultural bargains. Yet it is difficult to defend against these threats because policies designed to address the "social purpose" part of the compromise are equated with protectionism and marked for removal or excluded as options. This leaves governments constrained by a set of rules they themselves devised. The very policies that would provide *safeguards* against openness are targeted for dismantlement as *barriers* to openness. If we would acknowledge the sociocultural motivation for these cultural policies, as well as the limited relevance of theories of protectionism in these debates, we would be less inclined to discount cultural measures as veiled protectionism. In addition, we would be more likely to open up the discussion to the range of goals governments are trying to reach and the policy instruments they might have at their disposal in service of these goals. There is an overreliance on the language of protectionism in these debates. We are actually on the terrain of social and cultural policy, and not just trade policy. As such, the language of the embedded liberalism compromise expands the discussion by ensuring that the trade dimension of culture industries is not overemphasized. The following chapter examines how the Canadian government has contended with this dilemma in recent years.

Chapter 2

Canada and NAFTA

The greatest threat to Canada lies in the possibility (some might even say probability) that, as a result of the strong presence of American influences, our cultural development may be stunted. United States styles, ideas, and products are never far away. There is, alas, a well-grounded fear that as a consequence, our perceptions, values, ideas, and priorities will become so dominated by those of our neighbours that the distinctiveness of Canada will, to all intents and purposes, vanish.

John Meisel, former chairman of the Canadian Radio–Television and Telecommunications Commission (1986)

Successive Canadian governments since the early 1920s have used policy governing culture industries to contribute to the related goals of collective identity formation, nation-building, and more recently, the promotion of cultural diversity. As a result, a significant body of support measures favoring Canadian producers in film, television, and radio broadcasting; periodical and book publishing; and video and sound recording has developed. It is this body of policy that the Canadian government sought to keep intact by calling for the exclusion of culture industries from the Canada–U.S. Free Trade Agreement (CUSFTA) and subsequently from NAFTA. These support measures have generally been successful in creating and maintaining viable culture industries in Canada. Without the protection afforded by the exclusion clause in trade agreements, many of these measures would be challenged as unfair trading practices and, in all likelihood, either dismantled or rendered much more costly to employ.

It is widely believed in Canada that, without government support measures, culture industries would become nothing more than conduits for foreign producers of cultural goods. This is an undesirable outcome not for economic reasons (though these are not entirely irrelevant). During the long history of its communications policies favoring Canadian producers, as well as during CUSFTA and

NAFTA trade talks, the Canadian government repeatedly articulated a desire to strengthen Canadian culture industries as one of the key mechanisms for reproducing Canadian identity, and by extension, for distinguishing the Canadian political community from other national communities and promoting social cohesion domestically, as well as cultural diversity globally. This is not a protectionist agenda. Rather, the desire to embrace open trade on the one hand, while retaining some latitude for offsetting the cultural costs of liberalization on the other, is compatible with the logic of embedded liberalism.

With these factors in mind, I argue in this chapter that the history of culture industry policy in Canada is driven by a desire to achieve cultural goals, often in the face of protest from those inside and outside of Canada who would incur economic losses from measures designed to serve cultural purposes. The Canadian government's call for the exclusion of culture industries from CUSFTA and NAFTA was, therefore, not a protectionist ploy serving economic interests but a natural extension of the body of culture industry policy developed over the last several decades in response to the perceived challenges of Canadian nation-building. Canadian policy became particularly controversial in the 1980s and after as the reach of the trading regime expanded to encompass the culture industries. Canadian policy did not change. Rather, a long-standing set of national policies designed to achieve sociocultural purposes, previously outside the purview of multilateral trade agreements, collided with trading regime principles designed to serve commercial ones.

This study of the Canadian case, then, demonstrates that culture industry policy is one of the principal ways that the Canadian government seeks to cultivate collective particularity, in part by making Canadian cultural products available to Canadians. The extension of this strategy to the international arena illustrates that decisions about international trade policy can indeed be driven by predominantly noncommercial, cultural considerations. Interpreting the Canadian stance over culture industries during CUSFTA and NAFTA talks as veiled economic protectionism or as indicative of a slide toward autarky is certainly incomplete, if not entirely incorrect. Furthermore, it reflects a narrow understanding of the sociocultural motives for trade policy and precludes consideration of mechanisms at the level of the trading regime to accommodate these motives. Canadian resistance to liberalizing the culture industry sector does not reflect a government held captive by special interests. Rather, it is part of the federal government's strategy to cushion Canadian society from some of the cultural costs of economic liberalization.

In this chapter I analyze the Canadian emphasis on cultural goals in three sections. I begin by demonstrating the link made by Canadian policymakers between identity and culture industries. To underscore the ongoing preoccupation with identity and diversity as it relates to culture industry policy, I then survey the array of policies that have been instituted by the federal government over the years in response to these challenges. There are cultural policies at all levels of government in Canada. To date, conflicts with trade principles have concerned federal-level policies, so I focus on them here. I conclude by returning to the puzzle presented in the Introduction: namely, explaining the Canadian effort to exclude culture industries from the Canada–U.S. Free Trade Agreement and from NAFTA. Despite their reliance on trade and their willing participation in the global economy, Canadian policymakers seek to perpetuate "Canada" as a distinctive political community. Collective identity formation, greater national unity, and cultural diversity are the goals, and culture industries that showcase Canadian content and Canadian producers are a key means to achieving them. As a result, officials seek special protection for culture industries within the trading regime, not for commercial reasons, but for cultural ones.

Nothing in this argument is intended to suggest that economic considerations drop out of the equation—they do not. However, economic considerations have so dominated the discussion about culture industries to date that there has been little room for acknowledgement of the cultural considerations that are often as important as economic ones.

Canadian Identity

Nation building in Canada began in earnest in the mid twentieth century, much later than its advanced, industrialized counterparts. During the first half of the century, Canada drew on its colonial past as the foundation for its identity, appropriating many British symbols and traditions rather than attempting to develop its own. Many of the remnants of British colonial rule were only recently removed, and some still remain. Canadian lawmakers continued to send bills to the British Parliament for final approval until 1931. Only in 1965 did the Canadian government vote to replace the Red Ensign (featuring a Union Jack and a Canadian coat of arms) with the Maple Leaf as the Canadian flag. Until 1982, the document that served as the Canadian constitution—the British North America Act—was housed in London. While no former prime minister is honored with a holiday, the summer officially begins in all provinces but Quebec during the May long weekend that marks Queen Victoria's birthday, an event not even recognized in England. Queen Elizabeth's picture still adorns Canadian currency and, indeed, she remains the Canadian head of state.

Despite these modern manifestations of Canada's colonial history, recent changes in Canadian society have loosened Canada's long-standing ties with

Britain. Periodic resurgences in Francophone nationalism, waves of ethnic immigrants, as well as the emergence of a powerful movement for aboriginal rights, have greatly diluted the meaning that a Canadian identity celebrating British ancestry might have among contemporary Canadian citizens. In addition, the Canadian political economy has shifted from dependence on Great Britain for export markets and portfolio investment to dependence on the United States for export markets and direct investment, thus cementing the Canadian reorientation away from Britain (Marchildon 1995).

Proximity to the United States arguably exacerbates the difficulties associated with defining a Canadian identity. While many national communities distinguish themselves with their language, cuisine, styles of dress, and so forth, the United States and Canada are very similar in these attributes. As a result, some commentators have attempted to identify less tangible national differences, based on less easily discernible traits such as communication style or socioeconomic priorities, upon which Canadian identity might be founded. For example, Earle and Wirth (1995, 10) suggest that the greatest single difference between Canada and the United States is "the relative importance assigned to individual and collective rights." Lipset (1986, 114) adds that, "Canada has been a more elitist, law-abiding, statist, collectivity-oriented, and particularistic (group-oriented) society than the United States." Lipset goes on to argue that the distinctions between Canada and the United States stem from being on different sides during the American Revolution. As a result, "there is a greater conservatism in Canada—in the European sense of the word" (1986, 118).

> This political orientation, with its emphasis on the values of *noblesse oblige* and state responsibility, has meant, ironically, that Canada has provided a more favorable political and social climate for the development of welfare state policies than is found south of the border. (Lipset 1986, 118)

Canadians are generally supportive of government intervention in the economy and prefer policies promoting equal outcomes rather than equal opportunity. More Canadians are Roman Catholic or Anglican, religions that "are hierarchically organized and continued until recently to have a strong relationship with the state" (Lipset 1986, 125). Americans, notes Lipset, embrace a congregational tradition that grew out of opposition to the Church of England. There is also a distinctive legal culture in Canada.

> The explicit concern of Canada's founding fathers with "peace, order and good government" implies control and protection. The American stress on "life, liberty and the pursuit of happiness" suggests upholding the rights

of the individual. This latter concern for rights, including those of people accused of crime and of political dissidents, is inherent in the "due process" model, involving various legal inhibitions on the power of the police and prosecutors, characteristic of the United States. The "crime control" model, more evident in Canada, as well as Europe, emphasizes the maintenance of law and order, and is less protective of the rights of the accused and of individuals generally. . . . The Canadian government has greater legal power to restrict freedom of speech and to invade personal privacy. (1986, 128)

To be sure, such arguments are controversial and leave many unsatisfied, in part because these elements of the Canadian identity are evolving (see Nevitte 1996). Nevertheless, polls taken during the early stages of the CUSFTA talks showed that "89% of Canadians think Canada's culture and identity are different from the United States" (Audley 1994, 333). Indeed, Kymlicka (2003) identifies the need to distinguish Canada from the United States as a defining feature of the Canadian identity. He argues that

the nature of the contrast between American and Canadian identities is not a matter of primordial or essentialist differences. It is continually shifting. Yet it is universally taken for granted that such a contrast exists and will endure. Since the actual content of the contrast is not fixed, there is a constant need to redefine and reinforce the distinction. (2003, 364)

During CUSFTA talks, former Minister of Communications Flora Mac-Donald reminded Parliament that Canada is different, promising that free trade would not jeopardize this distinctiveness.

I represent Kingston, where many people loyal to the King of England came 200 years ago to escape the new United States of America. Old Fort Henry, built just over 150 years ago, still stands peaceful vigil on the St. Lawrence. It now invites American tourists to see Canada, and to remind them *and ourselves* that, though our histories are intertwined, we are a fiercely independent and *distinct nation*. No measure undertaken by Canada under this new trade agreement will alter our future as *a distinct people*, inhabiting the lands of this continent north of the forty-ninth parallel.[1]

---

1. "Notes for a Speech by the Honourable Flora MacDonald, M.P. for Kingston and the Islands, Minister of Communications, in the House of Commons," October 26, 1987, p. 17, Archival Records of the Trade Negotiations Office, file 5420–1. Emphasis mine.

The federal government has also attempted to identify the core values associated with Canadian identity. In 1990, following the failure of the Meech Lake Accord,[2] Prime Minister Brian Mulroney initiated the formation of the Citizen's Forum on Canada's Future. This body was charged with consulting Canadians through such mechanisms as telephone calls and town meetings to determine the direction they would like to see Canada take. After canvassing 700,000 citizens, the forum identified "seven universal beliefs as intrinsic to 'Canadianness.'"

- a belief in equality and fairness in a democratic society
- a belief in consultation and dialogue
- a belief in accommodation and tolerance
- a commitment to diversity
- an abiding compassion and generosity, including an attachment to Canada's social safety nets of universal health care and pensions
- a respect for Canada's natural beauty and environmentalism
- Canada's world image of being committed to freedom, peace, and non-violent change. (Canada 1991; Spicer 1995)

While these are all commendable attributes around which most Canadians would rally, so might also most Swedes. In other words, those values supposedly held most dear in Canada are not only held dear in Canada, again challenging Canadian efforts to distinguish the polity and society.

The Quebec secessionist movement has perhaps had the greatest, albeit arguably inadvertent, impact on Canadian identity formation in recent decades. In 1960, French-Canadian nationalists in Quebec initiated the Quiet Revolution. They sought to break free of the influence of both the Catholic Church and Anglophone Canada to celebrate and protect the heritage of the Francophone population. This prompted federal efforts to fashion a national identity that resonates with both the French- and English-speaking communities. In response to Quebec's continuing efforts to preserve its distinctive culture, language, and legal system, in 1968 the federal government initiated a policy of biculturalism. Rather than embracing one of the two dominant cultures, Canada chose officially to embrace both. In recent decades, the policy of biculturalism

---

2. The Meech Lake Accord sought to give Quebec entrenched status in the Canadian Constitution as a "distinct society." It also proposed an elected Senate and the extension of various rights to Aboriginal peoples.

has evolved into a policy of multiculturalism in recognition of the prominence of various unassimilated ethnic communities in Canada, many of which speak neither English nor French. The reality in Canada guarantees that there will be no tidy, traditional national identity, matching a single nation to a single state, despite the impulse to sometimes function as if it might be possible. Instead, the Canadian identity formation project requires forging a sense of unity and belonging amidst regional loyalties, a plurality of minorities, and multiple founding peoples (increasingly, Canadians are appropriately acknowledging three, not two founding peoples).

Rather than attempting to create a national identity that transcends the linguistic, regional, and ethnic divisions within the Canadian community, the federal government has co-opted these differences and made them synonymous with "Canadian." In some circles this has been applauded as progressive (Collins 1990); however, such a positive evaluation is rare. As John Ralston Saul (1997) argues, dominant thinking about identity springs from the notion that a successful and robust nation-state must be able to boast of a cohesive identity, as well as a single dominant language and culture. Canada—and perhaps a handful of other countries—is exceptional in that it does not conform to this model. For Saul, this need not imply that the Canadian identity is weak or imperiled. Rather, the complexity and fragmentation of Canadian society—the fact that it is "conceived as existing in permanent motion, more a sensibility than an ambition" (Saul 1997, 107)—merely fits poorly with traditional models of a monolithic nation-state mythology. This is described by most federalists and antifederalists alike as the failure of Canada.

> The failure to become like the others. To regularize a monolithic mythology. Some weep before the ever-retreating mirage of the unhyphenated Canadian. Others say its continued existence proves that the country is not real and cannot exist. For me, this failure to conform is in fact our greatest success. A proof of originality which we refuse to grasp as a positive. (Saul 1997, 8)

The tension between the Canadian experience and predominant models of the nation-state arguably makes culture industry policy that much more central to identity formation in Canada. Because Canadian collective identity is characterized neither by an effort to erase difference nor to freeze in place some preconceived notion of the Canadian self, an outlet for the dynamic and ongoing process of national (re)definition is desired. As I argue in the Introduction, culture industries provide one of the principal outlets.

Identity and Culture Industries

Like many national governments, the Canadian government counts among its responsibilities the promotion of a national consciousness, the preservation of space for domestic voices, and the safeguarding of cultural sovereignty. It goes on to operationalize cultural survival as the creation and maintenance of domestic culture industries. During CUSFTA negotiations, high officials in the Canadian government repeatedly invoked the notion that culture industries are vehicles of cultural expression through which identity is created and preserved. Not surprisingly, for example, Minister of Communications Flora MacDonald, whose portfolio included culture industries, expressed this position.

> The myriad of cultural instruments at our disposal is a powerful reason our country is as strong as it is today. . . . We recognize that they go to the very root of our identity. Across more than two centuries, thousands of talented men and women have known, lived in, and loved Canada. Their marvelous talents for showing—to us all—our people and our country have forged our identity—powerfully, invincibly, decisively.[3]

Minister of Trade Patricia Carney, whom one might expect to emphasize economic concerns, also acknowledged the cultural contribution of culture industries.

> Culture is an elusive and visceral concept because it is the way we know ourselves and each other. Cultural expression aims for excellence and self-knowledge, it is also the way we communicate among ourselves; Canada's cultural sovereignty is maintained and strengthened by the ability of Canadian cultural industries to produce, market, and distribute the products of our artists, our creative people; the dominance of U.S. firms of our sound recording, film, television and publishing sectors impinges upon our cultural sovereignty. This massive penetration of the Canadian market threatens the growth of Canada's cultural products which are the major demonstration of our identity as a separate nation.[4]

3. "Notes for a Speech by the Honourable Flora MacDonald, M.P., for Kingston and the Islands, Minister of Communications in the House of Commons," pp. 3–4. Ottawa, Ontario, October 26, 1987. Archival records of the Canadian Trade Negotiations Office, file 5420–1.

4. "Arts and Cultural Industries, Notes for Minister [Patricia] Carney's Briefing Book—Meeting with SAGIT's chairpersons," June 23, 1987. Archival records of the Canadian Trade Negotiations Office, file 5420–1.

The Office of the Trade Negotiator, acutely aware that this perspective would be unacceptable to the United States and would stall negotiations, defended the "cultural exception" strategy because of the contribution culture industries make to identity formation.

> Canada's cultural policy objectives are not to keep U.S. culture out of Canada. Their objective is to ensure Canadians an opportunity to maintain their own unique identity, through film, records, broadcasting and publishing. . . . The future of Canadian culture, the future of Canada, is secure as long as Canadian artists, performers and writers, Canadian broadcasters and publishers, have the opportunity to reach their fellow Canadians.[5]

The Trade Negotiator's Office used similar arguments in briefing Prime Minister Mulroney.

> It is critical to realize that open competition in a North American marketplace would threaten the ability (as well as the incentives) of our culture/communications industries to provide Canadian content to Canadian audiences. In this sense it would also threaten what gives us reason to call ourselves a sovereign nation.[6]

Not just during free trade talks, but for several decades, the Canadian government has pursued and defended policies that promote domestic culture industries not for their commercial value, but because they are perceived to be a site of national communication where a distinctively Canadian identity is registered and conveyed. This "cultural exception" policy accepts the commonly held belief that "the media" is one of the most powerful socializing agents in modern society. Hoskins, Finn, and McFadyen (1996) develop this argument with specific regard to Canadian culture industries.

> Pure entertainment goods would not result in external benefits. . . . Canadian drama programming and feature films may provide external benefits in the form of an increased sense of Canadian identity and greater awareness

---

5. "Overview of the Agreement," pp. 1–2. Archival records of the Canadian Trade Negotiations Office, file 5420–1.

6. "Notes for the Prime Minister on Cultural Industries," prepared by Trade Negotiations Office, October 23, 1986, p. 3. Citing Canadian Culture/Communications Industries Committee, September 1986.

of Canadian themes and values. Current affairs and news programming and documentary programs or films may promote a population more informed on Canadian institutions, events, and issues as well as a Canadian perspective in foreign affairs. (1996, 69)

Research has not confirmed that exposure to certain types of cultural products affects thinking or behavior (Liebes and Katz 1990). Still, there is a longstanding belief in Canada in the power of culture industries to play this role. Early on, the Massey Commission Report of 1951 professed that "television refashions us in its own image." Years later, in their study of measures taken by the Canadian government against Canadian editions of U.S. magazines, Litvak and Maule (1974) explain why U.S. split-run magazines might be problematic. *Reader's Digest* has traditionally had a high circulation in Canada. During the 1950s the magazine contained numerous articles supportive of the Taiwan regime, critical of mainland China, and critical of Cuba. At the same time, the Canadian government and many in Canadian society were trying to promote good relations with China and Cuba. Editorial content in Canadian magazines generally reflected or confirmed this government position. Litvak and Maule contend that U.S. periodicals might inject into the debate an opinion that runs counter to the one favored by domestic groups. More recently, Gathercole (1987) notes that Canadian children watching episodes of popular U.S. action programs see

left-wing Central American governments portrayed as bad guys, echoing the message promoted by the U.S. Administration. Studies done in the last decade have shown that Canadian school children think the FBI is a Canadian police force and know more about the laws, institutions and mores of the United States than those of Canada. (1987, 80)

These sentiments have been echoed by Canada's deputy chief trade negotiator for CUSFTA. Gordon Ritchie stated a preference for the Canadian courtroom drama *Street Legal* over U.S. programs such as *L.A. Law* because the former is set in a Canadian court context, thus potentially educating Canadians about their own institutions. Furthermore, Ritchie contends that access to U.S. media has fanned the debate over gun control in Canada, a country with considerably fewer incidences of violent crime in general and fewer crimes committed with firearms.[7]

The vigor with which Canadian negotiators tried to protect the array of cultural policy instruments during the CUSFTA and NAFTA talks leads one to

7. Conversation with Gordon Ritchie in the offices of Strategico. May 25, 1995. Ottawa, Ontario.

believe that government intervention has produced viable culture industries in Canada. However, the evidence for this contention is ambiguous. Oft-quoted statistics include the following: Canadians spend 80 percent of their viewing time watching foreign, mostly American, television programming (Canada 1982, 6). Canadian content comprised 41 percent of all television programming available in Canada in 1999; foreign content comprised 59 percent.[8] Sixty-two percent of all English-language programming available in Canada in 1999 was foreign.[9] Over 75 percent of the books sold in Canada are imported. Between 5 and 15 percent of the magazines on Canadian newsstands are Canadian.[10] Approximately 71 percent of the domestic periodical market is comprised of imported foreign products. Almost 90 percent of earnings in the sound recording industry accrues to foreign-controlled firms marketing imported music. Foreign films occupy close to 96 percent of screen time in Canada (Magder 1993, 6). Canadian films shown in theaters achieved a market share of 2.1 percent in 1999.[11] Most of the large film distribution companies operating in Canada are under U.S. control, and they earn 85 percent of all the revenue from distribution to movie theaters. In the overwhelming majority of instances, "foreign" means "American." Therefore, the inroads being made by these policies are significant but not stunning. Why then, does the government persist in this strategy?

The Canadian government suggests that even the small portion of the Canadian market given over to domestic cultural producers represents progress. "There were hardly *any* Canadian books, records or films around 1950. . . . In the three decades since, a steady build-up of creative organizations has taken place" (Canada 1987, 12). Similarly, Grant and Wood (2004, 203) credit government subsidies and quotas in the television industry with producing a Canadian program production industry. But in addition to this positive assessment, there is another implicit assumption underlying the Canadian policy strategy of implementing and protecting support measures for the culture industries that is unique to the Canadian experience: east-west integration of the vast and sparsely populated Canadian space *requires* transportation and communications technology. In Canada's early history, the Canadian Pacific Railroad (CPR) was the "space-binding technology" that facilitated state building in the face of threatened U.S. territorial expansion northward. In the modern period, the

---

8. "Broadcasting" Quick Facts (updated June 2002). Canadian Cultural Observatory Culturescope website (http://www.culturescope.ca), accessed July 17, 2004.

9. Ibid.

10. "Publishing" Quick Facts (updated June 2002), ibid.

11. "Film and Video" Quick Facts (updated June 2002), ibid.

CBC specifically, and culture industries generally, provide the "space-binding technology" that allows Canada to be constituted as a nation (Berton 1974; Charland 1986). Where the construction of the CPR facilitated the physical linking of Canadians, Canadian public broadcasting and, later, the full range of culture industries are thought to link Canadians at a more profound level of national consciousness. "The popular mind, like the land, must be occupied" (Charland 1986, 206). This outcome will only be achieved if domestic cultural producers can be heard.

Consensus has not always prevailed over government support measures in the cultural sector in Canada. Powerful groups inside and outside Canadian society have fought the economic cost associated with various policies. Within Canada, more often than not, intergroup agreement about the goals of government policy has emerged, but not about the strategies that might lead to their achievement. Culture industry policy reflects an effort to balance many interests, so the policy choice that might *best* serve cultural goals does not always prevail. But of decisive importance to the present discussion is the fact that the most economically logical choice does not always prevail either. In some cases, economic and cultural goals can be served by the same policy. Where this is not so, the government has shown a willingness to set aside economic goals to promote domestic culture industries that can contribute to the formation of a distinctively Canadian "imagined community."

Challenges Facing Canadian Culture Industries

Culture industries are high-risk industries in all countries. Individual project costs are very high, as is the failure rate for cultural products.[12] But the challenge facing Canadian culture industries goes beyond the risk inherent in this sector. Several related issues make it very difficult for Canadian producers of cultural products to thrive in their own market, thus limiting the degree to which culture industries can participate in identity formation.

First, the Canadian market is relatively small. The country's population is approximately 30 million. As far as cultural products are concerned, though, this market must be subdivided even further to account for the two major linguistic communities in Canada. Therefore, the market for English-language products is approximately 20 million and the market for French-language products only

---

12. Even in the large American market, eight out of ten film and sound recording releases will not turn a profit. (Canada 1987, 16). For more on the risk associated with these industries, see Vogel (1998).

7 million (a variety of ethnic communities account for the remaining numbers), making it very difficult to recover costs, not to mention, make a profit. UNESCO estimates, for example, that a minimum population of 10 million is required to sustain a viable publishing industry (Canada 1987, 29). As film production costs increase, even the U.S. film industry recognizes the need to expand its market beyond its nearly 300 million inhabitants by selling internationally (*Variety* 1997, 1). Therefore, Canadian producers are decidedly disadvantaged by their small domestic market. The challenge is particularly acute in English Canada. French Canada is somewhat insulated by a language barrier; however, the province of Quebec remains very supportive of the federal culture industry stance.

Many countries have markets that are comparable to Canada's in size. Nevertheless, the challenges posed by Canada's small domestic market are intensified by Canada's close proximity to the United States and by the similarity of the two cultures. In the past, geographical distance provided a natural barrier to terrestrial signal transmission across national borders. Various policies still in operation reflect creative efforts to compensate for the easy reception of U.S. radio and television signals in Canada. Of course, in recent years, satellite and internet technology have caused the world to shrink, thus introducing distant lands to what Canada has experienced for decades. Nonetheless, Canada remains a particularly easy market for U.S. cultural products to penetrate because the majority of Canadians speak English and are familiar with, even share many elements of, U.S. culture and society.

The periodical industry provides an example of the difficulties associated with close proximity to the United States. Periodicals depend, to a large degree, on advertising revenues. Many U.S. publications are imported into Canada. Consequently, subsidiaries of U.S. companies operating within Canada do not always use the domestic Canadian media as an advertising outlet because they can feel reasonably confident that advertising dollars spent in U.S. publications also reach Canadian consumers. Canadian periodicals lose out on the advertising dollars that could be provided by businesses operating domestically. Therefore, Canada's geographical location compounds the degree to which its small domestic market leaves its culture industries at a disadvantage.

There are various ways in which Canadian producers might attempt to compensate for the small size of the domestic market. They could obtain loans from commercial financial institutions; augment revenues by obtaining the rights to distribute foreign cultural products in Canada; and export Canadian cultural products. But it has only been possible to exploit these avenues to a limited degree because of the pervasive U.S. influence in the Canadian cultural sector, thus necessitating compensatory government support measures if viable culture industries are to be created and maintained.

In any national market, the high risk associated with culture industries makes it difficult to get financial backing from mainstream institutions. Some established artists and companies can obtain financing by trading on their assets and reputations. For example, major U.S. motion picture studios and recording companies can offer film libraries or recording rights as collateral. Recently, it has become more common to offer stock options against future earnings (Wasser 1995). But artists that are newcomers or highly leveraged are unlikely to be able to exploit these possibilities.

Canadian cultural projects can look even riskier to a financial institution because they must demonstrate the likelihood of success against formidable U.S. competition present in the Canadian market. American products typically have a lower per-unit cost because their initial standardized runs of items like books, for example, are so much larger. Similar economies of scale are difficult, if not impossible, to achieve in the smaller Canadian market. In addition, U.S. producers generally recover the cost of production in their home market, thus finding themselves able to underprice Canadian competitors in many culture industries, such as television program production. "The huge American market is the only one where a producer can spend $1 million or so per hour for a top quality drama series and make an expected profit on this investment from domestic sales alone" (Hoskins and Mirus 1988, 502). The exception to this may be the U.S. film industry. As costs continue to mount for special effects and big-name stars, U.S. filmmakers are turning to international markets to make profits.

Recently, corporate mergers leading to ownership concentration, as well as vertical and horizontal integration, have become the trend globally in the cultural sector. Therefore, Canadian firms are competing with huge multinational conglomerates that have substantial resources behind them. In this high-risk industry, large conglomerates can offset losses against gains elsewhere in the corporate family, something few Canadian firms are yet in a position to do. Some Canadian firms, like Canwest Global and Rogers Communications, are following this trend. But while this strategy makes good business sense, there is resistance to it in Canada because of the accompanying loss of heterogeneity. The publishing industry is especially concerned with this issue.

> The Canadian-controlled industry has gone to significant lengths in trying to avoid industry concentration in market share and location. In general, there is a commitment to the notion that the industry can contribute the most to society, in the generation of ideas, information and development of authors, when numerous firms across the country are all seeking titles and authors. . . . As a cultural policy, the encouragement of heterogeneity in the industry is a powerful device. (Lorimer 1996, 17)

The inference in the above quotation is that heterogeneity is a good *cultural* policy and not a good *economic* policy. Lorimer and O'Donnell (1992, 508) report that in Canada "the primary contributors to the publication of domestic fiction and poetry, especially by first-time authors, are the myriad of small to medium-sized, heterogeneously oriented publishing firms scattered all over the country." This cultural benefit would be lost if firms were encouraged to streamline their operations through mergers. Therefore, in Canada there is little finance capital available from mainstream institutions for risky cultural products. In addition, there is resistance in government and cultural circles to economically logical steps that might make Canadian companies less risky because they are thought to limit opportunities for domestic producers.

Traditionally, culture industries rely not just on revenue from sales of domestic works, but also on revenue generated from distribution rights to foreign products. But because so many foreign enterprises are active in the distribution of imported cultural products in Canada, much of the sales revenue on foreign products generated inside Canada flows out of the country. Therefore, revenues from sales of cultural products in Canada are not reinvested in Canadian culture industries to finance subsequent projects.

> Canadian companies do not usually become self-financing by dealing in Canadian products alone. They depend on their ability to benefit, as distributing agents, from the sales of imported cultural goods. However, most cultural products imported into Canada are distributed not by Canadian companies, but by subsidiaries of the foreign production or distribution company. (Canada 1987, 21)

This is not the case in other advanced industrialized nations.[13] The problem is particularly acute in the book publishing, sound recording, and film industries. Books reach the Canadian retail outlet in one of three ways: they are purchased from Canadian publishers; they are imported into Canada and sent to retailers by Canadian-based distributors; and they are sold directly to the retailer by the foreign supplier, thus bypassing the Canadian distributor. Statistics from the period of NAFTA negotiations show that the third category accounted for almost 50 percent of the Canadian book market (Canada 1987, 27). In

---

13. Canadian magazines attempting to penetrate the American market have discovered this. Carol-Anne Hayes, president of Toronto-based Where Magazines International, which publishes fifteen city magazines in the U.S., is quoted as saying: "There's a lot of wealth down there. But you can't go unless you work with American publishers or franchisers." *Folio: The Magazine for Magazine Management* 24, 17 (October 15, 1995): 32–34.

addition, subsidiaries of foreign publishers account for the majority of book sales in Canada.[14] Here we see specific evidence of how structural impediments restrict the ability of Canadian publishers to be self-financing because Canadian publishers have limited access to the revenues generated within their own home market.

Furthermore, Canadian publishers earn little of the revenue generated by distribution of foreign titles in Canada. It is common in the book publishing industry to view Canada as an extension of the U.S. market (Lorimer 1996, 14). Canadian publishers often find that they are not in the running for the rights to publish foreign titles in Canada because it is current practice to sell *North American* rights, rather than separate Canadian and U.S. rights. As such, Canadian publishers lose out on the revenue that could be reinvested in the domestic publishing industry.

In the sound recording industry, non-Canadian companies dominate the distribution of recordings. Sound recordings are generally made from master tapes. Subsidiaries of the major foreign recording companies—Warner Brothers, Columbia, RCA, PolyGram, MCA—commonly import the master tapes into Canada and turn them into the finished product in their local branch plants. In 1992–93, 81 percent of total industry revenues came from sound recordings manufactured in Canada in foreign subsidiary plants, based on imported master tapes (Straw 1996, 98). Non-Canadian recording companies set up branch plants in Canada to skirt tariffs on imported recordings that existed prior to the signing of the CUSFTA.[15] In so doing, they provided their own Canadian distribution service, thus leaving Canadian firms to the production and distribution of Canadian recordings, and the retail of Canadian and foreign sound recordings.

In the film industry, distributors play a pivotal role. In Canada, the distribution process is controlled by U.S. interests. As is the case in publishing, the Canadian market is considered to be an extension of the American one. Therefore, once again, the rights to distribute films in Canada are often sold as part of a package to distribute films within the broader North American market (Magder 1996, 152; Pendakur 1990, 258).[16] Canadian distributors that cannot survive by distributing Canadian films alone are deprived of supplementary income from their own film market. This, in turn, means less money is being funneled back into the production process.

14. In 1985, for example, Statistics Canada showed 201 publishing companies operating in Canada. Of these, 29 were foreign. These 29 accounted for 58 percent of book sales.

15. Tariffs have ranged from 10 to 15 percent on sound recordings. In the mid 1980s, prior to the signing of the Free Trade Agreement between Canada and the United States, the tariff was 14 percent. See Straw, 1996: 102.

16. A recent exception is the deal between the Canadian distributor, Alliance Communications, and Miramax, giving Alliance exclusive rights in Canada to release 50 Miramax films over five years.

Hollywood's international success, especially in the feature film market, is tied to the distribution activities of the major studios. . . . Because feature filmmaking is such a costly and risky venture, control over the circuit of distribution is vital to long-term financial success. (Magder 1996, 152)

In 1989–90, just before NAFTA talks opened, subsidiaries of U.S. firms operating in Canada accounted for 85 percent of the revenues from film and video distribution (Magder 1996, 152). If control of distribution is crucial to success in film production, then Canadian filmmakers are undeniably disadvantaged. The three stages inherent in the culture industries—production, distribution, and exhibition—are interrelated. The fact that Canadians have been unable to establish an indigenous distribution system in film, book publishing, or sound recording has consequences for the level of production in these industries, as well as the likelihood that what is produced will reach the public.

In other industries, export markets can be used to compensate for the small domestic market. Cultural products typically sell best in their home market. American success in marketing its cultural products abroad is the exception and not the rule.[17] For anglophone Canadian producers of cultural products, it would make most sense to penetrate the U.S. market, but they have had limited success. Recording artists and a select group of Canadian authors are exceptional in this regard. As far as Canadian films and television programming are concerned, Americans prefer stories set in the United States.[18] American producers prefer to copy the format of foreign films and programs, rather than importing the product itself.[19] Therefore, Canada is caught in a catch-22 situation. The government wants to promote exports of Canadian products so as to stimulate an indigenous industry that contributes to identity formation. But products with a more universal, as opposed to local, bent travel best.[20] The result is a two-track

17. In 1993, the U.S. film industry generated a $4 billion surplus, second only to defense and aerospace exports in its contribution to U.S. balance of trade. *Wall Street Journal,* March 26, 1993, R6.

18. Hoskins and Mirus call Americans "unusually intolerant of foreign programming." See Hoskins and Mirus, 1988: 504.

19. American viewers, in general, will not accept dubbing or subtitling and do not appreciate British accents. Therefore, rather than importing the British situation comedies *Man about the House* or *George and Mildred,* American producers created the American equivalents *Three's Company* and *The Ropers.* Indeed, in the 1970s the long-running British soap opera, *Coronation Street,* was offered free of charge to any American network that would give it a trial run of several months, but none accepted (*Variety,* Oct. 1986, 87) In film a similar approach prevails. For example, rather than importing the highly successful French films, *La Femme Nikita* and *Trois Hommes et Un Couffin,* American versions were produced and released as *Point of No Return* and *Three Men and a Baby.*

20. It is informative to note the Canadian movies that have had some success in the American market. They include *Porky's, Meatballs, Quest for Fire,* and various David Cronenberg thrillers, including *Scanners.* None of these films could be identified as Canadian by its content.

industry wherein some products are successfully exported, while others contribute to the cultural mission of the industry. Any overlap is often inadvertent.

Researchers have attempted to account for the limited appeal of culture industry exports. They differ from other exports because the country of origin of a cultural product appears to affect satisfaction with the product. The same cannot be said for the vast majority of export commodities. Hoskins and Mirus (1988) have introduced the notion of the "cultural discount." They argue that a

> particular programme rooted in one culture, and thus attractive in that environment, will have a diminished appeal elsewhere as viewers find it difficult to identify with the style, values, beliefs, institutions and behavioural patterns of the material in question. . . . As a result of the diminished appeal, fewer viewers will watch a foreign programme than a domestic programme of the same type and quality. (1988, 500)

Numerous qualifications must be made as the cultural discount will vary across genres of programming (Lorimer and O'Donnell 1992, 494). For example, the cultural discount will be much greater for news and public affairs programming than for drama. Nevertheless, overall, the value of many cultural products is greatest in their market of origin.

The cultural discount also varies across countries and this provides some insight into the relative success of U.S. culture industry exports compared with their Canadian counterparts. While U.S. exports lose their value, they do so to a lesser degree than the cultural exports of other countries. Hoskins and Mirus (1988) suggest that this has to do with the commercial philosophy that dominates the culture industries in the United States. Television broadcasting provides an informative example. The tradition in the United States has been to provide programming free of charge to the viewer and to finance the service by selling the audience to advertisers. Maximizing revenue means maximizing audience size, but programming with mass appeal makes a limited contribution to identity formation. Indeed, appealing to audiences comprised of various linguistic and ethnic groups requires neutralizing attributes of the product that are group-specific. American producers of cultural products are increasingly targeting not only their diverse domestic market, but also a global audience. Therefore, their strategy is to create cultural products with universal appeal (Wasser 1995).

Overall, then, U.S. cultural exports diminish in value as they cross national borders, but relatively less than cultural exports from other countries. A country like Canada is at a comparative disadvantage in exporting its cultural products because finance capital is limited and its most logical export market is relatively inhospitable to cultural products that clearly herald their Canadian roots. Canadian artists have had some success exporting to other markets besides the United States. But this success is limited to specific niches in which Canadian artists have distinguished themselves, such as children's programming (Collins 1990). In general, in more mainstream forms of cultural expression, such as feature films or television programs, Canadian producers find it difficult to compete against U.S. exports in third markets.

Canadian cultural producers, distributors, and exhibitors have limited access to their own market, and to foreign ones, for a variety of reasons. Classical economic theory would suggest that countries should allow competitively disadvantaged industries to perish so that valuable resources can be directed toward other, economically lucrative sectors. The Canadian government has not adopted this strategy with regard to the cultural sector. Instead, it has made a substantial and sustained effort to correct the structural impediments that restrict Canadian culture industries.

This is all the more interesting given that the Canadian government does not provide similar support to indigenous producers in other industries. For example, in the automobile industry, the Canadian government is content to have parts and assembly plants for U.S. companies, like Chrysler and Ford. At no time has there been an effort to design a "Canadian" car. Instead, over thirty years ago, the automobile industry was the first to be continentalized under the Auto Pact. Prime Minister Mulroney's words confirm the different way in which the car industry is perceived.

Under the Auto Pact, we have developed an industry in which 130,000 Canadians are directly employed, which accounts for 15 per cent of all our manufacturing, and more than one third, some $35 billion, of all our trade with the United States. That's more trade than we do with all the rest of the world. Since 1979, there's been seven billion dollars in direct new investment in the automotive and parts industry in Canada, mostly in Ontario for reasons of geography and proximity to U.S. markets. That was a tremendous boost for Ontario and Canada. And with that economic strength, our confidence in ourselves as a people has grown accordingly. *We're not any less Canadian because of it.*[21]

Yet in culture industries, the same approach does not prevail.

---

21. "Notes for an address to the Nation on the Trade Initiative by the Right Honourable Brian Mulroney, P.C., M.P., Prime Minister of Canada," Ottawa, June 16, 1986, p.3. Archival records of the Canadian Trade Negotiations Office, file 5420–1. Emphasis mine.

There is no question about it. Canada's cultural industries—including broadcasting, film production, sound recording and publishing—form one of the most difficult and sensitive areas in our relations with the United States. *The volume of bilateral trade in this sector is not particularly high*—imports and exports came to something over one and a half billion dollars last year including licencing fees, or less than one percent of our total two-way trade. But *this is not a sector like any other. . . .* Cultural industries are not just culture, they are by definition also industry. And as industry, they are subject to business factors like economy of scale and market dominance. Canada has a population and an economy just a tenth the size of our American neighbours. American products already dominate our television and movie screens, our book and record shops. Our cultural industries simply cannot compete directly across the board with their mammoth US counterparts, no matter how good our authors, filmmakers and other cultural figures are individually. Now, this would not be a problem if the industry in question was widgets. One widget is pretty much the same as any other widget, so it would not make sense for Canada to compete with the US in widgets unless we had an economic advantage of some kind. But *Canadian cultural products are emphatically not the same as American cultural products.* Cultural products express cultural identity, something individual to a given nation. Therefore, *you cannot simply let American cultural products substitute freely for Canadian, unless you are willing to put open competition for its own sake ahead of maintaining our cultural heritage.*[22]

Since the Canadian dollar fell in value relative to the U.S. dollar in the 1980s, cities like Toronto and Vancouver have played host to numerous U.S. film and television crews. In 1986, at the height of CUSFTA negotiations, the Alliance of Canadian Cinema, Television, and Radio Artists (ACTRA) reported that its eight thousand members earned $84 million the year before, up 21 percent from 1984. ACTRA's scriptwriters doubled their earnings in 1985 to $4.5 million ("Casting," 1986, 34). These increases were attributed to the emergence of "Hollywood North"—U.S. film and television crews flocked to Canada to take advantage of the favorable exchange rate. In addition, Canadian technical workers are highly skilled and eager and Canadian cities can very easily be made to look like American ones. This phenomenon created thousands of jobs and

22. External Affairs Canada Confidential Facsimile entitled "Notes and Speech Modules: Telecomm and Culture," pp. 10–11. Archival records of the Canadian Trade Negotiations Office, file 5420–1. Emphasis mine.

revenue for the provinces involved. But other statistics explain why the federal government insisted on exclusion of culture industries from CUSFTA. For example, in 1985, the film industry in British Columbia employed thirty-two hundred people and contributed $70 million to the provincial economy. But only two of thirty films produced there that year were Canadian. It is for this reason that the Canadian government persists in implementing measures to stimulate indigenous production of television programming and feature films despite the handsome economic benefits provided by Hollywood's presence in Canada. This film industry policy is emblematic of the broader approach to Canadian cultural policy. Cultural goals motivate the measures, making them examples not of conventional protectionism, but of embedded liberalism.

Overview of Federal Policies Affecting Culture Industries

In its 1982 report to the federal government, the Federal Cultural Policy Review Committee noted that the Canadian government uses a range of approaches to support culture industries (Canada 1982, 72–90). The government acts as *proprietor,* participating directly in the ownership and operation of cultural enterprises, such as the CBC and the National Film Board. It serves as *patron,* providing direct infusions of public money into cultural activity through such mechanisms as loans and grants. The government plays the role of *catalyst* by establishing tax incentives for private investment in and contributions to cultural activity. In addition, the Canadian government acts as *regulator,* making and enforcing laws governing the ownership and operation of cultural enterprises.[23] In general, all of these guises are guided by an overall desire to participate in culture industries "at arm's length" so as to ensure freedom of expression.

Of course, the government does not have unrestricted scope in implementing communications policy, regardless of its desire to use culture industries for cultural purposes. The need to ensure freedom of expression is just one limiting factor, dictated by the prevailing ideological climate in Canada. Even if the government were willing to restrict access to American cultural products, pragmatic considerations would sabotage such a strategy. Canadian voters have become accustomed to having access to U.S entertainment and would protest its loss. Furthermore, geography militates against any restrictive measures the government might introduce. The vast majority of Canadians live within a

---

23. The report adds another category that has little relevance for culture industries, suggesting that the government acts as *custodian* of sites and artifacts of cultural and historic interest, as well as the broader natural environment.

hundred miles of the U.S.–Canada border. Consequently, most can receive U.S. television signals, for example, with a standard roof antenna. Measures viewed as too stringent might cause Canadians to bypass the domestic cable system that currently makes television signals available, thus placing much of broadcasting beyond the reach of Canadian regulatory officials. In addition, within the culture industries there is disagreement on the role the government should play, and within the federal government itself, there are departments whose agendas conflict. Therefore, the government must work within certain parameters when it devises policies to aid domestic culture industries.

Nonetheless, despite these differences, overall intergroup agreement about the general cultural goals of communications policy seems to prevail. This has been noted with regard to the early history of television broadcasting policy, for example.

> General agreement on objectives was achieved because they reflected Canadian goals and aspirations. The declared national purpose of broadcasting was what reconciled proponents of commercial and public broadcasting, and produced at various times unanimity among political parties in Parliament. (Peers 1979, 414)

This notion is echoed by Jack Pickersgill,[24] minister in charge of broadcasting policy in 1958, when the Broadcasting Act was revised and made more explicit as to the connection between broadcasting and national identity. His observation has special relevance for radio policy: "I have a predilection for the free play of economic forces; indeed I belong to a party which has this predilection. But . . . there would be no distinctively Canadian content to radio broadcasting if it were left to undiluted commercial enterprise."[25]

More recently, Audley points to "the substantial measure of agreement which existed between government and the affected industries concerning the nature of the problems and the policy goals to be pursued" during the free trade talks (Audley 1994, 335). In addition, Doern and Tomlin (1991) report that one of the most powerful business lobbies in Canada, the Business Council on National Issues (BCNI), helped the Mulroney government in its efforts to exclude culture industries from CUSFTA. Made up of the CEOs of the most influential corporations in Canada, the BCNI were strong advocates of a comprehensive free trade deal with the United States. Nonetheless,

---

24. At this time, broadcasting was part of the portfolio of the Secretary of State.
25. House of Commons Debates, July 15, 1958, 2252–3, cited in Peers, 1979: 433.

BCNI also supported the government in its efforts to secure an exemption from the agreement of Canada's cultural industries. American business interests identified culture with the entertainment business, and saw only Canadian efforts to protect another industry. BCNI made a serious effort to convince its American counterpart that cultural issues were a sensitive and legitimate element in the Canadian political equation. (Doern and Tomlin 1991, 108)

Furthermore, in addition to the business, government, and cultural communities, Canadian voters support the cultural goals of Canadian communications policy. For example, a 1983 survey commissioned by the Department of Communications reported that 70 percent of Canadians (and 80 percent of Quebeckers) wanted television programming on Canadian stations to be more reflective of their lives (Gathercole 1987, 82). In addition, surveys taken before and during CUSFTA talks indicated a strong fear among Canadians that free trade would mean cultural homogenization of Canada. Therefore, it seems apparent that the desire to distinguish the Canadian imagined community is widely felt in Canada.

Some federal policies apply to the cultural sector as a whole, while others target specific industries, but all seek to correct the limitations on Canadian producers. For example, the Cultural Industries Development Fund, instituted in 1991 by the Department of Communications[26] in cooperation with the Federal Business Development Bank, targets the cultural sector as a whole. It makes investment capital and loans available to culture industry projects deemed too risky by mainstream financial institutions. This policy is in direct response to the difficulties encountered by viable Canadian producers in obtaining commercial financing to undertake cultural projects.

Perhaps the most prominent example of a measure designed for the entire sector are Sections 14 and 15 of the Investment Canada Act that seek to limit foreign ownership of culture industries. This is particularly illustrative of the preeminence given to cultural goals in the culture industries, since the Investment Canada Act was designed to stimulate foreign investment in other culturally neutral Canadian industries. "Recognizing that increased capital and technology would benefit Canada, the purpose of this Act is to encourage investment in Canada by Canadians and non-Canadians that contributes to economic growth and employment opportunities."[27]

---

26. Please note that the Department of Communications was replaced in 1995 by the Department of Canadian Heritage.

27. Section 2, Investment Canada Act, June 20, 1985, *Revised Statutes of Canada*, 1985, 1st Supplement, chapter 28 (Ottawa: Queen's Printer, 1988)

Section 14(5) of the act stipulates that proposed foreign purchases of "cultural businesses"[28] are "reviewable." Section 15 specifies that the federal government can review an investment by a non-Canadian if "it falls within a prescribed specific type of business activity that, in the opinion of the Governor in Council, is related to Canada's cultural heritage or national identity." Culture industries have special status in the act because there is a generally acknowledged link between Canadian ownership of culture industries and production and distribution of Canadian cultural goods. Recent statistics confirm this link. For example, in sound recording, "more than 250 small Canadian companies produce 90 percent of Canadian artists' recordings."[29] In book publishing, Canadian firms publish about 78 percent of Canadian-authored titles. In film, Canadian firms distributed 95 percent of the Canadian films released in 1983 (Canada 1987, 21).

What might qualify as a "Canadian" cultural good? The minister overseeing culture industry policy during the CUSFTA talks asserted the following:

Not all Canadian creators produce "Canadian" works, or would want to; nor do they all even create in Canada. Visual and performing arts are rooted in our human senses, beyond the call of place. Individual writers and filmmakers reach in essence for stories and insights that are universally significant. . . . But inextricably our culture and our life as a nation are intertwined. As the reflection of who we are, our cultural expression becomes the aggregate of our voices and creative energies. (Canada 1987, 7)

Therefore, Canadian government communications policy is evidently not founded on the assumption that every cultural product created by a Canadian must treat recognizably Canadian themes.[30] But each society ostensibly does have

28. "Cultural business" means a Canadian business that carries on any of the following activities, namely,

(a) the publication, distribution or sale of books, magazines, periodicals or newspapers in print or machine readable form, other than the sole activity of printing or typesetting of books, magazines, periodicals or newspapers,

(b) the production, distribution, sale or exhibition of film or video recordings,

(c) the production, distribution, sale or exhibition of audio or video music recordings,

(d) the publication, distribution or sale of music in print or machine readable form, or

(e) radio communication in which the transmissions are intended for direct reception by the general public, any radio, television and cable television broadcasting undertakings and any satellite programming and broadcast network services;

29. Department of Canadian Heritage, Fact Sheet—Canada's Sound Recording Industry, http://www.pch.gc.ca/special/tomorrowstartstoday/en-back-2001–06–26–fs1.html.

30. Still, a body of literature exists that suggests that certain recognizable themes do recur in one national literature, but not in others. See, for example, Atwood 1972; and Corse 1997.

a set of values associated with it, rooted in such things as its unique geography and historical experience. The perspective that an individual brings to her creative endeavors is thought to reflect, among other things, her national origins, and it is this element that might contribute to the creation of Canadian cultural goods. Indeed, this is, in many ways, a banal insight. *Only* Canadians can produce Canadian cultural products or, perhaps more accurately, Canadians can *only* produce Canadian cultural products. The same can be said for any other national group. Yet banal as this insight may be, it encapsulates the perceived tension inherent in sustaining a distinctive national community within an open, global economy. If only Canadians can produce Canadian cultural goods, then less costly, more efficiently produced, even higher-quality U.S. products cannot be substituted for them and make the same contribution to collective identity formation or a cohesive population. The logic of comparative advantage breaks down when applied to culture industries.

In addition to those policies that apply to the cultural sector as a whole, there are numerous other policies and programs that are designed to address the challenges of specific industries. Measures undertaken to benefit the film industry, the periodical and book publishing industries, sound recording, and radio and television broadcasting are examined below.

Film

The Canadian film industry is perhaps the weakest of all the Canadian culture industries. The Canadian government did not show the same zeal in developing support measures toward the film industry that it did in broadcasting, for example. At the same time the government was actively establishing a Canadian broadcasting system, it showed little effort to move away from foreign, mostly American, imports in film (Magder 1993; Pendakur 1990). Perhaps the one exception to this was the creation of the National Film Board of Canada (NFB) in 1939.

The original purpose of the National Film Board was to "make and distribute films designed to help Canadians in all parts of Canada to understand the ways of living and the problems of Canadians in other parts."[31] The NFB made films used in the recruitment of immigrants and for the war effort, thus inaugurating the tradition of documentary filmmaking for which it is known. Early in its history, feature films were seen to be outside the mandate of the NFB. John Grierson, the film board's founder and director until 1945, viewed feature

31. Website of the National Film Board of Canada, http://www.nfb.ca/e/mandate/mand1. html. Quoting 1939 enabling legislation for National Film Commission, later National Film Board.

film as popular culture that "pandered to the lowest common denominator" and eschewed it as a cultural form (Pendakur 1990). Grierson wanted to make the NFB the "eyes of Canada" to allow Canadians to, "through a national use of cinema, see Canada and see it whole: its people and its purpose."[32] His vision for the NFB was to make documentary films that would reinforce democratic ideals and good citizenship (Pendakur 1990). This focus on documentaries meant that no indigenous feature film industry would be cultivated by the NFB.

The federal government did not introduce legislation designed to stimulate feature film production until the 1960s. Evidence suggests that few interested groups sought such measures until the cultural climate in Canada changed, largely in response to the Quiet Revolution in Quebec (Magder 1993). During the 1940s and 1950s, the government reached an agreement with the major Hollywood studios. The agreement is widely viewed as a failure because it relied on the U.S. studios to distribute Canadian films voluntarily. The Americans made no firm commitments as to where or how many Canadian films would be distributed. In the end, the Americans did not adhere to the general agreement (Pendakur 1990), and Canadian filmmakers soon recognized that national legislation would be required to stimulate an indigenous film industry. Their lobbying convinced the federal government to develop film policy as they had developed support measures for other culture industries. But, by this time, U.S. companies already had a firm hold on the Canadian film industry that has proved difficult to loosen.

A Canadian feature film industry materialized in the 1960s, largely in response to federal policies designed to compensate for the challenges facing Canadian filmmakers in both the production and distribution stages of the filmmaking process. These early programs to aid the film industry, however, were geared specifically toward financing production, acknowledging that feature filmmaking is very costly and that investment capital is scarce. Attempts to redress the disadvantage in distribution came later and proved to be unpopular among powerful U.S. lobbies operating in Canada.

The federal government inaugurated The Canadian Film Development Corporation (CFDC) in 1967 with an initial budget of $10 million, marking the beginning of serious efforts on the part of federal officials to stimulate an indigenous film industry. The agency was renamed Telefilm Canada in 1984 to reflect its mandate to produce films for both theater and television audiences. In recent years, it has expanded this mandate even further, becoming "a cultural investor in film, television, new media and music."[33] Its stated mission is to

32. Website of the National Film Board of Canada, http://www.nfb.ca/e/index_about.html.
33. Website of Telefilm Canada, http://www.telefilm.gc.ca/01/11.asp.

provide "financial assistance and strategic leverage to the industry in producing high-quality works—e.g. feature films, drama series, documentaries, children's programming, variety shows and new media products—that reflect Canadian society, including its linguistic duality and cultural diversity."[34]

Telefilm Canada administers a number of programs, including the Canadian Broadcast Program Development Fund (CBPDF), the Feature Film Fund, and the Equity Investment Program, intended to help filmmakers and producers of programs for television finance their projects. The Feature Film Fund is perhaps Telefilm's most significant program for filmmakers, providing assistance for screenwriting, production, marketing, and promotion. In 2000, Minister of Canadian Heritage Sheila Copps, announced the new Canadian Feature Film Policy, entitled "From Script to Screen." Among other things, this new policy doubles the resources of the Feature Film Fund to an annual budget of $100 million (cdn). Copps justified the increase in the following terms:

> Thanks to the stories they tell, which represent our societies in all their diversity, filmmakers help bring Canadians together while providing us with a window on the world. . . . This investment demonstrates the government's continued commitment towards an industry that has made—and continues to make—a significant contribution to the cultural life of our country.[35]

This latest increase reaffirms the substantial growth in Telefilm funding over the years. In 1989–90, its budget reached $150 million (cdn) (Magder 1993, 5). By 2002, Telefilm's budget climbed to $230 million (cdn).[36] Of course, only Canadian productions are entitled to Telefilm assistance.

A point system enables Telefilm to determine whether applicants for funding are proposing film projects with adequate Canadian content. The ten-point scale varies by genre (animation, live action, etc.); however, in all cases, the director or screenwriter, as well as one lead performer, must be Canadian. Applicants then accumulate points if other key personnel are Canadian. In addition, they must ensure that 75 percent of production and postproduction services costs are paid to Canadians or incurred for services in Canada. Prior to 1996, Telefilm usually stipulated an eight-point score; however, there was no formal requirement to this effect. As of 1996, Telefilm formally committed to financing only those

34. Ibid.

35. "The Government of Canada Announces its New Feature Film Policy," News Release, Ministry of Canadian Heritage, October 5, 2000. http://www.pch.gc.ca/newsroom/news_e.cfm?Action =Display&code=0NR129E

36. Website of the Ministry of Canadian Heritage, Government of Canada, http://www.telefilm.gc.ca/01/11.asp.

productions obtaining eight or more points. Since that time, almost 90 percent of productions have received nine or ten points.[37]

The government revised its policy toward the feature film industry in 1974 because, although money from the Telefilm public fund significantly boosted the number of Canadian films getting produced, it did not get them on screen. Therefore, the federal government established the Canadian Audio-Visual Certification Office (CAVCO) to administer the Capital Cost Allowance (CCA).[38] The strategy behind CCA entailed stimulating private investment in Canadian film production, thereby increasing the budgets of Canadian films in the hopes that those produced would be more attractive to U.S. distributors (Magder 1993). The CCA gave investors a 100 percent deduction of investment in certified feature films, providing Canadians were employed in key creative and technical capacities. Before the CCA, investors in film projects of any national affiliation were entitled to deduct 60 percent of capital costs in the year the film was made (Pendakur 1990, 170). The boom in Canadian feature film production during the 1970s is widely attributed to the CCA. However the tax shelter was eventually scaled back in the 1980s once that boom slowed. At the height of the boom in 1979, sixty-six feature films were produced with an average budget of $2.6 million (Pendakur 1990, 172). Three years later, only thirty certified Canadian feature-length films were made, with an average budget of $1 million, in part because many of those produced during the boom were not distributed or were viewed as poor quality. Therefore, in 1983, the CCA was revised to allow capital cost deduction at a rate of 50 percent per year over two years. Five years later, the deduction rate returned to its pre-1974 level of 30 percent per year (Magder 1993).

In 1996, the Canadian Film or Video Production Tax Credit (CPTC) replaced the CCA. It provides a refundable tax credit of up to 12 percent of total costs on Canadian productions.

> The CPTC is available at a rate of 25% of eligible salaries and wages incurred after 1994. Eligible salaries and wages qualifying for the tax credit may not exceed 48% of the cost of the production, net of assistance, as certified by the Minister of Canadian Heritage. Therefore, the tax credit could provide assistance of up to 12% of the cost of production, net of assistance.[39]

37. "Canadian Audio-Visual Certification Office (CAVCO) 2000–2001 Activity Report," Website of the Ministry of Canadian Heritage, http://www.pch.gc.ca/progs/ac-ca/progs/bcpac-cavco/pubs/2000–01/english.htm.

38. CAVCO certifies the Canadian content of films and estimates qualified labor expenses.

39. Website of the Ministry of Canadian Heritage, http://www.pch.gc.ca/progs/ac-ca/progs/bcpac-cavco/progs/cipc-cptc/index_e.cfm.

In addition to the CPTC, the federal government administers the Film or Video Production Services Tax Credit to attract foreign productions to Canada. It offers an 11 percent tax credit for wages paid to Canadians or costs paid to Canadian companies.

The establishment of Telefilm Canada and the introduction of the CCA only partially addressed the problems associated with U.S. dominance of film distribution by replacing scarce finance capital and lost revenues on distribution rights. However, problems remained in getting the films produced with this money onto Canadian screens. In the 1960s, various film industry advocacy groups favored government programs targeting the financing of production, believing that the U.S. subsidiaries would distribute them (Magder 1996; Pendakur 1990). This did not turn out to be the case. In the 1980s, the Canadian film industry began calling for a fundamental restructuring of the industry in order to establish Canada as a distribution market separate from the United States, thus giving Canadian distributors greater access to the revenues from film rights (Pendakur 1990). The proposed legislation never did make it to Parliament for approval. The U.S. Congress threatened to vote down the Canada-U.S. Free Trade Agreement that was under negotiation between the two governments if the Canadian federal government went ahead with plans to restructure distribution.

More recently, the federal government has turned its attention once more to distribution, but to little avail. In early 1997, Canada refused to allow the Dutch firm PolyGram to distribute nonproprietary films in the Canadian market without a Canadian distributor. Polygram could distribute proprietary products, those films and videos for which Polygram holds world distribution rights or for which it was a majority investor in production. American firms would continue their distribution activity due to a "grandfathering" provision in the proposed legislation. The European Union challenged Canada before the World Trade Organization, arguing that this measure violates Canada's trading commitments, especially those pertaining to most-favored nation status.[40]

Although the Canadian government is ostensibly not content to have a "branch plant" arrangement prevail in the film industry, it has not followed through on efforts to restructure the domestic film industry, specifically the crucial area of film distribution. Given that Hollywood is such a key contributor to U.S. balance of trade, the Canadian government justifiably expects that such a restructuring effort would be met with potentially devastating retaliatory measures. In addition, there is some evidence in the records of the Department of Foreign Affairs and International Trade suggesting that the distribution restructuring proposal was used as a concession in the CUSFTA negotiations.

40. This suit was eventually dropped when ownership of Polygram changed hands. Canadian Seagram purchased Universal in 1995. Universal subsequently purchased Polygram in 1998.

Most recently, the Ministry of Canadian Heritage has taken a new approach. The new Canadian Feature Film Policy announced in 2000 "signals a major shift in the federal government's support of Canadian feature films—from building an industry to building an audience."[41] The press release announcing inauguration of the new policy puts it this way:

> The industry has arrived. Movies such as *I've Heard the Mermaids Singing, Jésus de Montréal, Margaret's Museum, The Red Violin, Les Boys* and *New Waterford Girl* stand as testament to the talent of Canadian creators and the strong foundation that has been laid. Despite the successes, Canadian films capture only a small share of total box office receipts. It is now time to refocus efforts from building an industry to building an audience at home and internationally.[42]

Restructuring of the distribution system is not part of this policy. Nonetheless, improving marketing and distribution is a central goal. Some money is earmarked for "alternative distribution networks," like film festivals. The lion's share, however, $40 million of the $50-million-dollar increase that the new policy promises, goes to the "Project Development, Production and Marketing Assistance Program." Some money will go directly to distributors to augment their marketing budgets, but more will go to producers to allow them to increase their average production budgets. In large part, this strategy equates likelihood of wide distribution with quality of film, which is, in turn, linked to size of production budget. Not just any film can qualify for assistance. Priority will be given to "culturally-relevant Canadian feature films."[43] The policy also includes funds for screenwriting assistance, "low-budget, director-driven feature film projects," as well as new filmmakers.

The target goal of the policy is a sobering one. This new policy, heralded with much fanfare and commitment of large sums of money, aims "to capture 5 percent of the domestic box office in five years and to increase audiences for feature films abroad."[44] Indeed, the government characterizes this as an "ambitious" goal. In 1999, Canadian films captured 2.1 percent of domestic box office receipts. That

---

41. "From Script to Screen: New Policy Directions for Canadian Feature Film," p. 1. Minister of Public Works and Government Services Canada, 2000. Available on the website of the Ministry of Canadian Heritage, http://www.pch.gc.ca/pc-ch/sujets-subjects/arts-culture/film-video/pubs/script-screen.pdf

42. "The Government of Canada Announces its New Feature Film Policy," News Release, Ministry of Canadian Heritage, October 5, 2000. http://www.pch.gc.ca/newsroom/news_e.cfm?Action = Display&code = 0NR129E

43. Ibid.

44. Ibid.

same year, domestic films captured 37 percent of the box office in Japan, 30 percent in France, and 14 percent in Italy and Spain.[45] Canadian numbers are unacceptable not only for commercial reasons, although these are clearly relevant. Rather, increasing the share of Canadian box office that Canadian films capture is desirable because "film matters" and because Canadians should have access to their own market.

> Film is a powerful and enduring medium that influences the way we see the world by offering compelling pictures of faces, places and experiences that we might not otherwise encounter. Film matters because it provides a window on history and a mirror of society, allowing us to reflect on the past and assess the present. . . . Film is a hub of cultural expression where print, music and image meet.[46]

Periodical and Book Publishing

Until the mid 1990s, the policy strategy adopted by the federal government in the periodical industry resembled that of the film industry in that the focus was on providing or freeing up capital. However, a 1997 decision by the World Trade Organization dispute settlement mechanism caused a policy reorientation. Early policy sprang from the notion that the periodical industry relies primarily on advertising revenues to finance its operations. For this reason, Bill C-58 amended Section 19.1 of the Income Tax Act,[47] stipulating that Canadian advertisers could not deduct the expense of advertising in foreign periodicals aimed at a Canadian audience, thus encouraging Canadian businesses to support domestic print media rather than advertising in U.S. periodicals that circulate in the Canadian market. To qualify as Canadian, a periodical had to be 75 percent Canadian-owned with 80 percent of its editorial material originating in Canada (Canada 1987, 38). "The intent was to redirect to Canadian magazines some of the considerable advertising revenues that had been flowing into multinational coffers" (Canada 1982, 225). While the Canada Council and the Social Sciences and Humanities Research Council (SSHRC) offer grants to literary, artistic,

---

45. Ibid.

46. "From Script to Screen: New Policy Directions for Canadian Feature Film," p. 3. Minister of Public Works and Government Services Canada, 2000. Available on the website of the Ministry of Canadian Heritage, http://www.pch.gc.ca/pc-ch/sujets-subjects/arts-culture/film-video/pubs/script-screen.pdf

47. Section 19, Income Tax Act, Revised Statutes of Canada. 1985, 5th Supplement, chapter 1 (Ottawa: Queen's Printer, 1992)

scholarly, and children's periodicals, the Income Tax Act provision made available substantial amounts of money for more mainstream Canadian periodicals.

Compounding the difficulties of Canadian magazines trying to compete with their U.S. counterparts are split-run magazines, those foreign periodicals that produce Canadian editions for the Canadian market. Commonly, little about the Canadian edition is different from the American one, except the addition of a few pages of reporting on Canadian events or personalities. But the Canadian edition does use Canadian advertisers, enticing their business with prices for advertising space that are below competitive rates. For example, in the mid 1990s, the split-run edition of *Sports Illustrated* charged $6,250 (Cdn) for a four-color page, while *Maclean's*, Canada's leading news magazine, charged $26,295 (Cdn) for the same (Newman 1994, 47). The split-run editions can underprice to such a degree because, in most cases, their costs have already been recovered in the American home market. This split-run strategy can divert a substantial amount of finite advertising dollars away from Canadian periodicals and has, over the years, provided a source of great friction between the United States and Canada.

Time and *Reader's Digest* have been the most prominent split-runs, beginning operations in Canada in 1943. By 1954, 80 percent of the Canadian periodical market belonged to U.S. publications, with *Time* and *Reader's Digest* enjoying the largest circulation among them (Litvak and Maule 1974, 30). Five years into operation, the two magazines accounted for 18 percent of the total advertising revenues generated by the twelve major magazines in Canada.[48] By 1955, this number had climbed to 37 percent.

Split-run magazines have been perceived to be such a threat to the Canadian magazine industry that their entry into Canada was actually outlawed in the 1960s. The federal government feared that the domestic periodicals industry might disappear because of advertising revenues being siphoned off by U.S. competitors. In introducing tariff legislation, the Liberal minister of finance offered the following explanation: "We have been considering this problem for some time, and we have decided that in this field, very exceptional measures can be justified—measures that certainly could not be justified in connection with any ordinary line of business" (Litvak and Maule 1974, 31).

Customs tariff 9958 prevented the "dumping" of foreign magazines containing minimal or no Canadian content. The only concession, granted at the insistence of the U.S. government, allowed *Time* and *Reader's Digest* to be "grandfathered" so that they could continue circulating in Canada.

---

48. This list of twelve included Canadian magazines in English and French, in addition to American magazines.

The strategy of outlawing split-runs ran up against technological innovation in the 1990s. Time-Warner used electronic transmission of text to skirt the ban on bringing split-run magazines across the border. As Grant and Wood (2004, 364) explain, "Instead of importing split-run copies of *Sports Illustrated* from a printing plant in the United States, the company simply beamed digital versions of the magazine's pages by satellite to a Canadian printing plant." Worried that other companies might follow suit, the Canadian government responded in 1995 by imposing an excise tax on split runs containing less than 80 percent original content. The tax, in the amount of 80 percent of the advertising contained in the issue (Bill C-103), prompted Time-Warner to shut down the Canadian edition of *Sports Illustrated* and sparked a trade dispute between the United States and Canada that went before the World Trade Organization in 1996.

The U.S. government objected to the 1995 excise tax, the original ban on split-runs, as well as postal subsidies that the federal government provided to publishers to offset the cost of delivering magazine subscriptions to far-flung locations. The WTO panel reviewing the three Canadian measures ruled that none were in compliance with Canada's trade commitments. As of June 1, 2000, in response to the WTO ruling, new measures govern the periodical industry in Canada. Whereas nationality of magazine or place of publication previously determined whether an advertiser could deduct advertising expenses, the new law stipulates that the level of original content is decisive. Therefore, 50 percent of advertising expenses in a magazine can be deducted if less than 80 percent of the editorial content is original. A full 100 percent of advertising expenses are deductible if 80 percent or more of the editorial content is original. In addition, foreign publishers are now permitted to sell up to 18 percent of their advertising space to Canadian advertisers.

The changes in policy necessitated by the WTO decision are significant. In order to compensate for some of the perceived losses to the Canadian periodical industry, the federal government introduced in 2000 the Canada Magazine Fund. This direct financial assistance to Canadian magazines to defray expenses has proven to be less offensive both to the United States and to the WTO.

Measures undertaken in the periodical industry illustrate the degree to which the Canadian government is constrained in its ability to implement policy favorable to domestic cultural producers. Even though there is a perception in official circles that culture industries play a sociological role fostering national identity, it is not surprising that the government is reluctant to subject other sectors of the Canadian economy to debilitating retaliatory policies emanating from American dissatisfaction with Canadian communications policy. Nonetheless, the prospect that some measures might be unpopular in powerful circles has not dampened the government's underlying commitment to cultural goals.

Like the periodical industry, the book publishing industry has also been on the receiving end of government support measures. The federal government introduced measures to aid this sector in the early 1970s, expanding federal publishing policy beyond copyright law. The sale of two publishing houses, Ryerson Press and Gage Publishing, to foreign buyers provided a wake-up call. At the same time, it became apparent that one of the larger trade publishers in English Canada, McClelland and Stewart, was failing and that the French house Hachette was having some success penetrating the French Canadian market (Lorimer 1996). These events sparked investigations into the publishing industry and proposals for government policy at both the federal and provincial levels. Among the initiatives that ensued, in 1972, the Canada Council introduced grant programs designed to provide financial support to book projects having cultural significance but unlikely to be fully financed by the market.

Seven years later, the Canadian Book Publishing Development Program (CBPDP) was launched by the Arts and Culture Branch of the Department of the Secretary of State and transferred to the Department of Communications in 1980 when the latter ministry assumed federal responsibility for arts and culture. The program was designed to provide support for the sales and marketing of Canadian books and to aid in "structural and professional improvements within the industry" (Canada 1982). The CBPDP complements the Canada Council grants to individual authors and book projects by subsidizing publishing companies. Furthermore, it goes beyond the Canada Council grants by stimulating the long-term economic viability of the publishing industry rather than providing annual infusions of grant money to keep publishers solvent.

In 1985, the federal government announced that foreign investors could establish or acquire publishing houses in Canada, but only in partnership with Canadians. If a Canadian publishing house is acquired as an asset of a foreign corporation undergoing sale, the foreign investor must divest itself of the publishing company by selling a controlling interest to Canadians within two years of acquisition. The same regulation applies to retailers of books, and the failed bid by Borders Books to enter the Canadian market has proceeded according to these guidelines. Borders announced its intention to open a superstore in downtown Toronto in the early 1990s. In anticipation of competing with the U.S. corporation, Canada's two largest booksellers, Coles and Smith Books merged, forming Chapters, a Canadian-owned and operated imitation of Borders, complete with arm chairs and Starbucks coffee. The difference, of course, is in the book list and in the nationality of the book suppliers. The *Washington Post* summed up the concerns of many Canadians at the prospect of Borders' entry into Canada.

> Books are not just any industry, but a fragile component of Canada's cultural fabric. Only a third of all books sold in Canada are by Canadian authors; the share of movies distributed in Canada each year that are Canadian-made is 4 percent. People inside and outside the book business here wonder: Will Canadian books go the way of Canadian movies? (Trueheart 1995, A33)

Others in Canada argued that Borders' presence in the Canadian market might provide Canadian authors with a vehicle to greater sales in the United States. Some assumed the superstores, both Borders and Chapters, would stock more Canadian authors, while others worried Borders would be inclined to streamline its booklist, dropping more obscure—often Canadian—authors.

In order to conform to the Investment Canada Act, which requires that foreign entities interested in participating in the culture industry sector join with Canadians in a partnership, Borders enlisted the help of prominent Toronto business executives Heather Reisman and Ed Borins to serve as majority stakeholders. Yet even the presence of Canadian nationals at the helm of the book conglomerate did not stem the tide of concerns. Canadian government officials, as well as those active in the Canadian bookselling industry, wondered if Borders would bypass Canadian suppliers in favor of their existing U.S. distribution and warehousing networks, effectively threatening the small domestic industry and many Canadian authors in the process. Ultimately, the Canadian government ruled that Borders' efforts to put Canadians in positions of power did not constitute Canadian "control in fact."

Blocking Borders' entry into the Canadian market was a controversial decision, as was the split-run excise tax that triggered the WTO dispute, and other measures designed to aid the periodical and book publishing industry in Canada. Nevertheless, the government bases such decisions on the cultural goal that "Canadians must have access to Canadian voices and Canadian stories."[49]

Sound Recording

In sound recording, the government's principal objective is to protect the Canadian-owned industry, which accounts for most Canadian-content recordings.[50]

---

49. "Book Publishing Policy," website of the Ministry of Canadian Heritage, http://www.pch.gc.ca/progs/ac-ca/pol/livre-book/index_e.cfm.

50. "Sound Recording (Film/Video)." Archival records of the Canadian Trade Negotiations Office, file 5420–1.

The Canadian recording industry benefits from the CRTC content requirements for radio, first introduced in 1971. Adherence to content requirements is a
condition of license issuance and renewal. In order to be designated as Canadian,
a recording must meet at least two of the four criteria outlined in the MAPL
system: (i) M (music)—the music is composed entirely by a Canadian, (ii) A
(artist)—the instrumentation or lyrics are principally performed by a Canadian,
(iii) P (production)—the musical selection consists of a live performance wholly
recorded in Canada or performed wholly in Canada and broadcast live in Canada, (iv) L (lyrics)—the lyrics are written entirely by a Canadian.[51] According to
the CRTC, the MAPL system has two objectives:

> The primary objective—a cultural one—is to encourage increased expo-
> sure of Canadian musical performers, lyricists and composers to Canadian
> audiences. The secondary objective—an industrial one—is to strengthen
> the Canadian music industry, including both the creative and production
> components.[52]

Regulations establishing Canadian content requirements for radio dating to
1970 initially mandated a 30 percent minimum. In 1986, content requirements
were revised, requiring varying percentages of Canadian recordings for AM and
FM stations. Depending on their format, stations were required to play between
10 and 30 percent Canadian music. By 1991, all stations on both the AM and FM
bands were required to play a minimum of 30 percent Canadian content. Furthermore, the Canadian selections had to be scheduled reasonably throughout
the broadcast day. For example, radio stations cannot fulfill content requirements
by concentrating Canadian selections in the wee hours of the morning. This has
been less of an issue in recent years since several Canadian recording artists,
including K. D. Lang, Alanis Morrissette, Celine Dion, Sarah McLachlan, Bare
Naked Ladies, and Diana Krall have earned widespread international popularity.
Nevertheless, in early 1998, the CRTC increased the minimum Canadian content requirement to 35 percent of musical selections aired between 6:00 a.m. and
6:00 p.m., Monday through Friday. Separate requirements exist for ethnic and
French-language stations. For example, in the latter category, at least 65 percent
of weekly, noninstrumental selections must be French-language.

The Sound Recording Development Program (SRDP) was established in
1986 to provide assistance on a project basis in the areas of production, marketing, and distribution of Canadian sound recordings. It grew out of a private

51. Website of the CRTC, http://www.crtc.gc.ca/ENG/INFO_SHT/R1.HTM.
52. Ibid.

sector initiative, spearheaded by the Foundation to Assist Canadian Talent on Record (FACTOR), taken in response to CRTC requirements that radio stations demonstrate support for local sound recording artists at the time of license renewal. Founded in 1982 by CHUM Limited, Moffat Communications, and Rogers Broadcasting Limited, in conjunction with the Canadian Independent Record Producers Association (CIRPA) and the Canadian Music Publishers Association (CMPA), FACTOR has an annual budget of $11 million (cdn). It disburses a range of funds, including contributions from its sponsoring broadcasters, as well as several of the components of the Ministry of Canadian Heritage's Sound Recording Development Program, to aid Canadian recording artists and songwriters in the production and distribution of their work.

In 2001, the Canada Music Fund absorbed the SRDP when the Ministry of Canadian Heritage announced a new sound recording policy, From Creators to Audience. This new policy goes beyond the project-based support of SRDP to a more comprehensive investment in all aspects of the sector. It includes a range of programs designed to enhance community building, collaboration, and skills development among songwriters and composers, funds for production and distribution, as well as aid to creators and entrepreneurs, including mechanisms for raising the profile of new and established artists. The new policy acknowledges the challenges to the sound recording industry of "a global digital economy," including new outlets for music such as the Internet. The new policy confirms its cultural motivations.

> Canadian music embodies the creativity and spirit of Canadians. It helps define who we are, and reflects the richness of Canada's linguistic and cultural diversity. Canadian music artists are among our best known cultural ambassadors abroad. Nelly Furtado, Natalie McMaster . . . and many others enrich the lives of Canadians and help to shape how we are perceived in the world.[53]

The same document goes on to note that Canadian artists "creat[e] a sense of common citizenship" and lists as its primary measure of success securing "a cultural return on the Government of Canada's investment."

Canadian copyright law has also been used as an indirect stimulus to the recording industry. For example, in 1988, the government introduced a plan to raise payments made to composers for the sale of recordings incrementally from 2 cents per composition to 6.47 cents by 1993. Tariffs have also been used,

---

53. Ministry of Canadian Heritage, "From Creators to Audience: New Policy Directions for Canadian Sound Recording." http://www.pch.gc.ca/progs/ac-ca/progs/pades-srdp/pubs/policy_e.cfm.

fluctuating between 10 and 15 percent; however, the Canada–U.S. Free Trade Agreement eliminated tariffs on imported sound recordings.

Radio and Television Broadcasting

Broadcasting policy in Canada dates back to the early 1900s. Notably, the Radiotelegraph Act of 1913 accorded the right to issue radio transmission licenses to the federal government, justifying this by characterizing the airwaves as public property, akin to natural resources. This principle has been reaffirmed, most recently in the 1991 revision of the Broadcasting Act. It underlies the notion of the "single system" that has oriented Canadian broadcasting policy since its inception. According to this principle, both private and public interests participating in broadcasting are considered to be parallel components of the same system.[54] It is, therefore, incumbent upon *both* elements to fulfill the stated objectives of the system as outlined in the Broadcasting Act. Central to these objectives is providing Canadians with a distinctly Canadian broadcasting system. The Broadcasting Act is explicit about the justification for this approach. As the primary law governing culture industries in Canada, it is worth quoting at length:

> It is hereby declared as broadcasting policy for Canada that the Canadian broadcasting system shall be effectively owned and controlled by Canadians;
>
> (a) the Canadian broadcasting system, operating primarily in the English and French languages and comprising public, private and community elements, makes use of radio frequencies that are public property and provides, through its programming, *a public service essential to the maintenance and enhancement of national identity and cultural sovereignty;*
>
> (b) English and French language broadcasting, while sharing common aspects, operate under different conditions and may have different requirements;
>
> (c) the Canadian broadcasting system should

---

54. Peers notes that the single system, operating parallel private and public elements, is one of a range of choices as to how a broadcasting system might be set up. Other choices include: a single system with the public element dominant; a private and a public system that are separately accountable, and a market-oriented system, dominated by the private component. See Peers, 1979, pp. 414–21 and appendix A.

(i) *serve to safeguard, enrich and strengthen the cultural, political, social and economic fabric of Canada,*

(ii) *encourage the development of Canadian expression by providing a wide range of programming that reflects Canadian attitudes, opinions, ideas, values and artistic creativity, by displaying Canadian talent in entertainment programming and by offering information and analysis concerning Canada and other countries from a Canadian point of view.*[55]

The above provisions apply to all broadcasters in Canada. The act goes on to stipulate further guidelines pertaining specifically to the Canadian Broadcasting Corporation (CBC) as the national public broadcaster.

the programming provided by the Corporation should
(i) *be predominantly and distinctively Canadian,*
(ii) *reflect Canada and its regions* to national and regional audiences, while serving the special needs of those regions, . . .
(vi) *contribute to shared national consciousness and identity.*[56]

Concern over U.S. influence in Canadian broadcasting also dates back to the 1920s. In 1923, the Radiotelegraph Act was amended to give only British subjects the right to hold broadcasting licenses. In 1929 the federal government established the Royal Commission on Broadcasting to look into broadcasting in Canada and, specifically, into U.S. predominance in Canadian radio.[57] Indeed, at this time, broadcasting was already recognized at the highest level as a powerful instrument in the nation-building process. In 1932, Prime Minister R. B. Bennett stated the government's position:

This country must be assured of complete control of broadcasting from Canadian sources, free from foreign interference or influence. Without such control, radio broadcasting can never become a great agency for communication of matters of national concern and for the diffusion of national thought and ideals, and without such control, it can never be the

55. Section 3, Broadcasting Act, February 1, 1991, government of Canada website, Statutes of Canada. Emphasis mine.

56. Ibid. Emphasis mine.

57. Broadcasting policy at this time refers to measures affecting radio. Television was first made available to Canadians in 1952 and the federal government did not begin consideration of measures to introduce it or to regulate it until the 1940s.

agency by which national consciousness may be fostered and sustained and national unity still further strengthened.[58]

Canadian radio and television broadcasting is somewhat unusual in that it is a hybrid system, incorporating both private and public components, more or less equally, under the same umbrella. As such, it stands apart from European and American systems, the former often characterized by a predominant public sector, the latter being a market-oriented system, with the private sector prevailing. Although the CBC dominated Canadian broadcasting during its early decades, the public and private elements have evolved since the 1960s to be on an equal footing.

At the center of broadcasting policy in Canada is the Broadcasting Act. In its first incarnation in 1932, it created the Canadian Radio Broadcasting Commission (CRBC), later to become the Canadian Broadcasting Corporation (CBC radio) in 1936, to provide Canadian broadcasting to Canadians. In addition to being designated as the national radio service, it had the power to decide on radio station numbers and locations. Therefore, the CRBC, and later the CBC, for a time played the dual role of national public broadcaster and industry regulator. National private radio outside of the CRBC was not permitted for several years, giving the CRBC and, by extension, the state, a national monopoly.

A similar situation prevailed for a time in television broadcasting. The CBC began television service in Canada in September 1952 (Peers 1979). The first privately owned stations did not appear until a year later.[59] Initially, the CBC established TV stations in Toronto and Montreal, extending the service to other major cities shortly thereafter. The CBC, in its role as industry regulator, only licensed private stations when it became apparent that it was not in a position to provide service to the majority of Canada's scattered population without help from private interests. Still, private stations would only be permitted in population centers where the CBC did not have a presence, following the "single-station policy." The single-station policy flowed logically from the notion of the single broadcasting system. Assuming that the airwaves are public property and that those using them are obliged to provide a service to Canadians, the single system policy dictated provision of basic broadcasting services to as many communities as possible before providing programming choices to areas of population concentration.

Private stations were not allowed to compete directly with the CBC until 1961. Furthermore, as part of a single national system, privately owned stations

58. House of Commons Debates, May 18, 1932, quoted in Audley, 1983: 184.
59. Sudbury in October 1953 and London in November 1953.

were charged with providing a public service to Canadians and, therefore, would be expected to provide a certain amount of Canadian programming. In fact, the CBC delayed licensing of private stations until it had established its own production operation so as to be able to supply private stations with CBC television programs. Commercial stations did little to resist this arrangement because the supply of CBC productions enabled them to survive in their lean early years. Therefore, it is not inaccurate to say that the early stages of broadcasting in Canada were driven by a governmental effort to ensure that cultural considerations—specifically, provision of a distinctively Canadian broadcasting system—did not lose out to commercial interests. Indeed, the notion of providing a public service was, in large part, synonymous with providing indigenous broadcasting.

> Underlying these and many other provisions is the assumption that broadcasting should not respond merely to the dictates of the market, but that it should serve certain national interests, some of them related to the strengthening of a sense of Canadian nationality and identity. This denotes a concern with community goals rather than the profit motive (substantially at variance with the American pattern). (Meisel 1986, 157)

In the intervening years, private broadcasters have come to play a more central role in Canadian broadcasting. The licensing of private stations coincided with a significant revision of the Broadcasting Act. In 1958, after protracted debate and a Royal Commission investigation into broadcasting, the CBC was stripped of its role as industry regulator. The CBC would, of course, remain the national public broadcaster, but a separate regulatory entity, the Board of Broadcast Governors (BBG), was created. Renamed the Canadian Radio and Television Commission (CRTC) in 1968, the regulatory body would assume responsibility for such tasks as license issuance and renewal and imposition of Canadian content requirements. The creation of a separate regulatory board, coinciding with the entry of private broadcasters, shifted the balance away from public predominance toward a greater role for the private component. Still, the BBG, and later the CRTC, instituted regulations reflecting a continuing commitment to the original objective of guaranteeing a Canadian broadcasting system.

CRTC initiatives designed to aid Canadian performers and broadcasting industries include licensing provisions, "signal carriage" regulations, and Canadian content requirements for television and radio programming, intended to ensure that television stations have adequate revenues to reinvest in costly program production. Signal carriage regulations stipulate that cable companies must provide simultaneous program substitution when a U.S. and a Canadian television station carry the same program at the same time. Therefore, a cable subscriber tuned to a U.S. station would actually see the same programming, including commercials, as the viewer tuned to a Canadian station. Mandating that the Canadian signal shall have priority over the American does two things: since advertising revenue is linked to audience size, signal substitution protects the advertising revenue of the Canadian private broadcaster by ensuring that audiences for a given program will not be split. In addition, signal substitution protects the investment of Canadian broadcasters who purchase "exclusive" distribution rights for specific programs.

As is the case for radio, the CRTC mandates minimum levels of Canadian content for television. "Simply put, it's about Canadian artists and Canadian stories having access to Canadian airwaves."[60] The CRTC certifies programs as Canadian providing the producer is Canadian; key creative personnel are Canadian; and 75 percent of service costs and postproduction costs are paid to Canadians. License renewal for broadcasters is tied to compliance with Canadian content requirements. Licensees must maintain a program log wherein they use CRTC certification numbers to distinguish Canadian content.

Canadian content requirements for radio and television are not as popular with private broadcasters, largely because adherence to them requires spending the revenue provided by Canadian priority signal carriage regulations. Nevertheless, content requirements have been viewed by the government as the best approach to ensuring the existence of a national broadcasting system, and not just a conduit for foreign programming. The BBG first introduced content requirements for television in 1960, calling for 55 percent of all broadcast time to be Canadian, averaged over a one-week period. Protests from newly licensed private stations led the BBG to suspend the quota for prime time hours temporarily and to extend the averaging period to four weeks. Furthermore, the BBG agreed to phase in the 55 percent requirement over a two-year period, imposing no Canadian content quota in the first year, followed by a 45 percent requirement in the second. The full requirement of 55 percent was to take effect in 1962.

The BBG definition of Canadian content was quite generous at this time, including the following: (i) any program produced by a BBG licensee and to be broadcast by the licensee, (ii) news and news commentaries, (iii) broadcasts of events taking place outside of Canada in which Canadians were participating, (iv) broadcasts of programs featuring "special" events outside of Canada but of general interest to Canadians (funerals of foreign dignitaries, the World Series), (v) programs, films or other productions made in Canada. In addition, programs

60. Website of the CRTC, http://www.crtc.gc.ca/ENG/INFO_SHT/b306.htm.

produced in Commonwealth countries or in the French language would receive half credit (Canada 1982, 286).

In fact, the 55 percent content requirement was stalled before it could take effect in 1962.[61] At this time, both the English- and French-language television services of the CBC were well over the allotted content requirements. However, the burgeoning number of private stations protested these restrictions as they were trying to establish themselves. New regulations were introduced in 1970, following the creation of the successor to the BBG, the CRTC. By this time private stations had become profitable and content requirements could be tightened. In addition, in the mid 1960s, a parliamentary committee had published a report on the state of Canadian broadcasting that sharply criticized private stations for making an inadequate contribution to the creation and maintenance of a distinctively Canadian system (Peers 1979, 317). The regulatory agency stipulated that 60 percent of programming both for the whole day and during the prime time hours between 6:30 p.m. and 11:30 p.m. must be Canadian, averaged over a three-month period. The CRTC further proposed restricting the maximum amount of programming from any one foreign country to 30 percent and eliminating the credit accorded to Commonwealth, French-language, and "special" interest programming.

In response to the bitter reaction of private broadcasters, the limit on programming from a single foreign country was raised to 40 percent and all content requirements would be averaged over a one-year period. In addition, the CRTC redefined prime-time to mean 6:00 p.m. to midnight. Regulations were eased further in 1972. The 60 percent Canadian content requirement for prime-time hours was retained for the CBC but reduced to 50 percent for private broadcasters. Limitations on imports from a single foreign country were canceled and credit for Commonwealth and French-language programs reinstated. Currently, private broadcasters must achieve a yearly Canadian content level of 60 percent overall, measured between 6:00 a.m. and midnight and 50 percent measured between 6:00 p.m. and midnight. The CBC must ensure that at least 60 percent of its overall schedule, measured between 6:00 a.m. and midnight, is Canadian content. Broadcasters can claim a 125–150 percent time credit for Canadian dramas aired during prime time hours between 7:00 p.m. and 11:00 p.m.[62]

While content requirements have not always been popular with private broadcasters, they remain in force. The Canadian content requirements illustrate

61. The quota was reduced to 40 percent and waived for the summer months. Commonwealth and French-language productions were given full credit and programs from Commonwealth and French-speaking countries dubbed in the other official language received one-quarter credit. Canada, 1982: 287.

62. Website of the CRTC, http://www.crtc.gc.ca/ENG/INFO_SHT/G11.HTM.

the degree to which the Canadian government, via its broadcasting regulatory agency, has maintained a commitment to cultural goals, even to the detriment of economic ones. By mandating Canadian content for television, the government is requiring television stations either to produce their own Canadian programming or to purchase it. Either way, the monetary investment is much higher than simply obtaining relatively inexpensive U.S. programs. Yet the return on investment is no higher, and it may be lower. Aware of the outcome that the market would produce, the government stepped in with a policy unpopular with those who deliver programming, but seemingly necessary for the identity formation process. Were nation building not a concern, it is safe to assume that policy more congenial to the commercial interests of radio and television stations would be implemented.

The highest court in Canada has been drawn into the debate over Canadian content requirements. In 1979, the CRTC required the CTV television network to present twenty-six new hours of Canadian drama in the 1980–81 broadcasting year and thirty-nine new hours in the following year in exchange for renewal of its broadcasting license (Canada 1982, 282). CTV challenged this stipulation in the courts but the CRTC directive was ultimately upheld by the Supreme Court of Canada. CTV claimed it did not have ample notification that such license conditions would be imposed. Chief Justice Bora Laskin delivered the judgment in favor of the CRTC, invoking provisions in the Broadcasting Act that establish programming guidelines for both private and public broadcasters and that empower the CRTC to enforce these guidelines.[63]

This court case drives home the difficulty involved in getting private broadcasters to present new Canadian drama. Dramatic programming is the most costly to produce, but it is also one of the most popular genres among viewers and generally assumed to make an important contribution to value formation. Private broadcasters prefer to fulfill the Canadian content requirements mandated by the CRTC by producing news, public affairs, and sports programs, however the CRTC has the authority to make provision of Canadian content in specific forms a condition of license renewal.

Even the CBC can only afford to offer its English viewers less than two hours of original Canadian drama a week. . . . As for the private broadcasters, their involvement in the production of Canadian drama is insignificant. One reason is obvious: they can acquire the rights to wildly popular

---

63. "CRTC v. CTV Television Network et al.," *Canada Supreme Court Reports*, part 3, vol. 1: pp. 530–552. (Ottawa: Queen's Printer, 1982)

American shows for very much less than the cost of comparable Canadian ones. It therefore makes very little *economic* sense for commercial broadcasters to try to program Canadian dramas.(Meisel 1986, 154, emphasis in original)

The fact that the Canadian government, through the CRTC, makes specific demands on private broadcasters concerning presentation of costly dramatic programming further underscores the preoccupation with identity formation and nation-building that drives broadcasting policy.

More recently, the CRTC has introduced some flexibility to its policies. In 1994, the regulatory body offered broadcasters a choice as to how they would contribute to the development of Canadian talent. They could either adhere to content quotas or they could agree to allocate a proportion of their spending to program development projects. Nonetheless, the goals remain the same. The CRTC justifies this new policy flexibility in the following terms: "Programming that reflects the views and values of Canadians, strengthens cultural sovereignty and national identity, that is designed for a competitive Canadian marketplace and is positioned for success in foreign markets, will depend upon a flexible regulatory framework."[64]

Specialty and pay-TV stations are not held to the same percentage Canadian content requirements, but they must "spend a specified percentage of their subscription revenues on Canadian programming. The percentage starts at 22 percent and increases to 32 percent as the number of subscribers to the service increases" (Grant and Wood 2004, 226).

In early 2002, Minister of Canadian Heritage Sheila Copps initiated a review of Canadian content regulations for television and film. "Today's definitions of Canadian content for film and television have been in place for 30 years. . . . We are asking Canadians to help us define what makes a film or television production Canadian. It is time to have an open discussion with the industry and all Canadians on this issue."[65]

Those involved in the production of films and television programs, as well as concerned citizens, were invited to submit reflections as to whether content requirements based on the nationality of owners and of key personnel, as well as location of key production expenditures, best serve the government's cultural goals.

Complementing content and signal carriage regulations are tax incentives similar to those struck down by the WTO for the periodicals sector. Section

---

64. Website of the CRTC, http://www.crtc.gc.ca/ENG/INFO_SHT/TV10.HTM.

65. "Minister of Canadian Heritage Launches Canadian Content Review," Press Release of the Ministry of Canadian Heritage, April 2, 2002.

19.1 of the Income Tax Act targets advertising revenues lost to U.S. competitors. These tax incentives for broadcasting remain intact despite mandated changes to magazine policy. The measure prohibits the deduction of expenses for advertising placed in foreign broadcast media but aimed at Canadian audiences. Also referred to as Bill C-58, this regulation encourages Canadian advertisers to support its national media rather than giving its advertising dollars to U.S. stations whose signals transmit into Canada. Enacted in 1976, Bill C-58 has been, to say the least, highly unpopular with the United States. It has been called "the most threatening irritant in Canadian–American relations" (Meisel 1986, 163). Both President Carter and Henry Kissinger personally intervened against it. The U.S. Congress passed very strong retaliatory measures in response to it.[66]

The U.S. response to C-58 was not proportionate to the economic effect of the Canadian legislation. Estimates suggest that approximately $15–$20 million were at stake in this dispute, money that would not be spent for advertising at U.S. border stations should Bill C-58 be passed into law (Hagelin and Janisch 1984, 45). By all accounts, this is not a substantial amount of money warranting intervention at the highest level. Instead, the disproportionate response suggests that something other than economic concerns may also be motivating the U.S. response to Canadian communications policy. The same thing can be said about the U.S. response to the exclusion of culture industries from CUSFTA and NAFTA. The extent of U.S. penetration into the Canadian cultural market suggests that barriers do not exist to flows of U.S. cultural products. While government support measures are intended to stimulate indigenous production and distribution of cultural products, they by no means impede access to the Canadian market. But suffice to say that the ongoing Canadian–U.S. conflict over the regulation of culture industries is grounded in philosophical differences about the role of the state in the two countries, especially as it pertains to culture.

Canadian policy on culture industries during CUSFTA and NAFTA can best be understood by examining how the Canadian government has treated these industries over the last several decades. The federal government enlisted culture industries in the nation-building process long before cultural products became lucrative commodities in international markets. Support measures for film, television, and radio broadcasting; periodical and book publishing; and video and sound recording have been implemented so that Canadian artists can compete against the strong U.S. presence in their own domestic market. In so doing, the government seeks to promote identity formation and internal communication

---

66. Congress retaliated by passing legislation that restricted the tax deductions allowed to Americans who attend conventions in Canada. The legislation was later repealed, but not before it reportedly cost Canada hundreds of millions of dollars in lost tourist income. Meisel 1986, 163.

among Canadians. If culture industries can fulfill this purpose, the Canadian state ostensibly moves closer to achieving the long-standing goal of distinguishing Canada from other national communities.

Equating culture industries with fostering cultural particularity is controversial and, in some cases, unreliable. Nonetheless, the Canadian government has consistently embraced this premise for the better part of a century, right up until the present day. These policies caught international attention in the 1980s and 1990s not because the Canadian government initiated some sort of radical protectionist policy reorientation that flew in the face of its trade commitments. Rather, the central manifestations of the global trading regime—the North American Free Trade Agreement and the World Trade Organization—expanded their reach at that time to subject the cultural sector to their trading principles. Commentators in the United States drew our attention to perceived Canadian protectionism. Framing the issue in this way obscured the much more profound tension between principles of open trade and Canadian efforts to mobilize culture industries in the pursuit of cultural objectives. Consequently, many missed the manifestation of the familiar dynamic associated with embedded liberalism. In addition, they missed an opportunity to expand our understanding of why states otherwise committed to open trade resist aspects of liberalization to preserve various sociocultural commitments to their citizenry. As I discuss in the next chapter, another opportunity to learn these lessons would soon present itself during Uruguay Round GATT talks.

Chapter 3

GATT, Europe, and Audiovisual Industries

If I could do it all again, I would begin with culture.

Attributed to Jean Monnet, architect of the European Community

During the closing days of the Uruguay Round of GATT talks, after seven years of negotiation, the European Union, led by France, threatened to scuttle the agreement unless audiovisual industries were left out. The U.S. Congress imposed a deadline of December 15, 1993, for the end of GATT negotiations. As the deadline neared, some major sticking points remained, among them disagreement between the United States and the European Union over agricultural and audiovisual policy. The parties were able to reach agreement on agricultural policy, but U.S. and European negotiators were unable to reconcile their respective interests with regard to television and film. In order to honor the deadline and avoid the collapse of the negotiations, the United States conceded to European demands that audiovisual industries remain unregulated by GATT. The treaty did provide for the sector to be incorporated into the evolving General Agreement on Trade in Services (GATS); however, this would give governments much greater flexibility to implement individual policies.

The European Union sought this outcome so it could continue support measures to the European television and film industries because of the contribution they are thought to make to enriching European society and to fostering European identity. The EU position in the Uruguay Round mirrored Canadian cultural sector trade policy, which emanates from a belief that culture industries can contribute to the establishment of shared meanings that underpin collective identity, social cohesion, and cultural diversity.

Within the European Union, France was the most visible and vocal supporter of the exclusion of audiovisual industries from the GATT agreement. In advancing their position, they invoked the threat posed to French culture by the influx of U.S. films and television programs, as well as the difficulty for European producers to find domestic outlets for their works in the face of U.S. competition, a difficulty that would be made greater by liberalization of the sector.

European insistence that audiovisual industries be left out of GATT converges with the Canadian case on some levels, but departs from it on others. It is more complicated because both national-level and supranational-level policymakers are implicated, but equally instructive with regard to the dynamics under consideration in this book—the appearance on the trading agenda of culture industry regulation and the ensuing tendency to mischaracterize a defensive effort to offset the perceived contemporary costs of liberalization as veiled economic protectionism. Once again, concerns about cultural identity, social cohesion, and diversity intervene to shape state interests with regard to trade policy. However, in the GATT case, audiovisual industries are being used not only to reinforce existing national borders—as was the case with Canada and NAFTA—but also to establish a bounded space over which the European Union has jurisdiction. The European stance sprang from the belief that audiovisual industries could help to evoke a transnational European identity that accommodates and transcends the collective identities of the EU member states. As the trading regime evolves to encompass services, European resistance to liberalizing the audiovisual sector is grounded in a desire to preserve and promote key components of European culture and society that would otherwise be threatened by economic liberalization.

Comparing the GATT dispute over audiovisual industries and the Canadian experience with NAFTA is particularly illuminating. However, it is also useful to examine the French and European perspectives independent of each other. European Union member states negotiate in GATT as a bloc, making the call for exclusion of audiovisual industries a European position and not strictly a French one, as it was often portrayed in the U.S. media. Since the early 1980s, European Union institutions have pursued policy measures to harmonize audiovisual industry regulation across the member states. Therefore, we can situate the audiovisual industry dispute during the Uruguay Round within a broader policy framework implemented at the supranational level.

Nonetheless, many audiovisual measures in place at the European level were initiated by France and are modeled on French policies. In addition, audiovisual policy at the national level in France and at the European level does not always serve the same goals. Therefore, the present chapter proceeds on two fronts to elucidate both the French and European agendas in the audiovisual realm to show how not only economic imperatives, but also cultural ones, led to the trade dispute over audiovisual industries. First, I show that in the period preceding the GATT negotiations, audiovisual policy had become a central element in the European project to bring about political union by promoting a European identity. In this regard, the GATT and NAFTA cases are similar in that both the European Union and Canada seek to promote social cohesion and diversity via culture industries.

Second, this chapter explores post–World War II audiovisual policy in France in order to contextualize France's championing of the "cultural exception" during the Uruguay Round of GATT. France, like Canada, rejects a purely economic approach to culture industries. Both countries assume that domestic culture industries can make a sociocultural contribution to the greater good of their respective societies. France has both a philosophical and a practical tradition of enlisting culture—including audiovisual industries—in the pursuit of broader sociopolitical goals. Therefore, many similarities between France and Canada brought them to reject incorporation of culture industries into international trade agreements. Both share a long-standing experience with a strong state. The French state played a central role in forging a nation out of the disparate groups that inhabit it. The French state "substituted for the absence of a shared image" (Flynn 1995, 4). Both countries have sustained robust public broadcasting sectors. In addition, as is true with Canada, the stance taken by France in the GATT talks is not new, but rather a continuation of the policies put in place to protect French television and cinema over the years and another installment in the story of Franco-U.S. disagreement over the regulation of culture industries.

American movies and television programs have a strong presence in France and all over Europe, as they do in Canada. As a result, local producers find it difficult to be heard among their own people. In France, 50 percent of the films shown in 1980 were French and 31 percent American. Ten years later, 31 percent were French and 59 percent American (Condron 1997, 210). In 2001, French films accounted for 39 percent of market share in France, the best showing in years. In 1990, France imported 600 million francs worth of television programming from North America and exported 35 million francs worth (Kuhn 1995, 239).

Nevertheless, Canada and France are also very different. In order to understand the French position vis-à-vis the cinema and television industries, it is useful to disaggregate them. Insomuch as an unprotected cinema industry threatens French identity, it is not only because it is a *means*, but because it is an *end*. A thriving French cinema industry does not only promote collective particularity by mediating values and norms that underpin it. French cinema *itself* is a pillar of French identity and a source of national pride because it is viewed as an art form in which the French have traditionally excelled. Television, on the other hand, can play the more instrumental role of promoting social cohesion that Canadian policymakers attribute to all culture industries. But it can also disseminate mass culture, something French elites have traditionally opposed and equate with the United States.

Ultimately, France, the European Union, and Canada can be grouped together, in opposition to the United States, because their approaches to culture industries are grounded in a set of normative and ideological assumptions that view cultural products as intrinsically valuable qua cultural products and able to contribute to broad sociopolitical and cultural goals. Nonetheless, within this grouping, Canada and the European Union must be distinguished from France. France does not enlist culture industries in the pursuit of identity formation in the same way (or to the same degree) that Canada and the European Union do. The French have a keen sense of what characterizes "Frenchness" and cultivate a more traditional national identity. Policymakers reject the infiltration of U.S. cultural products because it disturbs *clearly defined* notions of French culture and the French way of life.[1] Neither Canada nor the European Union cultivates a unitary "sense of self" reminiscent of more traditional national identities. Instead, both are working to define their respective multicultural identities. American domination of culture industries ostensibly interrupts efforts to use them as a means of identity formation by conveying a set of American ideas that are believed not only to challenge existing beliefs—as is the case in France—but potentially to substitute for weak notions of what it means to be Canadian or European.

Still, as much as French identity is strong, it is not settled. Identities are constantly evolving and their perpetuation requires ongoing attention. Certain elements are emphasized in certain historical periods. For example, while Roman Catholicism is no longer the central element of the French identity that it has been in the past, the purity of the French language remains definitive of "Frenchness." Therefore, as is the case in Canada, France wants to retain power to define what it means to be French. The French government attributes to audiovisual industries an ability to contribute to the preservation of France's distinctiveness as a cultural and political entity, to (re)create the *idea* of France at a time when national borders are becoming less meaningful. At the same time, the European Union works to move beyond economic union to political union. European officials see a central role for audiovisual industries in this process.

1. It is interesting to note that the debate over French identity concerns *when* it came into being, with particular attention given to whether a French national consciousness existed before 1789. See Bell 1996. Of course, debate over the Canadian and European identities centers on *if* they do indeed exist at all.

Therefore, the GATT trade dispute resembles the NAFTA one in that both provide examples of identity formation and cultural concerns taking center stage alongside economic considerations. But the GATT trade dispute moves beyond the straightforward nature of the Canadian case because it is happening at two levels simultaneously. Whereas the Canadian government uses culture industries to reinforce existing boundaries, the European Union, with the active participation of the French, uses audiovisual industries both to reinforce existing national borders *and* to rearticulate the boundaries of collective identity and the public sphere in Europe.

European Identity and Audiovisual Industries

The origins of the European Union date to 1952, when the European Coal and Steel Community (ECSC) came into being. Five years later, the Treaties of Rome, signed by France, Germany, Italy, and the Benelux countries, created the European Atomic Energy Community (Euratom) and the European Economic Community (EEC). These three entities joined in 1965 to form the European Community. In 1973, Denmark, Ireland, and Great Britain joined the original six members. Greece acceded in 1981 and Spain and Portugal brought the total to twelve in 1986. "The Twelve" were joined by Finland, Sweden, and Austria in 1995. At this writing, the EU has just welcomed ten new members, including several eastern and central European countries, to bring the total membership to twenty-five. The European Community was generally thought to be a way to keep France and Germany from entering into conflict with each other and to give Europe a voice in the emerging postwar, bipolar structure, dominated by the United States and the USSR. However, in recent years, it has evolved into something more ambitious.

The integration of Europe began in the economic sphere with the lowering of national barriers to the movement of goods and services. The founders assumed that political integration would naturally follow, but this has proved difficult. Events in recent decades signal an effort to encourage European integration at a more fundamental level. European participation in the Gulf War marked the first attempt to harmonize defense policy. The signing of the Maastricht Treaty in 1992 formalized efforts to create a common currency and to broaden our understanding of European integration as not just economic union, but also political union. Political union is particularly elusive, in part because of the variety of languages spoken across member states and because of the range of interests pursued by their governments. The Maastricht Treaty promises to "mark a new stage in the process of European integration . . . creating an ever closer union among the peoples of Europe." This means evoking among citizens of member states a collective consciousness of their status as Europeans.

As early as 1973, at the Copenhagen Summit, this issue was broached in terms of identity, with The Declaration on European Identity. Uniting Europe at the level of identity could potentially serve many purposes, including legitimating the institutions of the community as its jurisdiction expands, strengthening Europe as an international actor, and justifying economic transfers from richer to poorer member states (Garcia 1993). Originally based on the assumption that there is a (already existing) European identity to evoke, this strategy later evolved toward the notion that there is an identity to cultivate.

Defining European identity is difficult for many reasons. Most obviously, Europe is comprised of many national cultural, religious, and linguistic traditions. In addition, the European Union is still in the process of becoming, as pending accession applications from other Eastern and Central European countries, as well as Turkey, attest. Therefore any identity must be able to accommodate, at the very least, orthodox and Islamic religious traditions, as well as Communist historical experiences. Like any collective identity, the European is, or will be, socially constructed and need not mirror European reality. Nonetheless, before it can emerge, there must be some agreement on such basic issues as the geographical limits of the Europe to which it will apply.

The European Commission has argued that any European identity is predicated on difference. Political union in Europe evidently does not hinge on the promotion of a diluted European identity that supersedes national identities; rather, it is an effort to make sure that Europeans come to know each other in their diversity and to acknowledge the common European thread that apparently runs through the culturally and linguistically distinct member states. Ultimately, contend European officials, a homogenized European identity is not necessary (nor is it possible); instead, a loose consensus has developed that there is a common idiom shared by the members that distinguishes them from non-Europeans.

It is worth noting that European-ness in a cultural sense is assumed by the heads of government to be plural: there is no suggestion that there should be a move towards some kind of "federal" culture to parallel the moves that are taking place towards a more integrated—if not politically federated—Europe. The link between polity and culture is one in which diversity is seen as the fundamental characteristic of that culture: the ideal European citizen, then, will happily enjoy the artistic endeavors of a wide variety of national cultures other than his own; he will *not* be consuming "instant Euro-pudding." (Hutchison 1993, 439)

This perspective gives the European Union much in common with Canada. Both seek to incorporate multiethnic communities into the broader political community without compelling them to relinquish loyalties and attachments to ancestral cultures. These cultural groupings within Europe and Canada have already laid claim to the standard components of collective identity, specifically linguistic and cultural attributes that traditionally underpin national identity. In choosing not to trample on these, both Canada and the European Union must cobble together collective identities from the remaining, and often more nebulous, social attributes that can end up being unsatisfactory social glue. The EU is at a particular disadvantage because it does not (yet) evoke any of the emotional attachments that states do. At a minimum, the "aims of the EU's cultural policy are to bring out the common aspects of Europe's heritage, enhance the feeling of belonging to one and the same community, while recognising and respecting cultural, national and regional diversity, and helping cultures to develop and become more widely known" (Commission 2002, 3).

In order to promote European identity, the European Union has taken a number of cultural initiatives in recent decades. It has subsidized translations of major works of European literature and financed the preservation of architectural treasures. It has supported the ERASMUS program, which gives college-level students the opportunity to study in another member state. Since 1985, it has named one city annually as the European City of Culture. "But it is in the audio-visual sphere that the Community has made the most effort and had the most impact" (Hutchison 1993, 439). In fact, since the 1980s, there is a widespread belief that the audiovisual sector may be the key to bringing about "ever closer union" on which continued progress in the European Union depends. Theiler (2005) argues that the original hope among EU officials was to promote genuinely European, "denationalized" products. This did not materialize in part because of national resistance to EU activity in the cultural sphere. Instead, EU measures promoted greater national cultural production, as well as greater circulation of national cultural products within the EU.

The European perspective highlights the link between the economic and cultural importance of audiovisual industries—they must be economically viable in order to fulfill their cultural purpose.

Special consideration . . . must be given to the status of audiovisual production. Quite suddenly, technological progress in broadcasting and telecommunications turned television into a media that is not only dominant, but will also represent in the very near future the alpha and omega of social communication. . . . Broadcasting will soon be the principal instrument for expression. No one can be expected to deliver exclusive control of such an instrument to someone abroad. (Maggiore 1990, 38)

Jacques Delors, in his capacity as president of the European Commission, commented in 1989 at the European audiovisual conference, that "culture is not just another type of merchandise . . . we cannot treat culture as we would treat refrigerators or even motor cars. Laissez-faire, market forces alone cannot suffice" (in Maggiore 1990, 197). Delors goes on to specify the link between audiovisual industries and identity.

To our American friends, who took the opportunity three or four days before the conference to attack in the GATT . . . four countries which had signed the Council of Europe Convention [Eurimages], I would like to ask: do we not have the right to exist? Do we not have the right to perpetuate our traditions, our heritage and our languages? How can a country of 10 million inhabitants, faced with the universality offered by satellites, maintain its language which is a vehicle of its culture? Does not the defence of liberty so loudly proclaimed elsewhere include the effort made by each country, or group of countries, to preserve its identity by audiovisual means? (in Maggiore 1990, 197)

This perspective is echoed in European Commission documents.

Cinematographic and televisual programmes are goods unlike any others: as privileged vectors of culture, they retain their specific nature amid the new types of audiovisual product which are currently multiplying; as living witnesses of the traditions and of the identity of each country, they merit encouragement; only a strong European industry will be able to guarantee both the diversity of programmes and an increase in the international influence of European cultures. Given the position of the image in our society, much is at stake in cultural terms.[2]

The U.S. government has opposed this stance, accusing France and the European Union on separate occasions of cloaking a protectionist economic agenda in cultural arguments. Ironically, however, it would appear that European leaders have often done the opposite, cloaking what is actually a cultural initiative in economic language. European Union representatives are well aware of the ability

2. "First Report on the Consideration of Cultural Aspects in European Community Action," Directorate-General X, Information, Communication and Culture, Commission of the European Communities, part 3, section 2, 1995–96.

of the institutions they govern to trample on national policy terrain. In order to legitimize any measure they implement, "every directive, decision or regulation must refer to the appropriate Treaty (ECSC, EC, Euratom) and to one or more articles. This formality is taken seriously in order to ensure that the Community bodies do not legislate on something that does not fall within their competence" (Papathanassopoulos 1990, 111). The Treaty of Rome does not extend the jurisdiction of the European institutions to the realm of culture. Therefore there has been a "necessity for the Commission's actions in respect of culture to be presented as an exercise of Community jurisdiction in the economic, rather than cultural, sphere" (Collins 1994, 90). Jacques Delors echoed this difficulty in his speech to open the European Parliament as Commission president in 1985.

> Under the terms of the Treaty we do not have the resources to implement a cultural policy; but we are going to try to tackle it along economic lines. It is not simply a question of television programmes. We have to build a powerful European culture industry that will enable us to be in control of both the medium and its content, maintaining our standards of civilization, and encouraging the creative people amongst us. (In Collins 1994, 90)

This perspective is echoed in Commission documents.

> The weakness of Europe's most effective regulatory institution is the second "e" in "EEC." While Community regulation is the closest that international law comes to law without adjectives, its competences are limited to the realm of economic activity. Cinema and television can therefore only be handled as economic activities. (In Maggiore 1990, 107)

Theiler (2005) argues that to this day, EU officials must tread lightly around issues of culture. They continue to "economize" their initiatives—package them as contributing to the evolution of the single market or to economic policy where the EU has a clear mandate. Yet it is in the cultural realm that a sense of belonging to the European Union will supposedly be reinforced.

> European Union, the principal elements of which have been linked historically to economic and commercial activities, is thus required to deepen, over a wider basis, which is likely to increase citizens' involvement and reinforce the sense of belonging to the European Union, whilst respecting the diversity of the national and regional traditions and cultures involved. In this respect, cultural action has a major role to play.[3]

---

3. Ibid., "Introduction."

It is not surprising, then, that the Treaty on European Union, signed in Maastricht in 1992, includes a provision that expands the jurisdiction of the institutions of the European Union to the cultural sphere.

Section 128 of the Maastricht Treaty "is an expression of the Community's obligation to consider cultural objectives in all its activity."[4] It officially recognizes that it is not possible to develop a cultural policy within institutions designed to create economic union. It provides "a legal basis specific to culture [that] signifies that Community action with regard to culture will henceforth be of a permanent nature and become an acknowledged branch of community activity."[5] Article 128 includes the following provisions:

1. The Community shall contribute to the flowering of the cultures of the Member States, while respecting their national and regional diversity and at the same time bringing the common culture to the fore.

2. Action by the Community shall be aimed at encouraging cooperation between Member States and, if necessary, supporting and supplementing their action in the following areas:

— improvement of the knowledge and dissemination of the culture and history of the European peoples;

— conservation and safeguarding of cultural heritage of European significance;

— non-commercial cultural exchanges;

— artistic and literary creation, including in the audiovisual sector.

3. The Community and the Member States shall foster cooperation with third countries and the competent international organizations in the sphere of culture, in particular the Council of Europe.

4. The Community shall take cultural aspects into account in its action under other provisions of this Treaty.

The Maastricht Treaty came into force in 1992, shortly before EU negotiators would make the explicit link between cultural goals and audiovisual industries in the trade talks. The European commissioner responsible for audiovisual industries in the aftermath of the Uruguay Round affirmed the sociocultural significance of his portfolio.

Audiovisual industries play a crucial role in conveying culture both in terms of distribution and production. They also play an important part in

---

4. Ibid., "Summary."
5. Ibid., "Introduction."

the development of our societies. The average European spends more than three hours a day in front of the television and children spend as much time watching television as they do at school. *Preserving and developing the European social model means making better use of audiovisual capacities as a major means of communication, conveying information and knowledge and forming identity.*[6]

The European Commission explicitly stated before the Uruguay Round talks that it would only embrace liberalization of the audiovisual sector if it did not jeopardize the cultural importance of these industries.

> Cultural and linguistic identities . . . must be protected. . . . The Community is therefore approaching these negotiations with the firm intention of achieving international liberalization within the limits already achieved within the Community, i.e. by leaving intact the cultural specificity of the sector and the Community measures dependent on this specificity.[7]

EU policy documents from the 1980s and 1990s make clear the link between promoting European identity and strong audiovisual industries throughout Europe. These industries are thought to be able to contribute to the creation of a European identity or a collective consciousness that would underpin and strengthen the institutions of the EU, in part because Europeans produce and distribute the majority of European works (Maggiore 1990). Audiovisual industries are believed to play a socializing role and to contribute to social cohesion. One European Commission document contends that the disappearance of European programming would "leave the continent with no ink with which to write."[8] The European Council has asserted that audiovisual industries are the key to eliciting support from Europeans for further integration.

> The commitment of citizens to the European idea depends on positive measures being taken to enhance and promote European culture in its

---

6. Memo from Mr. Oreja to the Commission, "Audiovisual Policy: Progress and Prospects," p. 4, Marcelino Oreja, Commission member responsible for audiovisual policy, Records of Directorate-General X, Information, Communication and Culture, Commission of the European Communities. Emphasis mine.

7. Commission of the European Communities, "Communication from the Commission to the Council and Parliament on Audiovisual Policy," (COM[90]78final), Brussels, 21 February 1990, p. 64.

8. "First Report on the Consideration of Cultural Aspects in European Community Action," p. 41.

richness and diversity. In this context the European Council considers it essential to consolidate recent achievements and capitalize on the guidelines which emerged from the Audiovisual Conference in order to develop Europe's audiovisual capacity. (Commission 1990, 9)

The Council also notes that a European audiovisual space is necessary for cultural and political reasons. "The implementation of common technical specifications simplifies the broadcasting of television programmes in all countries of the Community and makes a significant contribution to European unification and to the development of a true European identity."[9]

The European Commission has argued that the commercial value of audiovisual industries is not the only, or even the most significant, measure of their worth. "The two hours a day which the average European spends in front of his television set and their impact on the general public in terms of news, consumer fashions and life styles are such that the sector's importance cannot be measured solely in terms of the contribution to GDP."[10]

This same document later refers to broadcasting as "a vector of cultural identities" (Commission 1990, 64). Elsewhere, the Commission has elaborated on this position.

The audiovisual sector is now seen as a strategic sector for the services industry in the European Community. Although relatively modest in economic terms, its growth is significant: put at ECU 25 billion in 1990, it should grow to around ECU 35 billion at the end of the decade. In addition to its potential for economic growth, the audiovisual sector is important because of its socio-cultural dimension: as a vehicle for the wealth and diversity of European cultures, its development gives expression to the very essence of the Community. It helps to shape public opinion and to establish references for both behavior and consumption.[11]

9. "Council Directive of November 3, 1986, on the Adoption of Common Technical Specifications of the MAC/packet Family of Standards for Direct Satellite Television Broadcasting,"http://europa.eu.int/ISPO/infosoc/legreg/docs/86529eec.html

10. Commission of the European Communities, "Conclusions of the Presidency: European Council," Strasbourg. December 8–9, 1989, in *The European Community Policy in the Audiovisual Field: Legal and Political Texts* (Luxembourg: Office for Official Publications of the European Communities, 1990), p. 29.

11. Commission of the European Communities, "Commission Communication to the Council Accompanied by Two Proposals for the Council Decisions Relating to an Action Programme to Promote the Development of the European Audiovisual Industry 'Media' 1991–95," in *Legal and Political Texts,*, p. 70.

More recently, officials at the Commission confirm this view. As one official in the Directorate General for Trade observed, "When we talk to Europeans about trade in audiovisual products, they don't think about the economic aspect, they think about their very souls."[12] Other EU sources explicitly note that developing Europe's audiovisual capacity by such measures as the enhancement of the free movement of programs "will contribute to a substantial strengthening of a European cultural identity."[13] Television is an instrument of integration that "will play an important part in developing and nurturing awareness of the rich variety of Europe's common cultural and historical heritage. The dissemination of information across national borders can do much to help the people of Europe to recognise the common destiny they share in many areas."[14]

Television is said to "help to develop a people's Europe through reinforcing the sense of belonging to a Community composed of countries which are different but partake of a deep solidarity."[15] Theiler notes that many on either side of the audiovisual debate in Europe attributed to television "an almost magical ability to mould popular attitudes" (2005, 87). Many in the Commission and the Parliament, in particular, had "too uncritical a faith in the ability of technology to act as a European identity forger" (Theiler 2005, 111).

In the report from the High Level Group on Audiovisual Policy, former Commissioner Marcelino Oreja argued that

the importance of the audiovisual industry therefore cannot be overestimated: for the vast majority of Europeans, it is the major source of information not only about events in their world, but also about the nature of that world. It plays an enormous role in developing and transmitting social values and influences not only what citizens see, but how they understand what they see. It is the single most important source of entertainment and culture.[16]

12. Interview with Julien Guerrier, Office of the EU Trade Commissioner, Brussels, July 2003.

13. "Conclusions of the Presidency: European Council, Rhodes, 2 and 3 December, 1988," in *Legal and Political Texts*, p. 7.

14. Commission of the European Communities, "Council Directive of 3 October 1989 on the Coordination of Certain Provisions Laid Down by Law, Regulation or Administrative Action in Member States Concerning the Pursuit of Television Broadcasting Activities," (Television without Frontiers) (89/552/EEC).

15. Commission of the EC, "Towards a Large European Audiovisual Market," cited in Morley and Robins, 1989: 12.

16. "Chairman's Message," Report from the High Level Group on Audiovisual Policy. Available at http://europa.eu.int/comm/avpolicy/legis/key_doc/hlg_en.htm#CHAIRMAN, accessed July 7, 2002.

The Report of the High Level Group on Audiovisual Policy goes on to state this in even stronger terms:

> However, the role of the media goes much further than simply providing information about events and issues in our societies or allowing citizens and groups to present their arguments and points of view: communication media also play a formative role in society. That is, they are largely responsible for forming (not just informing) the concepts, belief systems and even the languages—visual and symbolic as well as verbal—which citizens use to make sense of and interpret the world in which they live. Consequently, the role of communication media extends to influencing who we think we are and where we believe we fit in (or not) in our world: in other words, the media also play a major role in forming our cultural identity.[17]

These views have become even stronger with the accession of new members to the EU. In early 2004, a Commission report on the prospects for European citizenship in an EU of twenty-five or more members, observed:

> The coming decade will greatly increase the diversity of the Union. With the accession of 10 new Member States on 1 May 2004, it will undergo the most significant enlargement in its history. Further accessions are foreseen. . . . Moreover, our societies are undergoing major demographic change. . . . These developments make it more necessary than ever that Europe's citizens have an opportunity to experience a feeling of *belonging* to the Union and are able to identify with it. The reality is that many citizens experience the Union as merely a distant and remote political and economic entity. (2004, 5)

The same document goes onto specify that EU-level action can be significant by contributing to "the bottom-up development of a dynamic European identity," (2004, 10) assuming it has adequate *means* to make such a contribution. The audiovisual industry is among the favored means.

> The social and cultural impact of the audiovisual sector exceeds that of any other medium. This impact is its defining feature and is evident from the role of television alone. Household penetration of television sets in

17. "The Media and the European Model of Society," Report from the High Level Group on Audiovisual Policy. Available at http://europa.eu.int/comm/avpolicy/legis/key_doc/hlg_en.htm#CHAIRMAN, accessed July 7, 2002.

Europe is of the order of 98% and the average European watches more than three hours of television a day. For children the figure is even higher. The audiovisual media play a fundamental role in the development and transmission of social values. The audiovisual sector has a major influence on what citizens know, believe and feel and plays a crucial role in the transmission, development and even construction of cultural identities. (2004, 13)

Therefore, the European Union, like the Canadian government, equates culture industries with identity formation. Economic liberalization at the global level, but also at the regional level, promises immeasurable positive economic and political benefit for Europeans. But it also carries with it unique challenges to Europe's ability to promote national and regional identity and diversity. Meeting these challenges through support measures in the audiovisual realm is not protectionist. Rather, it is an effort to embrace liberalization while simultaneously offsetting its cultural costs, a dynamic we associate with embedded liberalism.

Challenges to European Audiovisual Industries

Across the European Union, certain countries have relied more heavily than others on imported audiovisual products, just as some have put more energy into developing domestic television and film industries. France, for example, is relatively well-off compared to some European countries with regard to film. In 1986, U.S. films accounted for 43 percent of screen time in France, compared to 92 percent in Britain (Dyson and Humphreys 1990, 22). In 2001, U.S. films accounted for 81.4 percent of the British market, with British films claiming only 12 percent.[18] In the mid 1990s, approximately 60 percent of all films shown in Italy were American, 77 percent of those shown in Spain, 82 percent of those screened in Germany, and 95 percent of the films exhibited in Greece and Portugal (Condron 1997). The share of the audience taken by U.S. films in EU countries increased from 46 percent in 1980 to 69 percent in 1991 (Hutchison 1993, 440). Ten years later, many in Europe ironically celebrated when U.S. films took "only" 66 percent of EU market share, down from 73 percent in 2000, thus reaching its lowest level in four years.[19] The market share of European films in the EU market rose in 2001 to 31 percent, up from 23 percent in 2000.[20]

---

18. *Focus 2002*, European Audiovisual Observatory, p. 36.

19. Ibid., p. 5.

20. Ibid., p. 20.

In television programming, the U.S. presence is equally pervasive. In the late 1980s, 40 percent of "telefilms" on European public service television channels were American.[21] "When the overall figures for television fiction are considered the non-dramatic presence is unmistakable: in 1990, 29 percent of television drama on ARD and ZDF was American and 53 percent German, while 32 percent on the BBC channels came from the US and 34 percent was British. Italy's public service channels derived 80 percent of drama from America and 7 percent from Italy, and the French public service channels 43 percent from America and 35 percent from France" (Hutchison 1993, 441). The European Commission reports that, during a five-year period in the mid 1980s, French-made prime-time programming was down 30 percent, while U.S.–made prime-time programming was up 60 percent (In Palmer and Tunstall 1990, 71). Overall, U.S. programs account for approximately one-quarter of broadcasting time in Europe and between one-third and one-half of fiction programs broadcast in Europe come from the United States (Dyson and Humphreys 1990, 19).

Of course the situation is very different in the United States, where more than 90 percent of all films shown are American. In 1997, "the European film industry [posted] its best results in five years," taking 3 percent of market share in the United States, compared to 1.16 percent in 1995 and 1.24 percent in 1996.[22] The market share for European films steadily rose to 4.51 percent in 2000 and 5.02 percent in 2001,[23] and while the trend is encouraging, the numbers do not come near U.S. showings in the European market. Indeed, according to the European Audiovisual Observatory, the deficit in audiovisual trade between the European Union and the United States has been growing steadily, reaching $8.2 billion in 2000, up from $7.2 billion in 1999.[24] In addition, for every twelve hours of U.S. programs shown on European television, less than one hour of European programs is shown in the United States, and this one hour is often available only on PBS or on cable channels catering to the Hispanic community.[25]

French and European industries have found it difficult to compete with this U.S. presence for a variety of structural reasons.[26] Among other things, they are

21. Commission of the European Communities, *The Audio-Visual Media in the Single European Market* (Luxembourg, 1988), p. 22.

22. "News: Market Share of European Films on the American Market Came to Three per Cent in 1997," Press release of the European Audiovisual Observatory.

23. *Focus 2002*, European Audiovisual Observatory, p. 5.

24. Ibid., p. 5.

25. Ibid., p. 24.

26. "First Report on the Consideration of Cultural Aspects in European Community Action," part 3, chap. 2; ibid., "Opening Speech by Jacques Santer . . . ," p. 3. Commission of the European Communities, "Commission Communication to the Council Accompanied by Two Proposals for Council Decisions Relating to an Action Programme to Promote the Development of the European Audiovisual Industry 'MEDIA 1991–95,'" (COM[90]132final), Brussels, May 4, 1990, 72.

disadvantaged with regard to market size, control of distribution networks, and availability of financing. As is the case with Canada, European countries cannot compete with U.S. producers who are often able to recover their costs, especially in television, in their huge domestic market. At the time of the Uruguay Round negotiation, the European cinema market was roughly half the size of the U.S. market, in terms of admissions per year, though this changed with the accession of ten new member states.[27] Nevertheless, even though the European market seems large, it operates as a collection of national markets because of linguistic and industrial differences. To the degree that European countries have been able to sustain viable television and film industries, it is due in large part to policy measures that have been put in place to help them.

All over Europe, television expanded rapidly in a relatively short period of time. In France, for example, there were less than 1 million television sets in 1958. Ten years later there were more than 10 million (Palmer and Tunstall 1990, 80). Only one channel existed until 1964, broadcasting sixty-five program hours per week, as compared to fifty-three hours a decade earlier (Palmer and Tunstall 1990, 80). With the addition of new channels and the expansion of programming schedules, this number jumped significantly by the 1970s and 1980s. Satellite technology will further increase the number of programming hours (Dyson and Humphreys 1990, 15). But the European Commission reports that production of fiction and feature films for television in the four largest original member states—France, Germany, Italy, and the United Kingdom—cannot meet this programming demand (Maggiore 1990, 42). Indeed, production of any type of programming cannot keep up with demand (Kuhn 1995, 241). Insomuch as content regulations allow, television stations purchase cheaper U.S. programs to fill airtime and to keep their costs down.

The Directorate General of the European Commission responsible for audiovisual policy identifies the European program industry's key weaknesses as "fragmentation into national markets which means that producers are too small to compete on European and world markets; a low rate of cross-border programme distribution and circulation; a spiralling and chronic deficit; inability to attract the financial resources for recovery."[28]

European distributors generally operate on a national scale, while U.S. studios are able to distribute across Europe. The European Union's Green Paper on

27. "The European Film Industry under Analysis: Second Information Report 1997," Directorate-General X, Culture, Information, Communications and Audiovisual, Commission of the European Communities, section 1.1.

28. "Audiovisual Policy," Records of Directorate-General X, Culture, Information, Communications and Audiovisual, Commission of the European Communities. See also André Lange, "The Ups and Downs of European Cinema," 8–11–2001, European Audiovisual Observatory. Accessed from EAO website at http://www.obs.coe.int/medium/film.html.en, June 10, 2004.

Audiovisual Policy notes that "only twenty percent of European films go beyond their national frontier." In 2002, the European Audiovisual Observatory reported that European films outside their national market accounted for 9.3 percent of the European market.[29] Those that are released outside their borders often suffer from poor promotional strategy (Hift 1994, 27). In addition, the exhibition of so-called nonnational European films—films that sell within Europe but outside of their national market—is uneven across Union member states. French audiences watch 23 percent of nonnational films circulating in the European market, while British audiences only watch 3 percent.[30] In other words, European films that do leave their country of origin are not circulating freely throughout the European Union. "With respect to the distribution of feature films, it is almost universally agreed that the difficulty of distributing European films is not so much due to their quality but rather to the weak and fragmented nature of distribution circuits."[31] European companies are starting to work together to create distribution networks that transcend national borders. For example, in 1997, French companies Pathé and Canal Plus agreed to share their European distribution networks.

Fragmentation of the European audiovisual industries also occurs at the subnational level. The predominance of numerous small production companies is a major structural impediment to film production in Europe. There is no "studio" structure to rival the Hollywood model. In fact, "the majority of European productions are made by small producers in a highly fragmented industry where 80 percent of companies produce no more than one film a year."[32] Many European countries have at least one company that is competitive internationally—Canal Plus and Gaumont in France, Sogepaq in Spain, Polygram in Holland—but there is, to date, limited interpenetration between them. As a result, European producers find it difficult to compete with U.S. studio productions that can invest millions of dollars in production and promotion.

The average investment per film in Europe in recent years is $3 million. However, the average cost of film production is well above this. In the United States, the average estimated cost per film is $12 million. This number is closer to $60 million if only major studios are considered; this includes $20–30 million for promotion alone.[33] The European Audiovisual Observatory reports that these figures, current for 2001, represent an increase in marketing costs, but a significant *drop*—to 47 million dollars—in production costs.[34] "The figures show that

29. *Focus 2002*, European Audiovisual Observatory, p. 20.
30. "The European Film Industry under Analysis," section 3.3.
31. Ibid., section 3.1.
32. Ibid., section 2.1.
33. Ibid., section 2.4.
34. *Focus 2002*, European Audiovisual Observatory, p. 11.

50 percent of the total budget of an American film goes toward marketing, compared to only 3 to 6 percent of a European film budget."[35] British films have the highest budgets in Europe, rising from 7.8 million euros in 2000 to 9.6 million euros in 2001. Italian film budgets also grew in 2001, from 2.1 million euros to 2.9 million euros. On the contrary, French film budgets dropped slightly, from 4.68 million euros in 2000 to 4.36 million euros in 2001.[36]

The revenue structure in the film industry is unusual. A very small proportion of the revenue from a film comes from its actual sale, that is, its exhibition in a cinema. The European Commission reports that only 6 percent of revenue comes from the box office.[37] Pay television and video are growing in importance as sources of revenue. The UK, Italy, and France require television broadcasters to invest in the film industry. In Germany, although it is not mandated by law, television channels finance 50 percent of television drama and are increasingly making a contribution to feature film production for cinema exhibition.[38]

Coproductions are another response to the lack of financing. Of the 610 films produced in the European Union in 1996, 44 percent came from coproduction arrangements.[39] American studios traditionally shy away from coproduction agreements, preferring instead to recoup costs through the sale of film soundtracks and other merchandise, as well as partnership deals with groups from outside the film industry, such as fast-food restaurants. Luc Besson's *The Fifth Element* is one of the first European films to try a U.S.–style merchandising campaign, but few others have embraced this approach.

European Audiovisual Policy

In response to the structural weaknesses outlined above, the audiovisual policy of the European Union has been driven by two major objectives: the establishment of a "European area" for audiovisual services so that "most of the work disseminated by European broadcasters is European," and the reinforcement of the European program production industry.[40] The publication of the Hahn Report[41] in 1983 is an early sign that audiovisual policy would play a central role

---

35. "European Film Industry under Analysis," section 1.3.
36. *Focus 2002,* European Audiovisual Observatory, p. 20.
37. "European Film Industry under Analysis," section 1.3.
38. Ibid., section 2.1
39. Ibid., section 2.4
40. "First Report on the Consideration of Cultural Aspects in European Community Action," part 3: Audiovisual Policy.
41. Officially known as the *Interim Report on Realities and Tendencies in European Television: Perspectives and Options,* COM(83)229, Final, European Parliament, Brussels, May 25, 1983.

in European unification strategy, pointing to transnational communication and audiovisual industries as the cornerstone of the cultural initiative toward political union (Collins 1994, 94). The report advocates an EU broadcasting policy and supports satellite technology to facilitate the establishment of European television.

If the Hahn Report was the first move toward European audiovisual policy, the 1984 Green Paper, which led to the 1989 Commission Directive, Television without Frontiers, remains the most important. Indeed, Television without Frontiers provided the major point of conflict between the United States and the EU during Uruguay Round GATT talks. The directive creates a single broadcasting market across European member states, establishes standards for advertising, and promotes independent production and distribution companies. As a "directive," it is enforceable by European Union law. However, implementation is at the discretion of each member state "where practicable." European officials explicitly acknowledge its potential contribution to European integration.

> Information is a decisive, perhaps the most decisive factor in European unification. . . . European unification will only be achieved if Europeans want it. Europeans will only want it if there is such a thing as a European identity. A European identity will only develop if Europeans are adequately informed. At present, information via the mass media is controlled at the national level.[42]

The preamble of the directive argues that free circulation of broadcasting programs within the European Union will contribute to "an ever closer union among the peoples of Europe, fostering closer relations between the States belonging to the Community."[43] It goes on to acknowledge that "co-ordination is nevertheless needed to make it easier for persons and industries producing programmes having a cultural objective to take up and pursue their activities."[44]

The most controversial provision of the directive is Article 4, section 1, which states:

> Member States shall ensure where practicable and by appropriate means, that broadcasters reserve for European works, within the meaning of Article 6, a majority proportion of their transmission time, excluding the time appointed to news, sports events, games, advertising and teletext services.

---

42. Commission of the European Communities, Television without Frontiers, pp. 2 and 28.
43. Ibid.
44. Ibid.

This proportion, having regard to the broadcaster's informational, educational, cultural and entertainment responsibilities to its viewing public, should be achieved progressively, on the basis of suitable criteria.[45]

Article 5 imposes a related requirement, mandating that broadcasters reserve at least 10 percent of their transmission time or 10 percent of their programming budget for "European works created by producers who are independent of broadcasters." Article 6 defines "European work."

1. Within the meaning of this chapter, 'European works' means the following:

a. works originating from Member States of the Community and, as regards television broadcasters falling within the jurisdiction of the Federal Republic of Germany, works from German territories where the Basic Law does not apply and fulfilling the conditions of paragraph 2;

b. works originating from European third States party to the European Convention on Transfrontier Television of the Council of Europe and fulfilling the conditions of paragraph 2;

c. works originating from other European third countries and fulfilling the conditions of paragraph 3.

2. The works referred to in paragraph 1(a) and (b) are works mainly made with authors and workers residing in one or more States referred to in paragraph 1(a) and (b) provided that they comply with one of the following three conditions:

a. they are made by one or more producers established in one or more of those States; or

b. production of the works is supervised and actually controlled by one or more producers established in one or more of the States; or

c. the contribution of co-producers of those States to the total co-production costs is preponderant and the co-production is not controlled by one or more producers established outside those States.

3. The works referred to in paragraph 1(c) are works made exclusively or in co-production with producers established in one or more Member State by producers established in one or more European third countries with which the Community will conclude agreements in accordance with the procedures of the Treaty, if those works are mainly made with au hors and workers residing in one or more European States.

---

45. Ibid.

4. Works which are not European works within the meaning of paragraph 1, but made mainly with authors and workers residing in one or more Member States, shall be considered to be European works to an extent corresponding to the proportion of the contribution of Community co-producers to the total production costs.

The definition of a European work resembles that of a Canadian work in that both are predicated on the nationality of participants. Neither definition suggests influencing content by requiring specific themes or categories of characters. Therefore, the Television without Frontiers directive parallels Canadian measures that rely on domestic nationals to infuse their works with certain values.

In 1997, the Television without Frontiers directive was revised to take into consideration such developments as "teleshopping," the desire to protect children, and the increasing prominence of digital technology. The definition of European works expanded to include coproductions with third countries where the major portion of the costs of production is covered by community coproducers and where production is not controlled by a producer or producers established outside the territory of the member states.

In 1986, the European Commission proposed the MEDIA program (Measures to Encourage the Development of the Audiovisual Industry) and launched it five years later as a complement to Television without Frontiers. MEDIA is designed to ensure that there is enough programming content to fill the quotas set by the Television without Frontiers directive. The program has since been renewed twice, as MEDIA II from 1996–2000 and as MEDIA Plus from 2001–2005. MEDIA responds to structural weaknesses in European audiovisual industries by promoting cooperation among Europeans in programming, financing, and distribution. It supports training initiatives, production assistance, promotion, and multilingualism of programming. It emphasizes the pre- and postproduction phases of creation and encourages production companies to improve their organizational structure and to seek European partners. "Priority is given to small- and medium-sized undertakings and to those countries whose languages and cultures are less widespread than others within the Community."[46] In the area of project development, MEDIA supports film and television drama, documentaries, and animation. In addition, it provides assistance for script writing, help with financing, and training.[47]

---

46. "MEDIA II (1996–2000), A Support-Scheme for Boosting the Competitiveness of the European Programme Industry," Documents of Directorate-General X of the European Commission, Information, Communication, Culture and Audiovisual, p. 3, and Hutchison 1993, 446.

47. Ibid., p. 1.

Among other measures, MEDIA supports pilot projects by providing up to 50 percent of the cost of the undertaking as seed money that must then be matched by professional institutions or private sponsors.

The MEDIA 92 approach to the question of providing an effective support to the European audiovisual industry consists of two basic assumptions: first, that the professionals themselves must determine the form that aid to production must assume; and second, that the support has to result in the establishment of independent agencies and/or structures. (Maggiore 1990, 63)

The pilot projects supported by MEDIA have included the European Film Distribution Office, based in Hamburg, which gave loans to offset distribution costs for low-budget European feature films; BABEL (Broadcasting across the Barrier of European Languages), which helped finance subtitling and dubbing; the European Script Fund, based in London, which focuses on preproduction assistance and the development of script ideas for feature film and television fiction, an area in which Europeans traditionally invest little as compared to the United States;[48] and, EAVE (European Audiovisual Entrepreneurs), which provides management training.

In the priority area of distribution (cinema, video, television), MEDIA II aims to encourage distributors to invest in the production of promising films to add to their catalogues and to enhance their chances of worldwide distribution by increasing the number of copies available and the amount spent on promotion. One of the best ways of doing this is to build strong and lasting links between distributors and to encourage multilingualism by means of dubbing and subtitling. Incentives are also being offered for the creation of networks of commercial cinemas with a policy of showing mainly European films. . . . MEDIA II is focusing its effort in the television sector on independent production companies. These are capable of producing high-quality works which can be shown outside their country of origin, provided they are backed from the outset by the various national television channels in Europe. Loans will be available for co-productions bringing together independent production companies and broadcasters who agree to show their programmes in their particular area.[49]

48. "The European Film Industry under Analysis," chapter 2, section 1.2
49. MEDIA II (1996–2000), pp. 1–2.

MEDIA promotes distribution of films within the European Union by offering incentives for several distributors to come together to promote a single film throughout Europe. In 1996, fifty films were distributed widely throughout the member states under this program.[50] The European Union further supports distribution by supporting film festivals. "The festivals play a prime cultural role as an alternative method of film distribution to the commercial cinema circuit, and enable the public to see films which would otherwise not have been distributed widely, if at all."[51] Festivals subsidized by the European Union generally show upward of 80 percent European content.

Among other initiatives taken by the European Union, the European Commission dubbed 1988 the European Film and Television Year. A year later it introduced the EUREKA program, dubbed the audiovisual 'marriage bureau' (Collins 1994, 97), to promote co-productions within Europe. Other proposals include the creation of a European Film and Television School and the establishment of a European "Oscars."[52] Of course, a rich tradition of public broadcasting also provides avenues for promoting sociopolitical goals via audiovisual means. In recognition of this, the 1999 Amsterdam Treaty contains a provision reinforcing the European commitment to public service broadcasting and confirming each member state's freedom to organize and finance its own system in ways that serve the public interest.

As Collins (1994) argues, there are threats to diversity that accompany a body of policy designed to promote unity. "A single market would tend to eliminate cultural production by producers whose linguistically or geographically peripheral status made them vulnerable" (Collins 1994, 95). MEDIA is a response to this. Indeed, even countries that dominate European audiovisual industries, like France, promote diversity because English language productions would probably be the norm in unity.

Great Britain does not oppose the single market, but it has been known to oppose some of the policies, in part because its tradition is generally more liberal than its fellow member states. In addition, it could benefit from open competition in broadcasting as the only other major producer of cultural products in English. Nevertheless, even groups within Britain recognize the benefit of throwing in their lot with Europe, as opposed to the Anglo-Saxon world, represented by the United States. As one former chief executive of British Screen asserts:

> Increasingly, we in the UK are coming to understand the cultural significance of being part of Europe. . . . There is plenty of evidence that

50. "European Film Industry under Analysis," section 3.4.
51. Ibid., section 3.6.
52. Ibid., p. 6

nationalism and insistence upon cultural individuality are as strong now as ever. . . . Yet young people in Europe are already spending more time in each other's countries, making friends, hearing and speaking each other's languages, watching television. . . . Out of this will gradually come a sense of "Europeanism," of belonging to Europe as well as to a particular country. And in due course, this new sense of identity will give rise to a distinctive culture—expressed by European stories, European humour, European stars, European music and, we must assume, European movies. Even the traditionally insular Britons should cease to regard the Continent as foreign. (Perry 1991, 1)

Perry goes on to note that British filmmakers belong to European cinema and not to English-language cinema. Indeed, Europe is Britain's home market and the United States is for British filmmakers a particularly promising export market. Consequently, maintains Perry, filmmakers in the UK must endeavor to mount coproductions with their European partners.

We are the losers as a result, effectively imprisoned in the Anglo-Saxon world, missing out on a European party which has been long underway on the Continent. French, Spanish, Italian, German and Swiss producers consistently co-produce films with each other. . . . There are economic arguments. . . . But there are also cultural imperatives which necessitate participation by British film-makers in European projects. (Perry 1991, 2)

Given these sorts of considerations, it is therefore not surprising that Britain, often the spoiler for many European initiatives that threaten its sovereignty, would support its fellow member-states during the GATT round by resisting deregulation of the audiovisual sector. Even this most liberal of European Union members acknowledges the links between the cultural sector and broader political integration of Europe.

The European Union points to successes coming from its various audiovisual policies. For example, the *International Herald Tribune* reported in 1996 that, for the first time, European programs, like the Italian Mafia series *The Octopus* and the French detective show *Julie Lescaut*, were moving previously dominant U.S. programs out of prime time. In Italy, the top five shows in 1996 were all Italian, and in France, seven of the top eight were French. Ratings indicate that there is "a natural demand for national products"[53] and "an enormous appetite among

---

53. Jan Mojto, programming director of the Leo Kirch Group, a Munich-based broadcaster, cited in the *International Herald Tribune*, October 15, 1996, p. 2.

viewers for their own stars, plots and characters" (Tagliabue 1996, 2). In other words, demand exists if obstacles to supply can be removed. Since France has been the leading advocate of support measures to the audiovisual sector, the next section surveys the origins of this French position.

France and Audiovisual Industries

France led the European Union in its pursuit of the "cultural exception" strategy during the Uruguay Round of GATT, and it has been a strong proponent of various audiovisual support measures implemented at the European level. France and the European Union have complementary, but not identical, interests. The European Union seeks to use audiovisual industries to promote European integration and France supports this. Yet French officials are also concerned with the threats posed by foreign (read: U.S.) penetration of European audiovisual industries to French culture broadly construed.

French policymakers and intellectuals have long viewed U.S. cultural products as a threat to the values of French culture and civilization. French elites and others often equate U.S. culture with mass culture and the materialistic pursuit of standardized, disposable consumer goods. The sweeping influence of things American is made all the more difficult for the French because the United States is a relatively young country, not yet believed to be intellectually mature enough to set standards for the Europe from which it sprang. Though many in France follow and consume U.S. culture, many also feel there would be a loss if it were the only choice, rather than one among many.

Hollywood films are the most visible incarnation of U.S. popular culture apparently threatening to debase French high culture with movies and programs that anesthetize audiences, rather than encouraging critical reflection. Only in France would public debate erupt about the interruption of televised films by advertisements, with many arguing that it would "harm the integrity of the programme" (Maggiore 1990, 34).

> Hollywood appeared to be the quintessential expression of American culture. The French tended to attack American film-making as an "industry" that produced meters of banal celluloid escapism for profit. Gallic reservations about mass culture were already apparent: Hollywood threatened true culture because it subordinated quality to box office receipts. (Kuisel 1995, 11)

In addition to contaminating the French language with English words, U.S. films threaten to overtake the French cinema, widely believed to take a more artistic approach to filmmaking. France is said to be fighting "la guerre des images," the "war of the image" or the "war of representation." This perspective unites politicians across the political spectrum (Kuhn 1995, 240). In the weeks leading up to the [GATT] talks, Francois Mitterrand is reported to have said, "What is at stake, and therefore at risk, in the current negotiations is every country's right to create its own images" (Condron 1997, 208).

There is no doubt that identity considerations influence France's opposition to inclusion of audiovisual industries in trade agreements. Flynn (1995, 1) identifies "a national preoccupation with French identity." He goes on to clarify:

> This national preoccupation does not imply that large segments of the French population have suddenly stopped feeling French, or are about to do so. There is no evidence that the French are beginning to identify more with other objects of loyalty, either at the subnational or supranational level, than with their national state. Indeed, it is not even clear that the average French man or woman is really spending a great deal of time pondering the nation's identity at all. At the same time, it is undeniable that over the past few years, concerns about French identity have surfaced regularly among political elites, in intellectual circles, and in the media, engendering impassioned debate over national political choices in both domestic and foreign policy. (1995, 12)

These debates over identity are fueled by various developments in the contemporary French experience. Like most other industrialized nations, France faces the challenges to national distinctiveness that accompany globalization. In addition, all the members of the European Union, despite their general support for European integration, periodically resist the loss of sovereignty that it brings. Furthermore, France faces the formidable task of integrating immigrants, especially from former colonies in West and North Africa, into French society in a way that enriches without diluting traditional notions of what it means to be French. Unlike Canada and other immigrant countries, France has not been willing to embrace multiculturalism, wishing instead to preserve the single dominant culture that it has cultivated over the last several decades. Therefore, France attributes to audiovisual industries a constitutive role in the ongoing project of French identity formation. Nonetheless, U.S. domination of French audiovisual industries has traditionally struck a more fundamental chord. It is believed not only to interrupt the nation-building process, but to threaten to disrupt "certain mythological constructions of how the world works" (Loriaux 1999, 20) prevailing in France, specifically pertaining to culture and the state's role in its cultivation. As Jean-Noel Jeanneney, former director of Radio France and Secretary of State for Communications,[54] put it, the dispute over audiovisual industries is a philosophical debate, pitting two models of the state against each other.[55]

The French state has a long tradition of intervention in its economy. State intervention in France has often had a paternalistic character. Flynn contends that the French commonly view "the state as the agent of assimilation; the state as the guarantor, as well as provider of last resort, of wealth and welfare; and the state as protector" (1995, 6). He goes on to note that "in France, the nation's sense of itself has also required the state to be the protector of the nation's status and the propagator of its values" (1995, 9). Nora concurs, noting that "other countries may owe the sinews of their cohesion and the secret of their togetherness to economics, religion, language, social or ethnic community, or to culture itself. France has owed them to the voluntary and continuous action of the state."[56] This perspective is echoed in government documents. For example, the 1992 report of the Planning Commisariat characterizes the French state as "the guarantor of social and territorial solidarity" (Loriaux 1999, 40).

Loriaux (1999) contends that France should be viewed as a *developmental* state, in part because it exhibits a certain kind of ambition. "That ambition is more than one of economic growth, but one of protection and promotion of national interests, as perceived or determined by the administrative elite" (1999, 1). He goes on to argue that

> aggregate economic growth is not the only nor even the primary ambition that animates the developmental state elite. Rather, the state elite is animated by a particular kind of ambition, the ambition to provide the national community with a kind of moral good. . . . I use the term "moral good" loosely to designate a good the pursuit of which cannot be justified purely in terms of economic theory. Such goods as "social stability," "social cohesion," and "self-sufficiency" are not valued solely or even primarily for the economic externalities they produce. Nor do such goods need to have any transcendental justification at all. They can be valued because they correspond to a customary good or social norm that has been constructed historically within a particular society. (1999, 19)

54. Radio France from 1982–1986 and communications from 1991–93.

55. Interview with Jean-Noel Jeanneney at the Institut d'etudes politiques in Paris, October 8, 1996.

56. Pierre Nora, *Realms of Memory,* vol. 1, cited in Bell 1996, 97.

One central element of the French state's moral ambition is to act as "creator and tutor of the nation" (Loriaux 1999, 23). The school system was, and is, a primary vehicle in the performance of this tutelary role, but the pursuit of the state's moral ambition has expanded to new domains, including cultural and audiovisual policy.

Citing Rioux, Looseley (1995) points out that France has always distinguished itself from other developed nations by "the secular effort that the state has given over to the transmission and enrichment of 'culture' broadly construed and the degree to which it perceives this activity to be firmly within the domain of the central government" (1995, 2, my translation).

Actors on both ends of the political spectrum in France justify state intervention in the cultural realm, albeit in different terms. The right has a history of state intervention in culture for political ends. Charles de Gaulle is perhaps best known for this. André Malraux, France's first Minister of Culture, appointed by de Gaulle, saw culture as a means of promoting national unity. "A shared, common culture, free of elitist strands, was, for him, a 'force for union,' part of the unifying myth" (Wachtel 1987, 13). Malraux's Ministry was one component in de Gaulle's program to restore "the grandeur of France" in the post–World War II period. De Gaulle believed strongly in "the superiority of French tastes and sensibilities" (Kuhn 1995, 132) and bristled at U.S. postwar dominance. Television could disseminate the glories of French culture to a mass audience and, in the 1950s and 1960s especially, classical French theater and novels provided the basis of many television drama productions. De Gaulle also used television to mobilize support for the institutions of the new Fifth Republic and policies over Algeria.

> Centralized state control of television by the Gaullists in the 1960s, for instance, was intended to reinforce the legitimacy of the one and indivisible (Fifth) Republic as the embodiment of the national will, just as the prefectoral system of 150 years previously had been used to bind the nation under the control of the Napoleonic Empire. (Kuhn 1995, 5)

De Gaulle's Minister of Information argued that "broadcasting is a means of communication between the state and public opinion; it would be absurd for the government to give it to those who, via the press or otherwise, seek merely to criticize its actions" (Palmer and Tunstall 1990, 80). President Pompidou later echoed de Gaulle, calling French television "the voice of France."

During the 1969 campaign, for example, Pompidou argued that "because we have a national radio and television service . . . they are in a sense the official voice of France, and there is a certain tone to be maintained which must be the tone of France" (Kuhn 1995, 142). Another unidentified Gaullist minister is quoted as saying that "television is the government in the dining room" (Palmer and Tunstall 1990, 80).

Many of the debates concerning television from the 1960s through the 1980s centered on how it acted as an instrument of the state. French television began as a public system in 1945, with an *ordinance* that gave the state monopoly on broadcasting to Radiodiffusion de France (later Radiodiffusion-Télévision de France [RTF]). Not until the late 1950s did a significant mass market begin to emerge.[57] Over the years, as was the case in Canada, French television evolved into a dual system with public and private elements. However, the arrival of private actors came later, and they have played a more limited role in France than in other countries. Only in 1982 did the government pass the Audiovisual Communications Act, officially encouraging a diversity of channels and the incorporation of new actors into broadcasting in France.

Socialists in opposition for many years criticized rightist governments for their control of the media, objecting to the use of television to define the political agenda and to promote political objectives. This created a conundrum for the Socialists when they gained power under Mitterrand and embraced the public service role of broadcasting. They advocated "controlled deregulation" (Kuhn 1995, 168) to ensure that cultural and political goals were not compromised by broadcast media expansion.

French Socialists have a history of viewing culture as more than entertainment. Socialists dating back to the 1920s developed a philosophy of culture as an agent for social change. The notion of *action culturelle* has a long tradition among French socialists, referring to a concerted effort to promote cultural activities at the local level, based on the assumption that ideas and institutions that foster cultural awareness and creativity can lead to the democratization of culture and, therefore, ease class distinctions in French society. This is especially about democratizing "an accepted 'national' culture" (Looseley 1995, 18). Presidential candidate Mitterrand wrote in 1974 that *action culturelle* is a component of political action, "tied in every way to the transformation of the social order" and not merely a "soul soother" (Wachtel 1987, 10).

Much of the debate over wresting control of the media from the governing right, while still preserving its public service function, played out in efforts to establish a regulatory body for broadcasting that operated at arm's length from the state. The great difficulty in getting left and right to agree on such issues as

---

57. Kuhn 1995, 109. Kuhn (1995) attributes this to a variety of factors. Low standard of living of many French people coupled with the initial high cost of TV sets; many intellectuals and opinion leaders showed distaste for TV, regarding it as a vehicle for the worst of mass culture; weakness of French electronics industry in production.

how much power should be given to the broadcasting regulatory body, what its status and duties would be, how its members would be appointed, led to the establishment of three bodies in less than a decade. Before that, however, in 1964, the RTF became the Office of RTF (ORTF), essentially giving broadcasting some independence from the government. Rather than a public company accountable to the Ministry of Information, the ORTF remained under government supervision, but it acquired wider range of motion. In 1974, Valéry Giscard d'Estaing made further moves toward relinquishing the tight grip of the state on broadcasting by splitting the ORTF into seven public broadcasting companies: TF1, Antenne 2, FR3, Radio France, TDF, SFP, INA. The first independent regulatory body, the Haute Autorité de la Communication Audiovisuelle, was established in 1982. It appointed the chief executives of the public broadcasting entities and issued licenses to radio stations and cable television operators. The Haute Autorité was intended to occupy an intermediate position between the public service broadcasting enterprises and the government. Members were appointed for nine-year terms by the government. Many were dissatisfied with the Haute Autorité, and in 1986, during the *cohabitation* of Socialist President Mitterrand and the center-right Assemblée Nationale, a new law passed through Parliament making further openings to privatization and replacing the Haute Autorité with the Commission Nationale de la Communication et des Libertés (CNCL). Two years later, yet another regulatory body would be established to replace the CNCL. This body, the Conseil Supérieur de l'Audiovisuel (CSA), remains the central audiovisual regulatory body in France. The duties of the CSA include ensuring compliance with content quotas by television channels; appointment of chief executives of public service broadcasting bodies; issuance of terrestrial and satellite radio, television, and cable licenses; and the establishment of advertising standards.

Although some power has passed out of the hands of public broadcasters in France, content quotas are in place to ensure that stations do not revert to the purchase of less expensive U.S. programs. In 1986, Socialists imposed quotas for French and European productions on both public and private television. Fifty percent of airtime was to be set aside for French productions and 60 percent for European productions. France has gone on to champion the imposition of television quotas at the European level. These mirrored, in many ways, the quotas that had been in place in France, although the percentage requirements were lowered to reflect the weaker audiovisual industries of smaller European Union member states. In 1989, French quotas were revised to coincide with the European Directive Television without Frontiers, which mandates 50 percent European programming. Commercial channels protested this, but are often fined for not respecting quotas. In fact, the CSA can revoke broadcasting rights temporarily or permanently if quotas are contravened. Quotas vary from channel to channel, with the publicly owned channels subject to the most stringent requirements.

The licensing of the private television station La Cinq provides an interesting case of the commitment to upholding the content quotas exhibited by the CSA. La Cinq has been described as a "commercial channel which was both loved and reviled as a bridgehead of American programming" (Emanuel 1993, 131). It has been argued that La Cinq was "allowed to go spectacularly bankrupt" (Emanuel 1993, 131) for precisely this reason. "Before it went bankrupt, the channel was fined frequently and heavily for failing to respect the legal quotas for French and European productions. . . . Suspicions ran high: did the government deliberately push the channel to its end?" (Perry 1997, 128).

The French government had two choices: allow La Cinq to go into receivership and keep intact the government's policy of protection of French culture, or save La Cinq by giving it wider parameters within which it would be expected to meet its legal requirements with regard to French and European content, thus seemingly abandoning its commitment to cultural goals. The government chose the former option and La Cinq ceased broadcasting in April 1992. It was replaced in the evenings by the publicly owned French cultural channel La Sept (La Société d'Editions de Programmes de Télévision), later the Franco–German ARTE, and educational channel La Cinquième in the daytime. La Sept and ARTE were promoted by the Mitterrand governments "as compensation for deregulation and privatization, and as a tool for building Europe" (Emanuel 1993, 131). ARTE, dubbed "télé-Maastricht," is a Franco-German bilingual television station launched in 1992 as a cultural alternative to commercial television. Programming is half in German and half in French. It began as a satellite network but, with the bankruptcy of La Cinq, it was awarded a coveted terrestrial frequency.

An agreement signed between the French and German governments in 1990 created ARTE from La Sept. Germans already had two cultural channels, transmitted by satellite to Eastern Europe especially. ARTE broadcasts a few hours a week in Poland, Hungary, Yugoslavia, and Czechoslovakia, and its programming includes mostly documentaries, great performances, art and foreign films, some news and current affairs, often packaged together in "theme evenings." No sports, variety programs, or popular drama serials (soaps) are presented.

The experience with La Sept and ARTE reveals much about European perspectives on privatization of broadcasting and on cultural policy more generally. Countries like France can apparently no longer resist the global forces that are causing communications policies in the West to converge. Nevertheless, European policymakers, products of a normative environment that values public service broadcasting and state aid to culture, are actively taking compensatory action to lessen the losses perceived to accompany a greater role for market forces.

In the time of Malraux, culture was understood as great works or high culture (*beaux-arts*). More recently, especially since 1968, culture is interpreted broadly as "the state of a society, its civilization, its morals, its way of being, of living, of thinking" (cited in Looseley 1995, 4, my translation). In keeping with this, "cultural industries were not just a means of *diffusion* but could be creative forms in their own right" (Looseley 1995, 123). It has been more difficult to view television as a cultural form than cinema. There is ostensibly a passivity associated with television viewing that is not attributed to the cinema. But French elites have recognized the potential for a "reorientation of television towards cultural and educational programming" (Looseley 1995, 62). Practically speaking, recent governments acknowledge that, in industrial society, most people have access to television. Rather than the democratization of high culture of the *action culturelle* age, it makes sense to advocate the invigoration of culture industries with imagination, creation, and meaningful content and to do away with distinction between "high" and "low" culture. Mitterrand's Minister of Culture, Jack Lang, especially embraced this approach. "Rather than batter heroically at the non-public's door as the Ministry had habitually done, Lang very soon began to look for another way in, tackling the problem of cultural inequalities not in terms of audiences but of creative forms" (Looseley 1995, 123). This led to ministerial recognition of "popular" arts—"mass-cultural, industrially produced forms which operate in a market economy and which have no public service mission" (puppet theater, circus, cookery, fashion). With state intervention, argued Lang, television could help democratize culture by bringing high culture to the masses and by exposing the masses to programs they might not choose to watch in a competitive system.

Socialist Minister of Culture Lang became the great champion of French cultural industries during Mitterrand's first term in office. Not surprisingly, audiovisual industries fit neatly into the Socialist's more populist notion of culture. Lang defined culture as "all of you in all your daily acts" (Wachtel 1987, 5). Audiovisual industries became a focus for the Socialist government with the introduction of private television in France. It became apparent that television stations would favor low-cost U.S. serials. Lang dubbed this "cultural imperialism" at the UNESCO conference in Mexico in 1982, arguing that the expansion of media technology had enormous implications for the terms in which U.S. influence could be discussed. In a speech that received much international publicity, Lang signaled the direction that Socialist cultural policy would take under his stewardship.

Yes, culture is universal, but we are careful not to put it all on the same footing. We know very well today that there is no such thing as a global culture. First among cultural rights is the right of peoples to make choices for themselves. All our countries passively accept, perhaps too passively, a certain invasion, a certain wave of stereotyped foreign images and standardized songs that naturally chip away at national cultures and promote a uniform way of life that we seem to want to impose on everyone. In reality, this can be called interference in the domestic affairs of states and even more seriously, in the very consciousness of the citizens of those states. Are we destined to become slaves to the enormous profit-making empire? (Forbes 1987, 144, my translation)

Lang spoke of the need for "decolonization" of the airwaves. He criticized mass culture, the lack of diversity, and the erosion of cultural differences that supposedly accompany U.S. dominance of the audiovisual sector. He sought to ensure that governments would retain some room for maneuver in policymaking in these areas.

Although Lang was considered to be a minister with a distinctive personal style, many of the themes that he evoked during his tenure still resurface. For example, Jean-David Levitte, director of Cultural, Scientific and Technical Relations at the Ministry of Foreign Affairs during the final months of the GATT negotiations, argues that strong audiovisual industries are central to France's international stature as a leading power. France is an economic power, a permanent member of the United Nations Security Council, a member of the G8, the "motor" (along with Germany) of European integration, and the center of the francophone world. Yet its distinctive power resides elsewhere.

France's image in the world, from Yokohama to Bogota, is as a country of high culture. There is an inheritance, stemming from the dissemination of our language, our culture, our science, and the values that underpin them. This exceptional cultural image—the very essence of France—isn't it an enormous asset today, as it will be tomorrow, in the era of the information society that each year moves our world closer to a global village? In the next century, emerging powers in Asia and Latin America will no doubt challenge France economically. Given this, only the European Union, through its continued efforts to reach its final form, will allow member countries to compete on an equal footing with the most powerful. In this new environment, in which the economic might of France on its own will count less and our large enterprises will take on a more European, even global cast, the dissemination of our culture and our science will be the key to affirming our identity and retaining our influence. (Levitte 1995, 194, my translation)

Having established the need to cultivate and maintain France's cultural power, Levitte goes on to identify how this might be done. Noting that the French state has a central role to play in this effort, he lists three pillars of French "cultural diplomacy:" promotion of the French language, research and educational exchanges, and the reinforcement of France's "audiovisual presence" (Levitte 1995, 206).

French policy initiatives to cultivate this audiovisual presence date back to the late 1920s when the Herriot Decree of 1928 established the first quota in the film industry. Already, these policies sought to combat the domination of the cinematic screen by U.S. films. In 1936, the French government imposed a ceiling of 150 dubbed U.S. film imports per year, a limit that was lowered sixteen years later to 110 films (Condron 1997, 209).

Over the years, the French government has implemented a substantial body of policy to aid domestic film producers. In 1946, the government formed the Centre National de la Cinématographie (CNC) to oversee the French film industry. It deals with all stages of film production, licensing companies operating in the French film industry, authorizing recipients of state aid, printing and issuing all cinema tickets, and inspecting the records kept by cinema exhibitors, among other duties. Grants offered by the state to the film industry pass through the CNC.

The CNC became active very quickly after its establishment in response to U.S. film exports to France. In 1946, the CNC initiated the Loi d'aide temporaire à l'industrie cinématographique. This legislation subsidized film production and distribution by levying two taxes, one on each new film produced and one on cinema tickets sold. The CNC used this tax revenue to finance new French films and to make improvements to cinema houses. The National Assembly made the temporary law a permanent one in 1953, thus establishing the Compte de soutien à l'industrie cinématographique. Currently, 11 percent of cinema ticket prices goes to the CNC fund. In the 1980s, the Ministry of Culture began contributing to the Compte de soutien as cinema attendance fell and production costs soared (Looseley 1995, 198).

> The bulk of the Compte goes to producers of existing full-length films who are willing to reinvest it in a further production. This aid is described as "automatic" in that it is available to all French producers planning to reinvest and is calculated on the basis of ticket sales of a previous film, irrespective of any judgment of quality. Although this inevitably favours those already successful, it has been a powerful instrument for maintaining the level of French film production at a time when that of other European countries has fallen off. (Looseley 1995, 197)

In 1959, the government launched the *avances sur recettes* (advance on receipts) policy. It gives more selective aid to production and is not automatic like the percentage of ticket proceeds. Interest-free loans are awarded by a commission of specialists who evaluate projects for aesthetic quality. Ultimately, this program subsidizes films that are artistically interesting, but unlikely to get financing from other sources.

In 1983, the Agence pour le développement régional du cinéma was established to help open and renovate cinemas. This body aids in distribution in a way the Canadian government arguably has not, in part by helping to get films to rural areas shortly after release by subsidizing the cost of copying. Distribution in France is monopolized by big companies, but not U.S. ones (Gaumont-Pathé). Their distribution decisions reflect commercial concerns. In 1982, the government passed a law that forced Gaumont-Pathé to split, curbing their domination of the market.

One implication of the central role of the state in promoting cultural life is that private or corporate patronage remains less common as compared to other Western democracies. Lang tried to integrate the private sector in the mid 1980s, but this is a relatively new phenomenon in France. In the early 1980s, the French government established SOFICAs (Société de financement de l'industrie cinématographique et de l'audiovisuel) in an effort to encourage private investment in French filmmaking. Private interests, including banks and film production and distribution companies operate the multiple SOFICAs by selling shares. The proceeds from the sale of shares are used to finance film production. Tax incentives make the SOFICAs appealing for investors. Individuals can place up to 25 percent of their taxable income into SOFICA investments and companies can write off 50 percent of total investment (Perilli 1991, 13). No one individual can account for the total investment of any one SOFICA. The SOFICAs fulfill a cultural purpose in that they can only invest in French or European productions, or other films approved by the Ministry of Culture.

France and the United States have disagreed on the regulation of audiovisual industries before. However, in the first instance, France was in a much weaker negotiating position. In May 1946, France and the United States signed the Blum-Byrnes Accord. The agreement was an early step in the U.S. effort to aid in the reconstruction of the French, and later the European, economies. The agreement proposed liquidation of French war debts and a low-interest loan of $650 million. In return, France would abandon all barriers to access of U.S. export products to the French market. The French government agreed to these terms, but made the film industry the single exception. At a time when many French industries were devastated by World War II and could benefit from protection, the French government sought special provisions for the film industry only. At a time when

France awaited badly needed loans from the United States, French government representative Leon Blum held up payment of these funds by engaging in protracted negotiations to restrict access of U.S. films to the French market.

Negotiations centered on film quotas. The United States wanted a maximum of three weeks in every thirteen to be reserved for French films. The French demanded six weeks in every thirteen. As would be the case in the Uruguay Round, the successful conclusion of negotiations seemed contingent on an agreement with regard to audiovisual industries.[58] Secretary of State Byrnes reportedly warned that the "whole financial negotiation would be 'handicapped' by the French insistence on [film] quotas" (Wall 1991, 115).[59] The two governments eventually consented to reserving four weeks in every thirteen for French films. The only annex to the Blum–Byrnes Accord concerns these arrangements governing the film industry.

There are important parallels between the Franco–American negotiations of the Blum–Byrnes Accord and of GATT. In both cases, the prevailing normative context favored the establishment of principles of open trade at the international level. In 1946, both France and the United States agreed that autarky had contributed to the occurrence of World War II, and both actively sought to institutionalize open trade. In 1993, once again, both France and the United States embraced liberalization of trade and the institutionalization of these principles in the World Trade Organization. Nonetheless, in both instances, audiovisual industries provided a formidable obstacle to conclusion of the talks.

Some analysts of the exclusion of audiovisual industries from the GATT agreement suggest that France favored this policy for economic reasons, because the cultural sector promises to show substantial growth in the years to come. Yet the French perspective on culture industries is a long-standing one. The French government took the same position that it embraced in 1993 over forty-five years before, at a time when film was not perceived to be an economic growth industry and before television had even arrived in France. But as one analyst notes with regard to the Blum–Byrnes Accord, "the often bitter and protracted negotiations over what appeared to be a minor matter, the motion picture industry, defy explanation in simple terms of economics" (Wall 1991, 56). Just as the French attributed greater importance to audiovisual industries during the Uruguay Round, so did they during the negotiation of Blum–Byrnes. "We cannot confirm what the effects of films are on peoples' minds nor that the cinema is an effective propaganda tool. Nevertheless, in 1946, many people were willing to assume that film had these powers" (Portes 1986, 319, my translation). Indeed, some have

---

58. Television obviously was not yet a force at this time.

59. Note that quotas were the only policy instrument considered because it is the only acceptable form of protection for cinema allowed under the GATT agreement negotiated the year before.

argued that appreciation of the cultural power of audiovisual industries explains not only French resistance to U.S. films in 1946, but also U.S. insistence on access to the French market for its filmmakers.

> One of the more curious aspects of the postwar period is the enormous amount of acrimony expended by both Americans and French over ostensibly superficial questions. Films and Coca-Cola . . . are a case in point. . . . At a time when basic essentials of food and coal were lacking, and the Americans were lending and then giving the French billions, both these nonessential items were pressed upon the French as exports for which they were expected to pay with their very scarce dollars. There is more here than frivolity, or the political clout of the companies in question, although both the Motion Picture Association (MPA) and the Coca-Cola Company carried an unusual amount of weight in Washington. Both items carried a symbolic importance as manifestations of the superiority of the American "way of life," which magnified their importance far beyond the few millions they were expected to earn. Fitting symbols of the consumer society, both were symbols of anti-Communism as well. (Wall 1991, 113)

American films had been banned by Hitler during the German occupation and Hollywood looked forward to renewed access to Western Europe.[60] In addition, major U.S. film producers were owed money that had not been collected before the war, but these outstanding franc balances totaled little more than $10 million (Wall 1991, 115). As would seem to be the case with regard to both the NAFTA and GATT experiences in the 1990s, the United States also had concerns in 1946 that went beyond commercial considerations. American efforts to export a maximum amount of films to France in the immediate post–World War II period may have had as much to do with a desire to avoid protectionist policy precedents at the international level and with the extensive campaign mounted by the United States government against communism in France[61] as it did with purely commercial considerations. Hubert-Lacombe argues that the Blum–Byrnes Agreement facilitated the entry into France of

60. It is important to note that Anglo-Saxon films had been banned between 1940 and 1944 in all German-occupied areas. Just as was the case in 1993, the French concern in 1946 was with American films specifically, and not with British films, for example. This reinforces the degree to which these disputes are infused with cultural considerations and not strictly commercial ones. The latter would imply protection not just from American imports, but from any that might compete with French producers.

61. See Wall (1991), especially pp. 204–18. Wall claims that the United States did try "to influence directly the shaping of the French mentality by the export of films" (p. 4).

U.S. propaganda film productions "financed directly or indirectly by the State Department or the Army" (Hubert-Lacombe 1986, 309, my translation). Hubert-Lacombe (1986, 313, my translation) further notes that "from the beginning of the Cold War, the United States enlisted the cinema in its efforts to reintegrate Europe."

The French did not get the outcome that it favored in 1946. Many groups mobilized in France against the annex to the Blum-Byrnes Accord, including members of the artistic, intellectual, and labor communities. Published manifestos, demonstrations, and press conferences eventually led the government to renegotiate the terms of the annex, increasing the number of weeks reserved for French films in every thirteen from four to five (Sellier 1993, 15). Furthermore, a quota limiting the number of visas for dubbed U.S. films to 121 per year was established (Condron 1997, 209). The experience has settled in the French psyche.

> As much as this Accord, fruit of difficult and laborious negotiations, put an end to the most contentious, post-war debates between the United States and France and set in action American financing of French reconstruction—a low interest loan of $650 million—it sometimes seems that the only thing that remains in the collective memory of the French is the annex to the agreement on cinema. (Portes 1986, 314, my translation)[62]

Indeed, during the Uruguay Round of negotiations, the precedent of Blum-Byrnes would be invoked on numerous occasions as justification for the French position on audiovisual industries within the context of GATT (Sellier 1993). During the debate over Blum-Byrnes, some of the same arguments that would arise during GATT talks were rehearsed.

> Must we add that the cinema today is the manifestation of a popular art that crosses national borders to touch, move, distract and teach thousands of people and, as a result, makes an important contribution to our prestige and influence in the world.[63]

The French position on audiovisual industries during the Uruguay Round makes sense as the extension not only of the body of policy that has been implemented in France over the last several decades to aid domestic producers, but

---

62. Wall also refers to the "legend of its [Blum-Byrnes Accord] catastrophic impact on French film," p. 116

63. René Naegelen, président de la commission presse, radio, cinéma, quoted in Portes 1986, 319. My translation.

also within the context of French thinking both about the role of culture in society and the perceived threat posed by economic liberalization to the government's ability to promote this role.

The GATT case of cultural exception, then, differs from the NAFTA case in fundamental ways. There are national level concerns, particularly in France, about the inundation of U.S. films and television programs. At the same time, the European Union is pursuing its own agenda at the supranational level in an effort to evoke unity where there is fragmentation and to build a sociocultural foundation under an economic and political project. Ultimately, though, the GATT case resembles the NAFTA case in that goals associated with identity formation and cultural diversity intervene where economic considerations generally prevail. In addition, as is true for Canada, this approach did not emerge during trade talks, but rather date back, in some cases, several decades. The policies associated with this approach allow Europeans to fulfill a set of sociocultural objectives, which are made all the more desirable in the face of European integration, economic liberalization, and the evolution of the global trading regime.

In recent years, European leaders have increasingly invoked a dynamic that reflects commitments associated with the embedded liberalism compromise, though they do not use this term. Perhaps most prominent among them is Pascal Lamy, EU Trade Commissioner from 1999 to 2004. Though the EU has not officially adopted his language, Lamy has taken to invoking the concept of "collective preferences" in his statements about the trade-off between market opening and domestic social contracts. As one of his economic advisors explains, the term gets at "the established, pre-existing social choices of different nations." These include a menu of issues, different for each country, ranging from views on the death penalty to an attachment to rural agricultural life.[64] Lamy (2002, 140) himself argues that the audiovisual realm is a prime example of collective preferences concerning cultural diversity that are under challenge by processes of globalization, thus necessitating a policy response.

Elsewhere Lamy (2004) expands on his thinking. It is worth quoting him at length since he was a central figure in shaping EU trade policy during expansion of the union, and he represented the EU both at the failed effort to relaunch trade talks in Seattle in 1999 and at the successful meeting in Doha in 2001, which marked the beginning of the current round. Interestingly, these excerpts come from a speech Lamy delivered to the European Parliament in early 2004 entitled, "Co-existence between Public Policy and Free Trade: Can We Achieve Good Protectionism?"

---

64. Interview with Edouard Bourcieu, economist in the research unit, Office of the EU Commissioner for Trade, Brussels, July 2003.

I should like to start by clearing up a common misunderstanding: the object of EU trade policy is not free trade but a sensible opening up of trade within a framework of multilateral rules. Both the approach and the aim are therefore quite different. We accept market opening for what it can bring in the way of growth, jobs, and development—for the developing countries as well. But we are not offering a blank cheque. We are aware of the potentially destabilising effects of market opening and the international division of labour on the fabric of society, and the danger that particular social choices may be undermined. Our trade policy therefore incorporates a regulatory dimension; this is essential if we are to manage trade globalisation, ensure equal treatment, integrate developing countries more fully and uphold social choices which may be at odds with commercial or mercantile logic.

Lamy continues:

So the real question is "How can we organise market opening in such a way as to uphold the varying collective preferences of different societies? How would we devise a trade system combining openness, universal acceptance and adequate safeguards for social choices?" . . . The WTO system is therefore an international instrument that should enable States to go on opening up their markets while still retaining the capacity to make public policy choices. It is up to us to help the system adapt as trade itself evolves.

Lamy and his EU team contend that we can distinguish between protectionist policies that masquerade as sociocultural imperatives and genuine social concerns of a citizenry.[65] As Lamy explains (2004):

Take for example our dispute with the United States over its extra tariffs on steel (which I'm glad to say have since been removed). These were clearly designed to protect an uncompetitive industry. Our refusal to import genetically modified maize or soya that we have not authorised, on the other hand, is not protecting a European industry (we do import soya and maize that are not genetically modified) but reflects our society's highly precautionary preference in this area.

Lamy's perspective represents an explicit effort by a high official to approximate the embedded liberalism compromise struck in the immediate post–World

65. Ibid., July 2003.

War II period, but in a way that recognizes the emergent challenges of the contemporary period. His perspective is compatible with the definition I quote in the Introduction, offered by Wolfe and Mendelsohn (2004, 262): "embedded liberalism is not a fixed bargain about levels of social spending or tariff bindings but a dynamic commitment to allowing countries to be different within a multilateral framework." Lamy's success in promoting his perspective outside of Europe has been uneven, as the following chapter explores, though this may change under his directorship of the World Trade Organization. Nonetheless, the EU has not relied solely on the powers of persuasion in this matter. It has also relied on its ability to influence countries that seek accession to the Union.

New members to the EU must adopt in its entirety the "acquis communautaire," the body of policies, legislation, rights, and obligations that have been adopted by the member states since its inception. Before new members can officially join the union, they must demonstrate that they have integrated the thirty-one areas of the *acquis,* among them audiovisual policy. The Union has reminded acceding states of this on various occasions when they have faced counter pressures from the United States. Several cases concerning Eastern and Central European countries serve as examples where they have entered into bilateral agreements with the United States or sought entry into the WTO. The United States has pressured these countries to open their audiovisual sector to liberalization and the European Union has countered by noting that such opening would contravene the EU *acquis,* thus precluding membership in the union. In the majority of cases, countries have not wanted to forego EU membership and have sided with Europe. Lamy (2002, 138) has referred to this EU strategy as "le travail de sentinelle" or sentry duty. The next chapter explores European efforts—in concert with the Canadian government and others—to move these issues outside of the trading regime completely and, in so doing, to ensure that other components of the global governance framework—especially those pertaining to domestic sociocultural concerns—are as well-developed as the trade component.

Chapter 4

Institutionalizing Cultural Protection

The evolution of the trading regime is creating new challenges for domestic cultural policymakers. As the two previous chapters demonstrate, the appearance of culture industries on the roster of sectors to be liberalized by multilateral trade agreements means that domestic cultural policy now intersects with international trade policy in new and often problematic ways. Until recently, the favored response to this was to exempt the cultural sector—either partially or entirely—from trade agreement provisions. However, since the WTO decision on Canadian periodicals policy, many consider such exemptions to be unreliable in allowing room for the promotion of sociocultural goals. This view has prompted the Canadians, the French, the EU, and others to initiate a new offensive strategy. This strategy removes the promotion of cultural diversity from the trading regime and creates a new institution whose principal purpose is the promotion of cultural diversity.

This chapter explores various efforts to shield the cultural sector from liberalization, from both inside and outside of the trading regime, in the post–World War II period. I show that contemporary trade agreement provisions fall short of providing the domestic regulatory policy autonomy required if governments wish to continue to promote domestic culture industries using measures they have traditionally favored. Devising new institutional forms, therefore, is desirable where culture is concerned. Yet *how* to do so is not so obvious. At a minimum, current efforts suggest that striking a new embedded liberalism compromise that can accommodate concerns about identity and cultural diversity will not happen *within* the trading regime. Instead, there is a movement afoot to erect a new international institution devoted to the promotion of cultural diversity *alongside* the institutions devoted to trade and market opening. Ideally, it will temper the tendencies emanating from economic liberalization that many perceive to be so threatening by according sociocultural purposes equal importance alongside commercial ones at the global level. This strategy recognizes that the mandate of the World Trade Organization is to promote open trade. Asking it to promote other values may be inappropriate and ultimately unsatisfying. Given the increasing importance of global-level policymaking, proponents of cultural diversity instead seek to fill in some of the perceived gaps in the global governance framework by establishing an international institution whose primary mandate is promoting cultural diversity. Before exploring this new institution, I consider the trade agreement provisions whose insufficiency generated demand for an innovative strategy.

The North American Free Trade Agreement

In the mid 1980s, the U.S. and Canadian governments began talks that would lead to a comprehensive free trade agreement. The two countries were already each others' largest trading partners and barriers were quite low between them. Nonetheless, the 1980s recession prompted the Canadian government to seek *assured* access to the U.S. market in the face of mounting U.S. protectionism. While the Canadian government sought a comprehensive trade pact, Canadian negotiators indicated from the outset that "culture was not on the table." This would mean negotiating an exemption for culture industries from the provisions of the agreement, which Canadian negotiators successfully accomplished.

Article 2012 of the Canada–U.S. Free Trade Agreement (CUSFTA) defines cultural industries as "an enterprise engaged in any of the following activities":

a) the publication, distribution, or sale of books, magazines, periodicals, or newspapers in print or machine readable form but not including the sole activity of printing or typesetting any of the foregoing,

b) the production, distribution, sale or exhibition of film or video recordings,

c) the production, distribution, sale or exhibition of audio or video music recordings,

d) the publication, distribution, or sale of music in print or machine readable form, or

e) radio communication in which the transmissions are intended for direct reception by the general public, and all radio, television and cable television broadcasting undertakings and all satellite programming and broadcast network services.

Article 2005(1) of CUSFTA provides a broad exclusion from trade obligations for these industries, stating that "cultural industries are exempt from the provisions of this Agreement, except as specifically provided in Article 401 (Tariff Elimination), paragraph 4 of Article 1607 (divestiture of an indirect acquisition) and Articles 2006 and 2007 of this Chapter." Article 2005(2) goes on to qualify this exemption by noting that "notwithstanding any other provision of this Agreement, a Party may take measures of equivalent commercial effect in response to actions that would have been inconsistent with this Agreement but for paragraph 1."

The North American Free Trade Agreement keeps the commitments made in the CUSFTA largely intact. Article 2107 of NAFTA preserves the definition of cultural industries. Annex 2106 of NAFTA states that "notwithstanding any other provision of this Agreement, as between the United States and Canada, any measure adopted or maintained with respect to cultural industries, except as specifically provided in Article 302 (Market Access—Tariff Elimination), and any measure of equivalent commercial effect taken in response, shall be governed exclusively in accordance with the terms of the Canada—United States Free Trade Agreement."

The cultural exclusion clause, especially its effectiveness in maintaining the federal government's capacity to implement cultural policy, was controversial. Some hailed the very achievement of a carve-out for culture as a victory. Others worried that it would provide limited protection. Why were those in the latter category skeptical? First, Article 2005(2) of CUSFTA gives parties perceiving themselves as injured by the cultural exclusion the right to take retaliatory action. While some thought it a victory to limit this retaliatory action to "equivalent commercial effect," given some of the overwhelming moves made by the United States in the past, retaliation was still possible. Indeed, in 1994, the United States invoked the right to retaliate in response to a CRTC decision to revoke the license of a U.S. country music cable station and reissue that license to Canadian interests.[1] The license had been issued to the U.S. company ten years earlier, when no Canadians had sought to provide a country music programming service. However, as Grant and Wood (2004, 369) explain, "If a

---

1. Note that, while the United States invoked the right to retaliate in NAFTA, it did not use official NAFTA dispute settlement mechanisms to pursue its grievance.

Canadian service were licensed in the future in a format competitive with an authorized non-Canadian service, the CRTC made clear that the latter could be dropped from the list, terminating the authority for it to be carried on cable." The threat of U.S. retaliation was enough to produce a compromise. The station remained Canadian, in terms of ownership and content, however the U.S. company was allowed to purchase a 20 percent interest in the channel, creating a partnership.

The experience with the country music channel challenges those who interpret the retaliation clause narrowly, finding it capable of providing protection. This optimistic perspective goes something like this:

> Carefully analyzed, the clause permits U.S. retaliation only for measures that otherwise would be inconsistent with the 1988 agreement. Since Canada made no national treatment commitments in the audiovisual services sector in the 1988 FTA, it is therefore free to introduce new measures affecting such services, including broadcasting, without triggering a right of retaliation. And, in fact, it has done so more than once. (Grant and Wood 2004, 361–62)

While it may be true that the clause has not prevented the Canadian government from introducing new measures, it has also given the United States legal grounds on which to contest Canadian measures. Ultimately, the debate captures the different ways in which U.S. and Canadian legal scholars interpret the clause. The possibility of multiple legitimate interpretations makes those who look to the NAFTA cultural exception for protection somewhat nervous. As Cahn and Schimmel (1997, 307) put it, "NAFTA allows Canada and the United States to exempt their cultural industries from its free-trade obligations. . . . Thus, in the cultural industries sector, Canada and the United States have the right to take unilateral actions, inconsistent with their otherwise binding obligations under NAFTA. . . . However, the degree of safety that safe harbor affords is hotly disputed."

The cultural exclusion in NAFTA is also controversial because of the very specific definition of cultural industries. On the one hand, a specific list of industries can reduce ambiguity. On the other hand, such a strategy requires that those defining that list demonstrate superhuman prescience. From a technological standpoint, cultural industries are evolving quite rapidly. This is especially true where the delivery of content is concerned.

> The cultural exclusion clause seems ill-suited to cover new technologies. For instance, in the area of CD-ROM technology, a CD embodying a painting or a literary work might not come easily under the definition of

article 2012 . . . it is unclear whether audiovisual programs on individual demand, such as pay-per-view services and video-on-demand are covered by the cultural exclusion. Because of rapid changes in the telecommunications field and the increased public demand for new telecommunications services, the language of the cultural exclusion will probably quickly become obsolete. (Cahn and Schimmel 1997, 291)

Perhaps even more central to the evolving culture industry sector are digital delivery systems and the Internet. While the European Union's use of the term *audiovisual industries* allows for the inclusion of these new developments, the specific list in NAFTA does not.

Many of these concerns about the content of the exclusion clauses became, to some extent, irrelevant in the 1990s when the United States sidestepped NAFTA dispute settlement arrangements completely, choosing to avail itself instead of the remedies afforded by the World Trade Organization. As I explain in chapter 2, the U.S. government took the Canadian government before the WTO to contest several measures supporting the domestic magazine industry. The "periodicals case," as it became known, convinced many in Canada that the cultural exception carved out in NAFTA was unreliable because it could do very little to prevent countries from opting to pursue their disputes in an alternative forum where similar protections are nonexistent. Indeed, in response to the WTO periodicals case decision, the Canadian government changed its strategy and, for all intents and purposes, abandoned the cultural exception, recognizing that, at best, it can be a limited, short-term solution. At worst, it may provide no protection at all.

The General Agreement on Tariffs and Trade

The treatment of culture industries in the General Agreement on Tariffs and Trade that emerged from the Uruguay Round is quite different from that found in NAFTA. Indeed, the GATT approach reflects some learning on the part of governments following the experience of the cultural exception in CUSFTA/ NAFTA. For example, the EU expressly chose not to seek a provision that would make exceptions for culture industries, yet also allow for the possibility of retaliation (Cahn and Schimmel 1997, 293).

Nevertheless, special GATT provisions for audiovisual industries did not begin in the Uruguay Round. In the earliest GATT negotiations in Geneva and Havana in the 1940s, "the United States conceded that cinematographic films were a special case that could not be left to the general provisions of the Agreement"

(Jarvie 1998, 38). As a result, Article IV of the GATT enshrines a screen quota that "sets forth an express limitation to the diffusion of U.S. motion pictures in Europe" (Cahn and Schimmel 1997, 284). This provision permits contracting parties to "require the exhibition of cinematograph films of national origin during a specified minimum proportion of the total screen time . . . in the commercial exhibition of all films of whatever origin" (GATT, article IV[a]), thus exempting films from principles of nondiscrimination. The United States has worked hard over the years to ensure that this article is limited in scope. For example, in the 1960s, a GATT working party was established in response to U.S. concerns that article IV might be interpreted to include television programs. Working groups again took up this question during the Uruguay Round of talks (Ming Shao 1995, 112).

The European Union spearheaded the move during the Uruguay Round to carve out a space for domestic policies promoting audiovisual industries. The EU had several options, including a complete exclusion of the audiovisual sector from the agreement and a cultural exception akin to that negotiated by Canada in NAFTA. In the end, "the European Union and the United States did not reach any substantive agreement concerning the audiovisual sector. The European Union and the United States merely agreed to disagree" (Cahn and Schimmel 1997, 297). This agreement to disagree meant that the EU could continue measures like the Television without Frontiers directive, as well as other existing subsidies and quotas, with no requirements to change current policies and no restrictions on the nature of future policies. "In other words, the European Union obtained an exemption from the application of the principle of non-discrimination" (Cahn and Schimmel 1997, 300).

While much of this was encouraging to the European cultural community, it would resemble the outcome in NAFTA in that the victory is partial and potentially short-lived. There is no explicit recognition that audiovisual products merit special consideration. Furthermore, within the context of the WTO system, the debate over audiovisual industries did not end with the Uruguay Round GATT agreement. Instead, it is ongoing, but now under the auspices of the General Agreement on Trade in Services (GATS).

The General Agreement on Trade in Services

The agreement produced by the Uruguay Round is the most comprehensive to date, amounting to a complete overhaul of the GATT system. In addition to the usual attention paid to trade barrier reduction, the Uruguay Round established the World Trade Organization, thus creating permanent institutions and governing bodies to supplement the periodic negotiating rounds. Members also sought, for the first time, to broaden the mandate of GATT (WTO) to include services and intellectual property. In 1992, world exports in commercial services totaled almost $1 trillion, representing more than one-fifth of all goods and services exports, and services exports have been expanding at a rate substantially higher than merchandise exports (Schott 1994, 99). By 2004, the value of world commercial services trade rose by 16 percent to $2.1 trillion.[2] The General Agreement on Trade in Services seeks to establish rules of nondiscriminatory trade in all services, including audiovisual services, though Article 1:3 (c) exempts services provided in the exercise of governmental authority, defined as any service which is supplied neither on a commercial basis, nor in competition with one or more service suppliers.

In many ways, the GATS is very similar to the GATT, which provides for trade in goods. For example, two key principles underpin the GATT regime: most-favored nation (MFN) and national treatment. MFN assures that no trading partner receives relatively better treatment than another. National treatment assures that trading partners and their imported goods receive the same treatment as local producers and their domestically produced goods. There are exceptions to both principles, though they remain the key concepts that animate the trading regime. These same principles form the basis of the GATS regime. Other concepts, like reciprocity and transparency, so central to GATT, also provide the foundation for GATS.

In other ways, however, the GATS differs from GATT. GATT signatories are obliged to liberalize all categories of goods covered by the agreement. The only exceptions to this come where specific exceptions have been negotiated. The GATS, on the other hand, obliges signatories to respect nondiscriminatory principles only in the sectors in which they have made commitments to liberalize. In other words, governments submit a list of sectors where they pledge to open market access and to adhere to the principles of MFN and national treatment. In general, where they have not pledged to do this, they are not obliged to do so, making liberalization commitments a matter of choice. There is some controversy around this, though, because it is generally recognized that services liberalization is an ongoing phenomenon. Official WTO documents confirm that making liberalization commitments a choice may only provide room for maneuver in the near term.

In looking at the GATS agreement, as well as at the significance of the specific services commitments undertaken by WTO members, it must be

---

2. www.wto.org/English/news_e/pres05_e/pr401_e.htm, accessed Aug 18, 2005.

borne in mind that the Uruguay Round services package is only a beginning. The GATS rules are not quite complete, and are largely untested. The process of filling the gaps will require several more years of negotiations, and experience will no doubt show a need to improve some of the existing rules. Each government's schedule of liberalization commitments for trade in services is also only a first step, comparable not with its GATT schedule of 1994, but rather with the initial limited tariff-cutting undertaken when the GATT was launched. Among the most important elements in the GATS package is the promise that successive further rounds of negotiations will be undertaken to continue opening up world trade in services. (WTO 1999, 1)

The same WTO document confirms this several pages later: "Article XIX is a guarantee that the present GATS package is only the first fruit of a continuing enterprise, to be undertaken jointly by all WTO members, to raise the level of their services commitments towards one another" (WTO 1999, 9).

As Grant and Wood (2004, 371) explain,

Built into the agreement on trade in services was a ticking clock. By setting up a variety of deadlines, expiry dates for exemptions and the presumption of future negotiating rounds, GATS is designed to maintain pressure on its members to progressively reduce all domestic policies that regulate trade to a theoretical null point. . . . Once the first set of commitments is locked in, the GATS framework contemplates the immediate resumption of negotiations in a new round of offers and requests. Any services not committed to liberalization under the current round will be vulnerable under the next.

To date, very few countries have made offers to liberalize their audiovisual services within the context of the GATS. Some question the motivation of those that have done so. For example, Baer (2003) notes that a number of developing countries recently requested that the European Union liberalize its audiovisual sector. Some of these countries have formidable audiovisual sectors that would likely benefit from such an opening (Brazil, Mexico, India). However, others are not known for their audiovisual industries (Mali, Peru, Nicaragua, Guatemala), leading some to wonder whether the promise to withdraw the request at a later date may be part of a broader negotiating strategy designed to gain leverage with the EU (Baer 2003, 23).

While there may be room for flexibility in requesting and offering market opening, there seems to be less flexibility once commitments to liberalize have been made, as New Zealand discovered "to its later regret" (Grant and Wood 2004, 359). In the late 1980s and early 1990s, the National (conservative) government in power undertook to commercialize and privatize New Zealand's state-owned broadcasting industry. As part of its overhaul, the government also made partial commitments at the GATS to open their audiovisual sector. Several years later, when the Labour Party came back into power, it inherited this arrangement, finding its capacity to pursue an alternative broadcasting policy, including local content quotas, greatly circumscribed. Prime Minister and Minister for Culture Helen Clark explained her predicament:

> We have unilaterally disarmed ourselves on trade but very few others have been so foolish. We're now left with perfectly legitimate calls for local content and people saying "You can't do that because of GATS." This seems a bit ridiculous so we're just working out the best way to handle it. (quoted in Kelsey 2003)

The New Zealand government is not without options, though many of those options do involve risking a WTO dispute. Nonetheless, the broader lesson of New Zealand's experience is that commitments to liberalize are not easily reversible.

Those who concede that the capacity for choice with regard to audiovisual liberalization in GATS offers greater range of motion than GATT where domestic cultural policymaking is concerned remain unconvinced that their interests can be adequately addressed inside the services trade regime. This skepticism lingers because cultural products defy straightforward definition as either goods or services. Is a television program, for example, a tangible good in the form of a videotape "that can be dropped on your foot?" Or is the service of transmitting the program over the airwaves its defining feature? As Ming Shao (1995, 124) explains, "Three characteristics commonly distinguish services from goods. First, production and consumption must be simultaneous in the case of services but not goods. Second, unlike goods, services are impossible to store. Third, services are intangible, while goods are tangible. Although the above criteria work well in distinguishing activities like haircutting from conventional goods, they have not proven very useful in classifying A/Vs." Nevertheless, reaching some consensus on this categorization is decisive in determining whether the cultural sector will be regulated by the more permissive GATS agreement or the more restrictive GATT, with important consequences for cultural producers and consumers, as well as cultural policymakers. Not surprisingly, the Americans have favored an interpretation of most cultural products as goods, while the Europeans and Canadians have made a case for defining them as services. More recently, the United States has introduced the term *virtual good* to capture audiovisual products as well as software and e-commerce in the hopes that recategorization in this direction might bring these sectors under the auspices of the GATT.

As was the case with NAFTA, many worry that whatever limited protections the GATS regime provides may be sidestepped completely. In particular, some analysts point to the inroads being made by the United States in bilateral agreements. The Central American Free Trade Agreement (CAFTA), for example, concluded between the United States, El Salvador, Guatemala, Honduras, Nicaragua, and Costa Rica contains no cultural exemption. Civil society groups worry that, in time, this may lead to a dismantling of media ownership laws, local content quotas, and subsidies in these countries.[3] Analysts also point to the agreements concluded by the United States with Australia, Chile, and Singapore. In the case of Australia, the agreement is structured around a "negative list." In many ways, this mirrors the cultural exception approach that Canada employed in NAFTA and which many perceive now to be discredited.

> In a negative list agreement, they represent a retention of rights to regulate. . . . But the rights named here are the only rights Australia has. The Australian negotiators seem to regard the outcome as a good one. They believe that they have retained the essential prerogatives for Australia for preserving an Australian presence in the audiovisual sector. However, from the cultural sector's viewpoint, there is a different story. Prior to this agreement, the Australian government's rights to regulate in support of Australian culture were completely unfettered. Now, it has only very limited rights, defined in this agreement. To assert any other rights will be impossible. (Letts 2004)

In the cases of Chile and Singapore, Bernier (2003b, 6) identifies what he calls a "top down" approach, but the effect is the same as the negative list. Each country retained some policy autonomy. Nonetheless, the bilateral agreements depart from the GATS approach to audiovisual regulation. In GATS, contracting parties have the choice of making no, full, or partial commitments to liberalization. However, in the free trade agreements with Chile and Singapore, the countries agree "to be fully committed, subject to the exceptions and reservations set out in their schedules regarding existing measures . . . or specific sectors" (Bernier 2003b, 7). Trade experts consider this to be a substantial increase in the level of commitment to liberalization that is, in many respects, incompatible with GATS.[4]

---

3. INCD Newsletter 5, no. 5 (May 2004). http://www.incd.net/docs/newletter41E.htm, accessed June 20, 2004.

4. Multiple interviews with Garry Neil, INCD executive director, and Peter Grant, lawyer for the CRTC and SAGIT member, March 2003, late 2003, and May 2004.

Bernier (2003b, 14–15) also points to another strategy deployed in the free trade agreements between the United States and Chile and Singapore.

The new strategy of the United States in the cultural sector rests quite clearly on the view that while measures that do not conform to national treatment, most-favored-nation treatment and free market access can be tolerated as they presently exist in the traditional audiovisual sector because they are bound one way or another to disappear with time, no such tolerance must be accepted for digitally delivered content which are the heart of the new communication economy and should therefore remain free of cultural protectionism.

This strategy is arguably made all the more effective by the fact that telecommunications services liberalization is proceeding apace. For a long time, many perceived this to be a separate realm; however, it is increasingly clear that cross-ownership of telecommunications and media concerns means that resisting liberalization of audiovisual industries alone will be insufficient to protect the right of governments to promote cultural diversity via culture industry policy.

These various developments make many uneasy about the degree to which we should rely on the trading regime to protect national governments' domestic policymaking capacity to promote cultural diversity. In addition, one thing is sure: incorporating an exception into trade agreements makes trade rules the benchmark from which cultural policies are deviations (Baer 2003, 9). This is especially true when dispute settlement panels made up of trade experts take as their guiding question whether cultural policies contravene commitments to the trading regime. This approach has real consequences for policy, but it also raises broader philosophical questions about whether we should refract our definition of culture through a commercial lens and whether we should limit our definition of legitimate cultural policies to those that are compatible with trade liberalization.

Embedding the Trade Regime in Shared Social Purposes

The pursuit of the cultural exception strategy in NAFTA and at the WTO represents an effort to institutionalize a new dimension of a contemporary embedded liberalism compromise. Through hard-fought (and ongoing) battles, Canadian and European officials, along with a steadily increasing number of their counterparts in other countries, have been working to reconcile sociocultural goals concerning identity, cultural diversity, and autonomy in domestic cultural policymaking with economic liberalization. While they have had some success, the arrangements they have created are not reliable in the long term. Why is this so?

In his former capacity as EU trade commissioner, Pascal Lamy said that "the WTO system is an international instrument that *should* enable states to go on opening up their markets while still retaining the capacity to make public policy" (Lamy 2004, emphasis mine). The embedded liberalism compromise of the 1940s represents one successful attempt at the simultaneous pursuit of these goals. Robert Wolfe points to another in the current period in an important book on agricultural policy and the trading regime. Wolfe (1998) analyzes the "farm wars" of the 1980s to show how GATT signatories were able to strike a compromise during the Uruguay Round of GATT negotiations—echoing the embedded liberalism compromise of the 1940s in many respects—*within* the context of the trading regime. This compromise limited conflict among signatories, introduced a new approach to reconciling domestic farm policy with multilateral trade in farm products, yet still allowed for limited liberalization of the sector. In recognition of various pressures emerging from structural and technological change in a declining industry, the negotiators created the Green Box in the Agreement on Agriculture, which identifies legitimate domestic support measures to farmers. "The creation of the Green Box is a recognition that being a farmer is a cultural and social not just an economic activity. Embedding the market in society means protecting farmers while allowing farming to adjust" (Wolfe 1998, 146). The agricultural compromise represents for Wolfe a tangible example of a larger truth:

> The GATT, and now the WTO, is the physical embodiment of the trade regime, a tool used by states in the governance of the global economy. The trade regime is part of the institutionalization of the double movement, which was the basis for the postwar "compromise of embedded liberalism." The GATT is not, therefore, and was never meant to be a "free trade agreement" aimed at the elimination of all barriers to commercial exchange. Free trade was the reference point not the objective for GATT. . . . The GATT does not act in opposition to the interventionist policies of states; it is rather the instrument by which national policies are reconciled. (1998, 10)

Wolfe's observation echoes Lamy's comment above. Both articulate a vision of the trading regime that seems elusive where culture is concerned, a vision that sees the trading regime as enabling national governments to fulfill social contracts, not working at cross purposes with them. Yet the outcome of the periodicals case suggests otherwise. Perhaps it was possible to reconcile sociocultural and economic concerns in agriculture because it is one of the few remaining sectors where traditional trade barriers, like tariffs, subsidies, and quotas, remain high. However, where culture is concerned, we have arguably moved into new territory. Dymond and Hart (2000) explain:

> The postwar model of multilateral trade policy—enshrined within the 1948 GATT—was erected upon an interlocking set of negative prescriptions by which governments undertook self-denying ordinances disciplining their capacity to impose trade barriers at the border and to discriminate among domestic and imported goods or among their trading partners. The object and purpose of the ensuing rights and obligations was to foster the expansion of world trade through the reduction of tariffs and other barriers to trade and the elimination of discriminatory treatment in international commerce. The WTO shifted the centre of gravity of international trade rules from negative prescription to positive rule-making. . . . The object and purpose of trade policy has been transfigured from trade liberalization through trade barrier reductions to positive rule-making aimed at ensuring the capacity of producers around the globe to fully contest the markets of member states. (Dymond and Hart 2000, 1–2)

This "paradigm shift" has had particular consequences for the ability of governments to continue long-standing domestic regulatory frameworks, "bring[ing] into question the deep social and historical roots which underpin systems of national or sub-national regulation and thus rais[ing] profound issues of national self-determination" (Dymond and Hart 2000, 6). Its consequences are particularly noticeable in services trade. "The agendas on services, investment, and competition policy are clearly not about trade liberalization. Rather, they are about the interface between the private economy and public regulation and the blurring lines between the domestic and global economies" (Dymond and Hart 2000, 12).

Dymond and Hart are not necessarily sympathetic to those who wish to promote cultural diversity. They do not mention this movement specifically. However, they do point to the "social agenda" being pursued around environmentalist and labor rights issues as "a minefield." Their pessimism about meeting the new social demands, coupled with their articulation of the new paradigm animating the trading regime, leads them to conclude that there is no longer consensus about the fundamental questions of global economic governance: "Who governs, what is being governed, and to what purpose?" (Dymond and Hart 2000, 12).

Embedding the liberal trading order in broader social purpose, therefore, will likely require approaches unfamiliar to those who crafted the embedded liberalism compromise of the 1940s. While this fact has not yet been fully acknowledged where trade and culture are concerned, it clearly informs the Global Compact, the most fully developed effort to think through how we might update and reconfigure the embedded liberalism compromise in the current period. According to United Nations secretary general Kofi Annan,

> The problem is this. The spread of markets outpaces the ability of societies and their political systems to adjust to them, let alone to guide the course they take. History teaches us that such an imbalance between the economic, social and political realms can never be sustained for very long. The industrialized countries learned that lesson in their bitter and costly encounter with the Great Depression. In order to restore social harmony and political stability, they adopted social safety nets and other measures, designed to limit economic volatility and compensate the victims of market failures. That consensus made possible successive moves towards liberalization, which brought about the long post-war period of expansion. Our challenge today is to devise a similar compact on the global scale, to underpin the new global economy. If we succeed in that, we would lay the foundation for an age of global prosperity, comparable to that enjoyed by the industrialized countries in the decades after the Second World War. (Annan 1999)

The Global Compact that emerged from this observation "enlists the corporate community in promoting human rights, labor standards and environmental sustainability in its global domain" (Ruggie 2002, 1). It represents "a new institutional form for 'embedding' global markets in shared social purposes" (Ruggie 2002, 6). By encouraging businesses to adopt socially responsible practices while they simultaneously reap the gains from economic openness, the Global Compact offers an innovative way of offsetting some of the social costs of liberalization. However, it takes a form that would be unfamiliar to the architects of the original embedded liberalism compromise. The United Nations sidesteps national governments and engages directly with corporate actors and nongovernmental organizations. The UN cannot compel companies to act in a socially responsible manner, but it provides incentives and resources to facilitate the evolution of socially responsible corporate cultures.

Originally, nine key principles in the three broad areas of human rights, labor rights, and the environment animated the compact. More recently, anticorruption has been added as an area that might benefit from inclusion in this undertaking, bringing the total to ten key principles, including a commitment to uphold human rights, to abolish child labor, and to promote greater environmental responsibility. To date, the Global Compact includes no principles that tap into the concerns about identity and culture. That this is so is not surprising. Of course, it is only appropriate that early efforts to confront the contemporary costs of liberalization would focus on areas where human life and well-being are threatened. Hence, the emphasis on human rights, labor standards, and the environment. What is surprising, however, is that few people have recognized that efforts by the Canadian, European Union, and other governments to continue their cultural policies while they simultaneously promote a liberal trading order represent components of an evolving and reconfigured compromise of embedded liberalism and not the return of protectionism in a new guise. As such, any current debate about how to cushion societies from the contemporary costs of liberalization is incomplete if it ignores cultural concerns.

Proponents of cultural diversity at the global level have already started pursuing an innovative strategy that reflects this conviction. In recent years, they have begun an effort to move the cultural question outside of the trading regime to an institution constructed specifically for the purpose of promoting cultural diversity. Such a strategy is in line with Lamy's vision of the trading regime.

> The WTO system is therefore an international instrument that should enable States to go on opening up their markets while still retaining the capacity to make public policy choices. It is up to us to help the system adapt as trade itself evolves. It is not the WTO's job to regulate everything under the sun; the regulatory dimension requires a strengthening of the other pillars of global governance as well, and the WTO then has to respect the rules they lay down. (Lamy 2004)

The International Instrument on Cultural Diversity represents one of the "other pillars of global governance" of which Lamy speaks.

International Instrument on Cultural Diversity

Efforts to recognize the unique sociocultural contribution of culture industries from within NAFTA, GATT, and GATS have left many unsatisfied that national governments will indeed be able to retain the capacity to implement the traditional range of cultural policies in the face of economic liberalization. The multilateral trade agreements, as well as a handful of bilateral agreements, use various strategies to shield the cultural sector, but none seems fully reliable. This was brought home to Canadians following the WTO decision in the periodicals case. The Canadian government was obliged to alter its magazine industry policies to bring them into conformity with their trade commitments, as understood by the dispute settlement panel. But they also did something else. Minister of Canadian Heritage Sheila Copps, whose portfolio included culture industries, invited several culture ministers to Ottawa for what would be the inaugural meeting of the International Network on Cultural Policy (INCP).

Copps used the opportunity to express her concerns about likely future occurrences of what the Canadian government had just experienced with magazine policy. She also introduced to her counterparts an idea that had been presented to her by a panel of Canadian industry experts, assembled by the Department of Foreign Affairs and International Trade, called the Cultural Industries Sectoral Advisory Group on International Trade (SAGIT). Among the recommendations articulated in the SAGIT report is the belief that the Canadian government should move away from the cultural exception strategy toward promotion of a "new international instrument"—a convention, a treaty, perhaps even a brick-and-mortar institution—whose mandate is the promotion of cultural diversity.

> According to the SAGIT's analysis, there is growing concern worldwide about the impact of international agreements on trade and investment on culture. Canada has reached an important crossroad in the relationship between trade agreements and cultural policies. The tools and approaches used in the past to keep cultural goods and services from being subject to the same treatment as other goods and services may no longer be enough. As is clear from events over the past few years, the cultural exemption has its limits. It is time for Canada to make some crucial decisions. Do we define ourselves simply as the producers and consumers of tradeable goods and services? Or are we prepared to step forward and reaffirm the importance of cultural diversity and the ability of each country to ensure that its own stories and experiences are available both to its own citizens and to the rest of the world? Members of the SAGIT believe it is time to step forward. (SAGIT 1999, ii–iii)

The SAGIT report made clear that this instrument should not be declaratory. Rather, it should be a binding instrument.

> A new cultural instrument would seek to develop an international consensus on the responsibility to encourage indigenous cultural expression and on the need for regulatory and other measures to promote cultural and linguistic diversity. The instrument would not compel any country to take measures to promote culture, but it would give countries the right to determine the measures they will use (within the limits of the agreement)

to safeguard their cultural diversity. A kind of blueprint for cultural diversity and the role of culture in a global world, the instrument would clearly define what was covered, and stress the importance of cultural sovereignty. The new instrument would identify the measures that would be covered and those that would not, and indicate clearly where trade disciplines would or would not apply. It would also state explicitly when domestic cultural measures would be permitted and not subject to trade retaliation. (SAGIT 1999, 31)

Official statements on behalf of the Ministry of Canadian Heritage identify the shifts that make such a change in strategy necessary.

New technologies combined with industry convergence and consolidation (mega-mergers) and the globalization of the economy are increasingly exerting pressure on cultural policies that have served to create a strong diverse Canadian culture. These trends are blurring definitions in international trade agreements and can limit the impact of the traditional exemption approach Canada and other countries have taken regarding cultural industries.[5]

Such an instrument would bring cultural diversity squarely onto the international agenda, alongside economic liberalization, the environment, sustainable development, human rights, and other key goals. The instrument would require governments to recognize cultural diversity as an integral value to be taken into account in global-level policymaking activities and also to confirm the legitimate right of national governments to implement domestic cultural policy in the public interest. In October 1999, the Canadian government committed publicly to pursuing a New International Instrument on Cultural Diversity (NIICD) as its official policy position.

Copps convinced her counterparts that a new international instrument is a worthwhile undertaking. The membership of the INCP has grown to more than seventy members. As of 2003, UNESCO agreed to house the instrument, giving the endeavor important institutional backing from a respected UN agency devoted to cultural diversity. A UNESCO expert panel mulled over the specifics of the instrument and issued a handful of statements about their key challenges. Though it continues to be known by many as the Convention on Cultural Diversity, its official name is the Convention on the Protection and Promotion of the

5. Website of the Ministry of Canadian Heritage, http://www.canadianheritage.gc.ca/progs/ ai–ia/ridp–irpd/03/index_e.cfm

Diversity of Cultural Expressions. As negotiations on the nature of the instrument evolved, many hoped for "a binding instrument that would establish rights and responsibilities for all countries and legitimize their right to preserve or implement national cultural policies supporting the production and dissemination of cultural content" (Bernier 2003a, 1). It would "provide a frame of reference, a code of conduct, and a discussion forum for all countries that consider the preservation of distinct forms of cultural expression and of cultural diversity more generally as essential aspects of globalization" (Bernier 2003a, 3).

At least three texts circulated among the communities interested in the contents of the new instrument—one written by the Canadian SAGIT, one by the INCP, and one by the civil society group, the International Network on Cultural Diversity (INCD). Some of the most pressing issues were conceptual, others technical. In the former category lies the definition of the key term, *cultural diversity*. The various participants in the process understand this term differently. For example, the Europeans and Canadians who experienced the battles over the cultural exception in NAFTA and GATT want, at a minimum, local culture industry producers to have access to their home markets, as well as a diversity of national voices circulating internationally. Minority groups in some of the affected countries wonder if this definition is inclusive enough.[6] Does such a conception promote the coexistence of groups *within* countries as well as globally? Can it capture issues of diversity that extend beyond culture industries? Does it allow developing countries that have not yet built their culture industries to do so, or does it privilege those who already have capacity in this area? What about INCP members from the former Soviet bloc who worry about enshrining in an international institution the state's legitimate right to make cultural policy? Their experience suggests that state-sponsored cultural policy is not always a benign activity. Will a notion of cultural diversity that can accommodate all of these concerns become so diluted as to be meaningless?

Tyler Cowen, the economist who represented the United States on the UNESCO expert's panel, introduces yet another conception of cultural diversity in his writings (2000; 2002). He notes, for example, that there are multiple notions of cultural diversity, some of which are being enhanced by economic liberalization, some of which are being threatened. On the one hand, he identifies diversity *across* societies. "Diversity across societies asks: 'Is one society like another society?' . . . I think we find in this regard that the world is becoming less diverse. You can see a poster of Michael Jordan in Bali, Indonesia, in South America, in Scandinavia, and of course in Chicago in the United States" (2000, 14). Cowen

6. Interview with James Early, INCD Steering Committee member and Smithsonian Institute, OAS Experts Seminar on Cultural Diversity, Halifax, NS, March 2003.

goes on to explain why he still believes that cultural diversity is being enhanced by market opening.

> Another notion of diversity is what I call 'diversity within society.' Diversity within society refers to the menu of choice. What do we have to choose from? What options do we have? What kinds of opportunities do we have with our lives? When we ask ourselves, 'does globalization bring more of this kind of diversity?', we find that the answer is usually yes. (2000, 15)

Cowen's answer, then, is to allow the market to run its course, a prescription that finds few supporters among the countries working to establish a binding international instrument on cultural diversity. Nonetheless, people like Cowen raise thought-provoking issues that cannot be ignored in the important debate over key conceptual definitions, a debate whose outcome will, in many respects, determine the effectiveness of the instrument to fulfill its mandate.

Other challenges were of a more technical nature. What is the scope of the instrument? Will it incorporate its own dispute settlement mechanism? Given the general assumption that the United States will not participate in the convention on cultural diversity, to what extent will nonsignatories be bound by the principles enshrined therein? From the perspective of international law, how will the convention interact with WTO agreements in cases where both are implicated?

Proponents of the convention were particularly concerned about this final issue, given that there would be no great gain if the WTO continues to prevail in disputes over culture industries. As the INCD executive director puts it, "How can we ensure that future disputes about trade in cultural goods and services will be judged under this convention rather than the trade agreements?"[7] Much of this debate hinged on whether or not a nonderogation clause would be included in the final text. The United States and others favored a clause stating that nothing in the Convention on Cultural Diversity would nullify existing rights and obligations that parties have to each other under other international treaties. On the other hand, governments and civil society groups hoping for a strong and binding convention argued that such a clause could make the convention irrelevant in key respects. A nonderogation clause could be interpreted by some as subordinating the convention to other international treaties. It could also make it likely that future disputes over cultural products, like the periodicals case, would be adjudicated at the WTO and not under the auspices of the convention on cultural diversity.[8]

---

7. Interview with Garry Neil, INCD executive director, May 2004.
8. Ibid.

In October 2005, the UNESCO membership voted to adopt the convention by a vote of 148 to 2 (the United States and Israel voted against; Liberia, Nicaragua, Honduras, and Australia abstained). It will come into force after thirty countries have ratified it. The draft does contain a nonderogation clause that reads: "Nothing in this Convention shall be interpreted as modifying rights and obligations of the Parties under any other Treaties to which they are parties." However, it also contains language saying that signatories are not subordinating this convention to any other treaty, as well as a clause that states: "when interpreting and applying other treaties to which they are parties or when entering into other international obligations, Parties shall take into account the relevant provisions of this Convention."[9] This combination of provisions makes predictions about how the convention might be applied in conjunction with the GATT very difficult indeed.

Observers and participants in the process have offered a range of responses to the adopted convention. Some hail the very appearance of such a treaty as a great accomplishment. The International Network of Cultural Diversity, the civil society group that has been leading the charge, called the convention a "rather weak shield against continuing pressure in the multilateral and bilateral trade negotiations to eliminate or amend policies and measures which promote a diversity of cultural choices."[10] At the same time, they note that the convention could have value as a "political tool" that could "become a rallying point for civil society groups and governments that remain concerned about how the trade and investment agreements are being used to stifle cultural policies."[11] For its part, the United States offered a scathing attack of the convention. The U.S. delegation issued the following statement about the draft convention: "The draft convention produced by this Working Group is deeply flawed and fundamentally incompatible with UNESCO's Constitutional obligation to promote the free flow of ideas by word and image." The statement goes onto say that "it could impair rights and obligations under other international agreements and adversely impact prospects for successful completion of the Doha Development Round negotiations. In so doing, it will set back progress toward the economic liberalization that has done so much to increase prosperity throughout the world."[12] United States Secretary of State Condoleezza Rice echoed this view in October 2005.

9. INCD Newsletter, 6, no. 6 (June 2005). http://www.incd.net/docs/newsletter54.en.htm, accessed July 5, 2005.

10. Ibid., 6, no. 5 (May 2005).

11. Ibid.

12. "Final Statement of the United States Delegation," The Honorable Robert S. Martin Paris, June 3, 2005, available at http://www.amb-usa.fr/usunesco/index.htm, accessed August 18, 2005.

Resolving the remaining issues discussed above so that a robust international institution devoted to cultural diversity can be established is one—albeit central—aspect of striking an updated embedded liberalism compromise that acknowledges concerns about identity and cultural diversity. Nonetheless, this step requires an accompanying effort at the domestic level to reform cultural policy measures. Just as the Convention on the Protection and Promotion of the Diversity of Cultural Expressions represents an innovative effort to think creatively about global governance in the realm of cultural policy, so must domestic policies recognize the evolving context in which cultural policy is now being made. Many countries have already taken up this challenge. For example, the Ministry of Canadian Heritage recently launched a review of Canadian content policies, focusing in particular on how Canadian content has been defined in the past. Similarly, European Union renewal of the MEDIA program reflects an effort to think through how best to constitute these policies in light of developments in industry structure, as well as technology. This effort at the domestic level will ensure that the new Convention on Cultural Diversity will both preserve the best practices that have proven effective in the past as well as promote new approaches necessitated by the rapid changes in the political, economic, and technological dimensions of culture industries.

In recent decades, governments sought to offset the cultural costs of liberalization by excluding the cultural sector from the provisions of trade agreements. This strategy proved unreliable, prompting new efforts to forge a global treaty that would establish the right of national governments to promote cultural diversity and collective particularity within their respective borders. The existence of the cultural diversity movement provides further confirmation that cultural goals are central, alongside economic goals. Furthermore, it illustrates the need for serious public debate about how we shall go about offsetting the cultural costs of liberalization in a context that presents new challenges. The following chapter confirms the urgency of such a debate by showing that similar sorts of concerns have surfaced in a range of sectors unrelated to culture industries.

Chapter 5

Beyond Culture Industries

Cultures of Agriculture and Health Care

So far this book has focused primarily on the perceived need to reconcile sociocultural and economic objectives where trade in cultural products is concerned. This challenge, which I argue is part of an evolving, contemporary embedded liberalism compromise, presents itself very clearly in the cultural sector. However, it does not only appear there. In fact, as the trade regime expands to include services, intellectual property, investment rules, and competition policy, this tension will be all the more central in a variety of sectors. Among them are agriculture and public services, which have much in common with the cultural sector. These sectors produce goods and services that have both commercial and sociocultural value. The desire to shield these sectors from economic liberalization has little to do with conventional protectionism.[1] The safeguards built into trade agreements to ensure that national governments can continue to regulate these industries in the public interest are, in the estimation of many, insufficient. In addition, these sectors are bound up with collective identity in the sense that traditions and practices that have come to be imbued with meaning in certain national and regional contexts are implicated.

The cultural sector is not the only site of intersection for commercial and sociocultural objectives, confirming the need for public discussion and creative

---

1. Liberalization of agriculture is fraught with controversy. It would be naïve to suggest that aspects of this debate do not reflect traditional protectionist concerns. However, as I explain below, my focus for the present purposes is on those (often overlooked) aspects of the debate that *do not* reflect traditional concerns.

policy responses to a growing challenge. In this chapter, I examine the manifestation of this challenge in the debate over the regulation of genetically modified organisms (GMOs) and the liberalization of health care services. Both issues are new to the trade agenda. Both exemplify situations in which national governments are faced with constraints on domestic regulatory autonomy—constraints they themselves created when they established the trading regime—making it difficult to offset new costs of economic liberalization. As is true for the cultural sector, GMOs and health services have commercial value. However, resistance to their liberalization is not based solely on economic considerations. GMOs tap into European views on such issues as scientific risk and environmentalism. Similarly, Canadians argue that their single-payer, public health system goes to the heart of what it means to be Canadian.

The GMO and health care services sectors are growing in commercial importance and liberalization of these sectors would be beneficial to many. Yet like culture industries, these sectors are also central to the identities and social bargains that governments have struck with their citizens. As such, their regulation cannot be based solely on their compatibility with trade commitments. Nor can resistance to their liberalization be understood strictly in terms of traditional protectionist rationales.

GATT, Agriculture, and Genetically Modified Organisms

In the early 1990s, the European Union introduced a range of policies designed to ensure full disclosure on the part of operators dealing in products containing genetically modified organisms. These measures require special product labels, as well as monitoring or "tracing" of products once they have found their way into the market. Later in the decade, the EU stalled its approval process for a time to update and complete its GMO labeling laws. In part, this was prompted by studies confirming the fatal consequences that certain strains of GM corn have for species of the monarch butterfly (Krenzler and MacGregor 2000, 297). But it also responded to a general unease among Europeans about the food supply in the wake of the mad cow disease scare.

Between 1991 and 1998, eighteen GMOs were authorized for release onto the European market (Bates 1999, 8). No further authorizations were granted after 1998, though several applications were pending. In response to concerns by citizens and member governments, the EU essentially froze its GMO approval process in 1999 pending reform of GMO regulations, a move designed to increase the confidence of the European consumer and to ensure the existence of an environment in which Europeans could make independent and informed choices about food purchases.

New EU legislation on GMOs has three main requirements: approval and registration; labeling; and "traceability." Directive 90/220/EEC, the original EU legislation governing GMOs, established a multistep approval process through which any GMO or product containing GMOs must successfully pass before entering the European market. A new directive, 2001/18/EC, which came into force in October 2002 and repealed 90/220/EEC, updates and strengthens the approval process.

The Regulation on Novel Foods and Novel Food Ingredients (Regulation [EC] 258/97), as well as a handful of other provisions, complement Directive 2001/18/EC. They provide for mandatory labeling of foods and food ingredients that contain or consist of GMOs. They also mandate that GMOs be traceable through all stages of production and distribution, or "from the farm to the fork." Producers and dealers in GMO products must have procedures in place to identify from whom the products were obtained and to whom they are made available. This legislation also requires that GM and non-GM products be fully segregated. More recently, legislation passed by the European Parliament in the summer of 2003 extends current labeling and traceability laws and streamlines the authorization process. Among the provisions enacted by this legislation are labeling requirements for feed to complement those for food, as well as more specific traceability obligations for business operators. The clearer and more stringent labeling laws paved the way for a reactivation of the GMO approval process. Indeed, by May 2004, two new strains of genetically modified maize had been authorized for import into the EU market.

From the perspective of the largest producer of GMOs, the United States, these policies meant closure of the European market to new strains of genetically modified American goods. In 2003, this led the United States, along with Canada and Argentina, to activate the World Trade Organization's dispute settlement mechanism by requesting consultations with the European Union over its GMO regulatory framework. They have continued the suit in protest of labeling laws, despite the fact that, in 2004, two new GMOs gained EU approval. After short consultations, the parties apparently concluded that they would not themselves find a satisfactory solution and requested that the WTO establish a panel to consider the dispute. At the time of this writing, the panel has just rendered a decision apparently in favor of the United States; however, the panel decision has not yet been made public.

Some parties to the dispute have argued that a desire to shield the European agricultural and biotech industries from foreign competition inspired the European GMO laws. Such a standard interpretation of this debate, in narrow terms of free trade versus protectionism, that suggests that the economic interests of a specific sector are motivating the policies, obscures the ways in which European

GMO regulations are bound up with general concerns about food safety, "food sovereignty," and identity. As Cook, Crang, and Thorpe (1999, 223) put it, "Everyday practices of commodified food provision and consumption involve the production and consumption not only of foods but of social imaginaries." It is difficult to identify a specific, commercial group in Europe that has sought, and derives, economic benefit from GMO regulations. Instead, the policies are motivated by broader, citizen concerns over food security, identity, and national self-determination.

The European Union defines GMOs (and genetically modified micro-organisms (GMMs)) as "organisms (and micro-organisms) in which the genetic material (DNA) has been altered in a way that does not occur naturally by mating or natural recombination. . . . It allows selected individual genes to be transferred from one organism into another, also between non-related species" (Commission 2002b). European consumers have loudly and vehemently opposed the introduction of GMOs into the European market. Polls suggest that between 70 and 80 percent of Europeans oppose GMOs in their food (Ford 2001). Whereas consumers in other parts of the world are only now questioning the costs and benefits of GMOs, Europeans very early on resisted their unregulated use. They do so for a variety of reasons. Some oppose the use of biotechnology for food on traditional moral and ethical grounds. The European experience with mad cow and hoof-and-mouth disease brought consumer safety issues to the fore and made Europeans skeptical about the reliability of their governments' risk assessment mechanisms. From a cultural standpoint, many citizens do not want culinary traditions and customs compromised. As Cadot, Suwa-Eisenmann, and Traça (2001, 16) argue with regard to Europe, "Nowhere have the ideas of free trade and economic efficiency less legitimacy than in the agri-food sector, as food is considered in countries like France as part of culture and something that ought to escape industrial logic, at least to some extent." Additionally, a desire to maintain the autonomy to respond to citizen preferences rather then to impose a universal standard that may be out of sync with domestic experiences is a key motivator. Europeans maintain that they do not want culinary habits imposed from without. Furthermore, they want to maintain the right to establish a higher domestic standard for GMOs than international agreements require, especially given that their long-term effects are not yet fully understood. Strong environmentalist traditions also play an important role here, including concerns over biodiversity and the consequences for wildlife and insects of introduction of GMOs into the ecosystem (Cohen 1999; Ford 2001; Krenzler and MacGregor 2000).

One of the better known European voices speaking out against GMOs is José Bové. Bové entered the public consciousness in August 1999 when he participated in the partial dismantlement of the McDonald's franchise in Millau, in the

Aveyron region of France. The European Union had recently renewed its ban on the entry of hormone-treated beef into the European market. The United States retaliated by setting tariffs on a range of European products, including Roquefort cheese, one of the main exports from the Aveyron region. Bové and fellow farmers were enraged by the harm done to Roquefort producers in their home town. In addition, they disagreed vehemently with the effort to redefine European resistance to hormone-treated beef as a trade issue, rather than an issue of quality, health, choice, and cultural identity. In response to actions taken against them, they proceeded to dismantle McDonald's as the global symbol of industrialized foodstuffs. Describing McDonald's fare, Bové (Bové and Dufour 2001, 55) remarks, "The food is completely uniform; the hamburgers have the same shape and content all over the world. In fact, it's 'food from nowhere.'"

Bové's fellow leader in the Confédération Paysanne, François Dufour, asserts that "people understood that agriculture is not a separate sector, that it can't be reduced to just another aspect of production. Eating habits, quality, gastronomy, cultural identity and social relations all depend on farming, and define what we refer to as agriculture" (Bové and Dufour 2001, 26). In the course of Bové's activities in response to U.S. tariffs, he has employed the term *malbouffe* to capture one of his primary concerns. The term has no good translation into English. It is typically rendered using "junk food" or "foul food"; however, Bové (Bové and Dufour 2001, 53–54) himself explains why this is insufficient.

The first time I used the word was on 12 August, in front of the McDonald's in Millau. . . . "Malbouffe" implies eating any old thing, prepared in any old way. . . . For me, the term means both the standardization of food like McDonald's—the same taste from one end of the world to another—and the choice of food associated with the use of hormones and GMOs, as well as the residues of pesticides and other things that can endanger health. So there's a cultural and a health aspect.

Dufour (Bové and Dufour 2001, 54) adds, "Today the word has been adopted to condemn those forms of agriculture whose development has been at the expense of taste, health, and the cultural and geographical identity of food."

Not only farm workers, civil society groups, and consumers have expressed such misgivings. Former European Union trade commissioner, Pascal Lamy, routinely defended "specific traits of European civilization—the insistence on high-quality foodstuffs, cultural identity in a world without barriers, and a reluctance to see some activities reduced to a commercial footing" (Hornblower and Beech 1999). At the WTO Ministerial in Seattle in 1999, he said, "The EU position on agriculture is extremely clear. Agriculture is not an economic activity. Agriculture has other functions such as protecting the environment and rural family circles, and these functions should be taken into account" (quoted in Mullarkey, Cooper, and Skully 2001, 35). He has also on many occasions alluded to a European approach to risk. Lamy's position reflects a broader sentiment in Europe—a sentiment that has now entered EU language and legislation—that agriculture is "multifunctional." This term is shorthand for the fact that the agricultural sector has commercial importance, but it also has an impact on the environment, the rural landscape, culture, identity, and in the case of GMOs, food safety. As a result, EU legislators have established strict regulations that, for a time, amounted to a ban on newly approved GMOs entering the EU market.

The fact that the United States, Canada, and Argentina are using the WTO dispute settlement mechanism to protest the European GMO regulatory framework effectively defines the debate as a trade issue. The regulatory framework comes to be understood primarily as a barrier to trade (with all the attendant negative connotations) rather than as a broader effort to promote a set of sociocultural goals revolving around food security, policy autonomy, and European identity. This effort is more appropriately understood in terms of the embedded liberalism compromise, based on the notion that governments simultaneously embrace openness while seeking to offset its costs.

Indeed, this broader characterization might have provided a framework for producing a more satisfactory outcome in the GMO trade dispute. As Falkner (2003, 34) correctly observes, "European consumers will not start eating GM food because of a WTO ruling," potentially creating a conundrum for EU officials. If faced with an unfavorable final WTO ruling, they will likely find it quite difficult to comply. This drives home the fact that, as is the case with cultural policy, European GMO laws do not conform to a traditional understanding of protectionism. Domestic interest groups do not benefit economically from the regulatory measures. The particular interest groups that benefit from conventional protection are usually producers; economists demonstrate that consumers generally benefit from free trade. Yet these oppositions are reversed in the GMO controversy. Producers must assume the cost of complying with traceability and labeling laws. Consumers may incur higher prices as a result of this, but they seem willing to do so for the peace of mind that comes with the regulatory regime. Rather than pitting the economic interests of a specific domestic group against those of their foreign counterparts then, or against the aggregate economic interests of the community, GMO legislation in Europe sets up oppositions unfamiliar to trade scholars (but quite familiar to those caught up in cultural diversity debates).

The American biotech industry claims that it loses as a result of European GMO laws. The ban on approvals did restrict the access of non-European producers to the European market. However, during the period of stalled approvals, European producers of GMOs ran up against the same restrictions that Americans and others did. It is not that no new *American* GMOs were approved during that period; no new GMOs were approved at all. Meanwhile, some foreign producers benefited from the regulations. Brazilian farmers, for example, who produced non-GM soy crops, were able to increase their exports to Europe under the moratorium. Indeed, the EU holds this up to demonstrate that the GMO regulations are nondiscriminatory and, therefore, in line with European commitments at the WTO.

The policy framework does not protect those who produce organic or non-GMO foods either. These producers do not need protection since GMO products do not tempt European consumers. Who benefits, then, in Europe? These measures protect consumers who wish to be informed about the content of their food purchases. GMO regulations exist to preserve a way of life, a range of choices, and an identity. They are designed to cushion the effects of liberalization in the face of consumer skepticism, making them examples not of protectionism but of efforts to strike a new embedded liberalism compromise. As Kristin Dawkins, from the Minneapolis-based Institute for Agriculture and Trade Policy, explains: "Fundamentally, this battle is also about the rights of nations to set up their own regulatory systems to protect human health and the environment. Instead of working through the U.N. to set an international floor of minimum standards that must be met around the world, the U.S. is pushing for a ceiling at the WTO which would restrict nations from setting more rigorous safety standards" (quoted in Raffensperger 2003, 12).

The difference between the American and European perspectives is illuminated by their opposing views on the precautionary principle. The dynamic is very similar to that found in the culture industry debate. In the cultural sector, the United States makes an argument in terms of free trade and protectionism while Canada and the EU make an argument in terms of cultural diversity. The United States rejects the cultural diversity argument as veiled economic protectionism. In the GMO debates, the United States makes an argument from free trade and protectionism, but also science, while the EU invokes the precautionary principle. Once again, American commentators reject the EU position as "high-minded rhetoric and convoluted reasoning . . . nothing more than another creative, non-scientific justification for national product distinctions that are susceptible to manipulation as disguised trade barriers" (Kogan 2004, 96). The United States has itself made policy based on the precautionary principle. Nonetheless, the precautionary principle has come to be understood in the current period as "essentially a European ethos" (Kogan 2004, 94). Even analysts that oppose the European approach note that Brussels "redefines both risk and risk regulation in terms not of science but of cultural values" (Kogan 2004, 93), that the European position springs from a "cultural aversion" (Kogan 2004, 95). They concede that European policy in this area "will not be the policy of a nation-state, based in national interest and realpolitik, but a policy suitable to its transnational identity and universalist aims. Environmental protection will therefore be high on the agenda, and policy will be guided by principle rather than expediency, and shared concerns rather than national self-interest" (Scruton 2004, 148).

This sort of analysis is curious because it acknowledges that there is "something cultural guiding policy-making" (Dobbin 1994, 1). It also observes that European traceability and labeling regulations, recently emulated in places like Japan, Korea, and China, are "costly and burdensome," potentially harming the competitiveness of the domestic biotech industry (Scruton 2004; Kogan 2004). In other words, cultural issues seem to be taking precedence over economic concerns, echoing the pattern in culture industries. Yet rather than concluding that rival societal goals are in play, which the trading regime may be ill-equipped to accommodate, opponents brand the European perspective as "irrational" (Scruton 2004) or "Luddite psychobabble," a "grave assault on entrepreneurial capitalism" (Kogan 2004, 99), and of course, protectionism. As I show in chapter 1, such conclusions do not follow from the evidence at hand. Only a willingness to take seriously the cultural claims of these governments, and to step outside of the confines of the free trade-protectionism dichotomy, can lead to more satisfying conclusions.

Taking GMOs Outside of the Trade Regime—The Cartagena Protocol on Biodiversity

The sorts of issues and responses that have emerged in the realm of cultural diversity have also emerged in the realm of GMOs and biodiversity. Again, a familiar tension is in play—a desire to regulate an industry domestically for sociocultural reasons and the accusation that such efforts at regulation are nontariff barriers or unfair trading practices. This tension, in turn, generates a demand for a global institution that might secure the domestic regulatory capacity of national governments in a specific sector and fill in the gaps in the evolving global governance framework. In the biotechnology sector, particularly the manufacture and sale of GMOs, that global institution is the Cartagena Biosafety Protocol.

The Cartagena Biosafety Protocol came into force on September 11, 2003, ninety days after Palau became the fiftieth country to ratify it. The protocol establishes "a right for parties to take precautionary measures at the national level" (Graff in Bail et al. 2002, 419). Article 1 defines its objective:

> In accordance with the precautionary approach contained in Principle 15 of the Rio Declaration on Environment and Development, the objective of this Protocol is to contribute to ensuring an adequate level of protection in the field of the safe transfer, handling and use of living modified organisms resulting from modern biotechnology that may have adverse effects on the conservation and sustainable use of biological diversity, taking also into account risks to human health, and specifically focusing on transboundary movements.

The protocol is not exhaustive in its coverage. For example, Article 5 excludes from the agreement "the transboundary movement of living modified organisms which are pharmaceuticals for humans that are addressed by other relevant international agreements or organisations." Where it does apply, however, the protocol ensures that signatories have adequate information to make decisions about importing "living modified organisms" (LMOs). In addition, the protocol takes the important step of enshrining the precautionary principle, allowing parties to the agreement to define what constitutes acceptable risk and protection within their respective societies.

As Cameron (2002, 288–90) puts it, the precautionary principle "provides the philosophical authority to take public policy or regulatory decisions in the face of scientific uncertainty. . . . [T]he precautionary principle stipulates that where environmental risks being run by regulatory inaction are in some way uncertain but non-negligible, regulatory inaction is unjustified." Under the protocol, governments can refuse the entry of the relevant GMOs into their market, a move that, for some, amounts to a nullification of key market access principles underlying the trading regime, including most-favored nation and national treatment. However, by enshrining the precautionary principle, the protocol does not endorse protectionism. Rather, it strengthens the ability of national governments to make judgments about how to define potential threats to their respective societies and to make policy accordingly. It reflects a perspective compatible with embedded liberalism as defined by Wolfe and Mendelsohn (2004, 262): "embedded liberalism is not a fixed bargain about levels of social spending or tariff bindings but a dynamic commitment to allowing countries to be different within a multilateral framework."

Unlike the experience in the cultural realm, where the Convention on Cultural Diversity emerged after the WTO decided in favor of the United States in the periodicals case, the need for a biosafety protocol did not emerge from a challenge to long-standing regulations by the trading regime. Rather, it emerged from a recognition that *new* biotechnology products were about to enter the market and regulation would be necessary to lessen any threat to human health or the environment. As executive secretary of the Convention on Biological Diversity, Hamdallah Zedan (2002, 23) says, "As far back as the 1970s, the international community recognized that . . . biotechnology might not be without its problems." He (2002, 23–25) further notes that "it was felt that advances in technology and ideas for applications were proceeding in a regulatory vacuum. . . . [M]any felt that public regulatory systems needed to be put into place in every country in order to identify and monitor any potential environmental impacts and adverse human health effects of new biotechnology." The result was the initiation of talks on biosafety many years before the mass marketing of GMOs occurred.

Indeed, the biosafety talks were unique precisely because the Cartagena Protocol was negotiated before evidence appeared that the release of GMOs would result in environmental damage (Falkner 2002, 4). Therefore, the initiative for the Biosafety Protocol emerged before the trading regime struck down domestic biosafety regulations. Nonetheless, the tension between domestic measures and trade soon became a pivot on which Protocol negotiations turned, and trade disputes would indeed materialize during the run-up to its ratification.

Countries in the developing world were especially interested in establishing a biosafety framework, in part because they were "concerned about becoming the testing ground for potentially unsafe biotechnological developments" (Falkner 2002, 6). They led an effort to include comprehensive biosafety provisions in the Convention on Biological Diversity (CBD) that emerged from the Rio Earth Summit in 1992. The European Community supported this effort in principle. However, the United States, with support from Japan, strongly opposed these proposals on the grounds that special rules for biotechnology were neither necessary nor desirable, especially since they would interfere with international trade in biotech products (Falkner 2002, 6). As a result, the Rio Earth Summit concluded without any biosafety provisions in the CBD. Article 19 (3), however, committed signatories to consider such measures in the future.

> The Parties shall consider the need for and modalities of a protocol setting out appropriate procedures, including, in particular, advance informed agreement, in the field of the safe transfer, handling and use of any living modified organism resulting from biotechnology that may have adverse effect on the conservation and sustainable use of biological diversity.

Three years later, a formal negotiating mandate for a biosafety protocol emerged. Though negotiations began in 1995, they soon stalled due to opposition by a group of agricultural exporting countries, later known as the Miami Group.

The Miami Group emerged from a meeting of states concerned with the potential trade implications of a biosafety agreement, held in Miami in July 1998 and initiated by the United States. Argentina, Australia, Canada, Chile, and Uruguay, along with the United States, all professing an interest in trade in GMOs, comprised the Miami Group by the time of the Cartagena meeting (Falkner 2002, 17). La Vina (2002, 42) contends that the Miami Group saw a risk to trade in the Biosafety talks: "as one high-ranking official from the United States told me then, 'This is not an environmental negotiation. This is about trade.'"

Arrayed against the Miami Group were countries that wanted to *establish* and to *maintain* GMO regulations. In the former category were developing countries seeking to control risk and, in some cases, to leave open the possibility of developing their own biotechnology capacities. Allied with these were developed countries that wanted to safeguard existing regulations, including labeling requirements. These groups shared the desire to keep some range of motion in domestic food safety regulation. Ultimately, the effort to create a biosafety protocol revealed the same lack of confidence in the trading regime's ability to provide national governments with the desired policymaking autonomy in the area of GMOs as we saw in the area of cultural diversity. This is particularly interesting given that arrangements exist at the multilateral level within the trading regime that deal with food safety and accept the precautionary principle. Yet for many, these safeguards are unsatisfactory.

For example, the 1994 WTO Agreement on the Application of Sanitary and Phytosanitary Measures (SPS) establishes rules on food safety and animal and plant life. The SPS agreement does allow governments to set their own standards within certain parameters. Further, Article 5.7 states that "in cases where relevant scientific evidence is insufficient, a Member may provisionally adopt sanitary or phytosanitary measures on the basis of available pertinent information." The agreement points to the Codex Alimentarius Commission, run jointly by the Food and Agricultural Organization and the World Health Organization, as the benchmark for international food safety standards and encourages harmonization of domestic regulations to reflect Codex guidelines. The Codex Alimentarius Commission does reflect many of the concerns that emerge among supporters of the Biosafety Protocol. Nonetheless, its suggested best practices do not reflect the concerns prevalent in some countries, largely because they are founded on a commitment to scientific risk assessment and nondiscriminatory trade.

The SPS Agreement permits WTO members to maintain SPS measures that are necessary to protect human, animal, or plant life but subjects these measures to three main disciplines. Firstly, the measure must be "necessary," meaning that it is not more trade-restrictive than required to achieve the appropriate level of protection (Articles 2.2 and 5.6). Secondly, the Agreement has as its objective the avoidance of discrimination based on the origin of a product and the inconsistent application of SPS measures in comparable situations (Articles 2.3 and 5.5). Finally, the SPS Agreement prohibits the adoption or maintenance of SPS measures that are not scientifically based. (Krenzler and MacGregor 2000, 309)

While none of these requirements may seem unreasonable, they do seek to accommodate the health and safety rules to the trade regime rather than the other way around. As a result, the SPS agreement does not satisfy many who fear that trade concerns may trump food safety ones. As Berger (2000, 3) explains, "domestic regulatory requirements based on Codex standards are generally presumed to be consistent with the [SPS] Agreement, but regulatory requirements that exceed Codex standards may be challenged before the WTO as trade barriers. As one commentator aptly stated, "The danger lies in the fact that, whenever a Codex standard is more tolerant . . . than a national standard, consumers in that country face an increased risk that the national standard will be lowered to prevent a trade controversy.'"

The U.S./Canada/Argentina trade dispute against the EU does indeed allege that the European GMO regulatory framework is in violation of the SPS Agreement. The dispute also maintains that EU measures contravene the Technical Barriers to Trade Agreement (TBT). The TBT Agreement establishes that technical regulations and product standards cannot be deployed as obstacles to trade. The agreement does not prohibit such regulations; rather, it establishes parameters and best practices so that divergent regulations do not intentionally or inadvertently discriminate against foreign producers or limit market access. In the case of the dispute between the United States and the EU concerning GMOs, European labeling laws, as well as the implicit requirement that GMO products be segregated from non-GMO products, may fall under TBT.

We must await release of the final decision of the WTO dispute panel for a definitive answer regarding which trade provisions and agreements may be implicated in national GMO regulation. Similarly, analysts cannot predict with certainty how the Biosafety Protocol will play into the WTO decision. According to the WTO (WTOa, n.d.), "If a dispute is brought to the WTO, the panel can only judge compliance with WTO Agreements. In doing so the Cartagena Protocol would presumably be taken into account as a relevant international treaty. The relationship of the protocol with the SPS Agreement and other international agreements is not clear." Indeed, it would likely be unwise for WTO officials to disregard a convention signed by more than one hundred countries.

The Biosafety Protocol does contain a nonderogation clause, offering some guidance on its relationship with the WTO. Nonetheless, echoing the Convention on Cultural Diversity, this guidance is not clear. According to Pollack and Shaffer (2000, 53), "the preamble provides that 'this Protocol shall not be interpreted as implying a change in the rights and obligations of a Party under any existing international agreements.' The next phrase, however, states that 'the above recital is not intended to subordinate this Protocol to other international agreements.' As an EU representative stated, the two clauses effectively 'cancel each other out.'"

In addition, the United States has not ratified the biosafety agreement, so it is not bound by it. Berger (2000, 1) notes that the "United States has no official standing in Montreal [home of the Biosafety Protocol Secretariat] because the United States Senate has not ratified the convention. The United States is therefore not technically bound to honor the Biosafety Protocol. Nevertheless, United States industry will have to comply with the rules of the Biosafety Protocol when exporting to nations that have ratified the treaty." Indeed, the many questions that remain regarding the interaction of the trade and biosafety treaties may have led the U.S. government to launch its suit against the EU when it did. Raffensperger (2003, 12) argues that "Washington was actually short-circuiting larger legal problems by initiating the challenge days before the Cartagena Biosafety Protocol was ratified by the 50th nation, Palau. If the United States had waited much longer the Biosafety Protocol would govern the trade dispute over genetically modified foods."

GATS and Health Care Services

International trade can affect the achievement of domestic goals in the health sector in a variety of ways. For example, enforcement of patent protection under the agreement on Trade-related Aspects of Intellectual Property Rights (TRIPS) can raise costs and diminish access to medications, especially in the developing world. The issue crucial to this book is the effect that the liberalization of services may have on the character of national health care provision arrangements—on the range of policy choices available to governments both to continue and reform welfare state programs. Though this issue may have far-reaching effects for all GATS signatories, I examine Canada as a representative case.

The liberalization of health services is unlike that of culture industries and GMO regulation in that much of the debate is currently taking place in the realm of the hypothetical. Unlike the cultural and agricultural sectors, where trade disputes are occurring, generating a demand for new international treaties, health services liberalization is in the very early stages. Discussion is centered primarily on what *might* happen, rather than what *has* happened.

Since 1994, the health care industry has fallen under the purview of the WTO, specifically the GATS. As part of the "built-in agenda" of the Uruguay Round Agreement, WTO member states are committed to a progressive liberalization of all services sectors. Before that, efforts at services liberalization within the context of NAFTA negotiations signaled the intersection of health care provision policy and trade policy. In 1996, Canadian trade minister Art Eggleton and health minister David Dingwall issued a statement assuring Canadians that "Canada's publicly financed, universal health care system is not in any way jeopardized by the NAFTA" (DFAIT, 1996). The government has taken specific steps in the context of both NAFTA and GATT/GATS to ensure that participation in the trading regime does not jeopardize the health care system, in large part because of sociocultural concerns, including the fact that a majority of Canadians view comprehensive health care as a social value, part of shared, collective understandings of what it means to be Canadian. Canadian officials have since indicated that these sociocultural considerations will cause them to opt out of talks to liberalize the health care sector. However, merely identifying health care services as a sector in which Canada will not make GATS commitments to market opening may amount to a strategy parallel to that of the cultural exception for culture industries, which has proven unreliable.

The Canadian system is a mixed system. It is public in the sense that a single public authority in each province—the provincial government—pays for insured services. The list of insured services is not exhaustive. Rather, it contains a range of "medically necessary" in-patient and out-patient services. The system also has private components in that private entities supply and deliver insured services, according to a price list set by provincial law. In addition, private insurers can legally provide coverage for the various health services that are not insured by the provincial government. The federal, provincial, and territorial governments share responsibility for the health system. According to Health Canada, the federal government sets and administers national principles or standards for the health care system and assists in the financing of provincial health care services through fiscal transfers, among other things. The provincial and territorial governments, for their part, manage and deliver health services, and plan, finance, and evaluate the provision of hospital care, physician, and allied health care services.

The system is governed overall by the Canada Health Act, passed in 1984. According to Health Canada, the act "establishes the criteria and conditions related to insured health care services—the national standards—that the provinces and territories must meet in order to receive the full federal cash transfer

contribution under the transfer mechanism, that is, the Canada Health and Social Transfer (CHST)."[2] The five principles of the Canada Health Act are as
follows:

1. Public Administration, meaning that "health care insurance plans are to
be administered and operated on a non-profit basis by a public authority,
responsible to the provincial/territorial governments and subject to audits
of their accounts and financial transactions";

2. Comprehensiveness, requiring that "health insurance plans of the provinces and territories must insure all insured health services (hospital, physician, surgical-dental) and, where permitted, services rendered by other
health care practitioners";

3. Universality, mandating that "one hundred percent of the insured residents of a province or territory must be entitled to the insured health services provided by the plans on uniform terms and conditions";

4. Portability, entitling citizens "to receive necessary services in relation to
an urgent or emergent need when absent on a temporary basis, such as on
business or vacation"; and

5. Accessibility, ensuring "reasonable access to insured health care services
on uniform terms and conditions, unprecluded or unimpeded, either directly or indirectly, by charges (user charges or extra-billing) or other
means (age, health status, or financial circumstances)."[3]

As Vellinga (2001, 138) notes, "this sector is not just another form of commercial activity." He goes on (2001, 145–46):

There is overwhelming evidence that health care is *not* a normal market
commodity; and health care markets are *not* ideal. No major developed
country treats health care like just another market commodity, or distrib-
utes it through normal market mechanisms. Chief among the reasons are:
   —the fact that health care is based on needs, not wants; and access to
health care should not be based on ability to pay;
   —the unpredictability of need for health care and the relatively high
burden of payment in the absence of insurance, as well as incentives for

2. Health Canada website, http://www.hc-sc.gc.ca/medicare/chaover.htm, accessed March 1,
2002.
   3. Ibid.

private insurers to avoid high-risk patients or limit insured coverage for costly care; and

—the asymmetry of knowledge and information that favours care providers (physicians) and requires patients to rely upon their advice and approval for care.

Similarly, in recent debates in Canada over health care reform, representatives of the federal opposition party, the Canadian Alliance, intimated that it favored changes that would reduce the federal government's capacity to penalize provinces that do not live up to the five principles of the Canada Health Act. Prime Minister Jean Chretien immediately discounted the idea, countering, "I am telling you there will be no more Canada" (Adams and Laghi 2000), demonstrating to what degree the character of the Canadian health care system is a defining feature of the Canadian identity. Lewis, Donaldson, Mitton, and Currie (2001, 926) echo this sentiment in asserting that Medicare is "an icon of Canadian values."

In 2001, Chrétien asked former Saskatchewan premier, Roy Romanow, to chair the Commission on the Future of Health Care in Canada. The commission report, delivered in November of 2002, echoes these sentiments:

provinces, territories, and the federal government need to make it clear to our trading partners that Canada's health care system will continue to be designed, financed, and organized in a way that reflects Canadians' values. . . . There is international agreement that countries must have significant room to adopt social policies, including health care policies that build the "social capital" of their societies in meaningful and productive ways. (Romanow 2002, 241–42)

In December 1999, *Maclean's* Magazine (1999, 48–49) reported that 79 percent of those surveyed ranked "our health care system" as "very important or somewhat important in what makes us Canadian," on a par with such things as the Canadian flag and the achievements of prominent Canadians around the world. Interestingly, the health care system garnered a full 10 percent more than "English and French national heritage" and 16 percent more than "public broadcasting," areas where the Canadian government has traditionally concentrated its identity-formation efforts.

It would appear that, on the face of it, the Canadian health care system (and similar systems) may be at odds with the principles of the trading regime. It is essentially based on a system of subsidies; it requires the establishment of a monopoly in each province, and by requiring a public authority to pay for insured health services, it has the effect of excluding private insurers from this market. None of these features, however, are a problem at the moment, thanks to specific clauses in the NAFTA and GATT/GATS agreements that allow for maintenance of the system as it is currently constituted.

As Ouellet (2002) explains, the strategy employed in each case is not identical and they may not be compatible in the long run. In NAFTA, the Canadian government relies on a series of reservations. The agreement requires the signatory governments to provide market access, to provide treatment no less favorable to signatory partners, and so on. However, Annex I grandfathers all nonconforming measures in effect as of January 1, 1994. In addition, Annex II shields from any investment or national treatment provisions in the agreement health services maintained for a public purpose.

GATS, of course, employs a different strategy. Rather than negotiating liberalization in all areas, then making specific exceptions, GATS only liberalizes those areas where signatory governments make explicit commitments. Canada has made limited commitments in the health sector. Specifically, it has listed life, accident, and health insurance services as an area in which it would allow greater market access. At first glance, this appears to open the health care system up to challenges; however, many argue that it does not because Article I: 3(c) of the GATS agreements shields "services supplied in the exercise of governmental authority." As such, publicly provided health insurance, the cornerstone of the Canadian health care system, is not subject to the liberalizing effects of the agreement.

Nonetheless, the WTO was moved by the outcry against prospective health care liberalization and its implications to post a notice on their website, entitled "GATS: Fact and Fiction: Misunderstandings and Scare Stories." One installment, entitled "The GATS and Domestic Regulation," speaks directly to the liberalization of health. This memo comes in response to an article that appeared in the British medical journal *Lancet* in 2000, which charged that GATS would lead to a fundamental overhaul—for the worse—in health service delivery. The WTO responded:

> This is a false account of the work on domestic regulation, seriously misleading in three respects. First, Member Governments will not have to submit regulations to the WTO for approval. Nor will they have to show that they are employing least-trade-restrictive practices, unless asked to justify a specific regulation in the event of a dispute with another Government. Second, none of the measures said to be at risk of being "outlawed" has ever been considered or even mentioned in the Article VI:4 negotiations. . . . Third, services supplied in the exercise of governmental authority are in any case outside the scope of the Agreement. (WTO 2001)

Despite these assurances, many analysts argue that the system may still be threatened. In general, GATS mandates a progressive liberalization of the services sector. Therefore, some of the safeguards in place may not have lasting effects. Even the Secretariat of the WTO has acknowledged that expanding the reach of the trading regime to new sectors will inevitably create tensions, perhaps exerting an unwelcome influence over national policy choices. As the GATS "extends to all forms of international trade in services . . . because such a large share of trade in services takes place *inside* national economies, . . . its requirements will from the beginning necessarily influence national domestic laws and regulations in a way that has been true of the GATT only in recent years" (Cited in Vellinga 2001, 138).

More pressing are concerns related to the possibility—some would say the necessity—of reform within the Canadian health care system. There is a general recognition across social democratic systems that governments cannot sustain welfare state policies in their current form. Rising costs as well as demographic changes make reform necessary. Canada is no different and recent public debates confirm that the health care system requires reform to ensure the principles of the Canada Health Act can be achieved efficiently and effectively. Most agree that infusions of money are not sufficient, nor is tweaking at the margins of the system.

Third Way scholars like Anthony Giddens (1999, 2000), as well as prominent students of the French social welfare system (Rosanvallon 2000), often hailed as the most efficient public system, concur that creative reform that explores a variety of public and private solutions must be considered. Communities in Canada are increasingly entertaining this argument, largely in frustration with long wait times for certain medical procedures. Yet reform seems likely to produce inadvertent consequences given the arrangements that have been struck within the context of the trading regime. The following two sections aim to illustrate why expansion of either the public or the private elements of the Canadian health care system is fraught with challenge. The NAFTA and GATS trade agreements allow the maintenance of the status quo. However, efforts at reform may unleash influences that make it difficult for governments to determine the exact direction reform of the system may take.

Health Care Services and Alberta—Expanding the Private Component

The province of Alberta spends one-third of its total budget on health, and this number is growing. The province claims that it can no longer sustain the level of health care provision to Alberta residents without further infusions of federal money and/or reform of the system. Alberta premier Ralph Klein has been calling for health-care reform. Many fear this means a greater role for the private sector, accompanied by a "delisting" of some medical services and the imposition of "user fees (charging people for services previously covered by the public funds of national health insurance)." In March 2001, Klein's government introduced Bill 11, entitled the Health Care Protection Act, legislation that would permit privately owned, for-profit surgical facilities. Many fear that Premier Klein is on the leading edge of a movement to introduce a "two-tier system" to Canada that would no longer have as its guiding principles universality and equitable provision of health care, but rather link speed of service delivery to ability to pay.

Perhaps more important, Klein's efforts could open the floodgates to an irreversible change in the Canadian health system, a change over which both the provincial and federal governments could lose control. Although the Klein government is careful not to refer to their proposed for-profit surgical facilities as "hospitals," there is enormous potential for countries, led by the United States, to invoke provisions of the North American Free Trade Agreement (NAFTA) and/or the General Agreement on Trade in Services (GATS) and insist that they have the right to deliver similar services in Canada.

> Canada protected health care from foreign intrusion by tucking it into a so-called reservation clause to exempt it from key provisions of the treaty. But the protection only applies 'to the extent that they are social services established or maintained for a public purpose.' Because treaty reservations are always interpreted narrowly, that should set off alarm bells: the United States has argued that when private providers enter a social service sector, that sector becomes a commercial service. (Janigan 2000, 46)

According to this logic, the protection offered by the national schedule at the GATS may not apply and foreign providers could be accorded the same right to compete as the Canadian providers have. In 1995, the office of the United States Trade Representative noted that "where commercial services existed, that sector no longer constituted a social service for public purpose" (quoted in Dutta 2001). Johnson (2002, 12) argues that "the province departing from the Canada Health Act principles would have to treat U.S. insurers no less favorably than domestic insurers. However, the treatment by the departing province would not constitute the treatment benchmark for any other province." Nonetheless, not all agree, suggesting that only a test of the provision after the fact will provide a reliable answer. As a joint study by the WTO and WHO attests regarding whether the exception for services provided in the exercise of governmental authority will be sufficient to safeguard public health systems: "Because none of these issues has yet resulted in a dispute between WTO Members, there is no definitive interpretation" (WHO/WTO 2002, 119).

Is there any indication that foreign investors might like to make their way into the Canadian system? It is not only the momentum at the WTO and GATS to liberalize services that has opened the question of liberalizing the health sector. As Health Canada official Jake Vellinga (2001, 138–41) notes, "the potential dollar value of international trade in health services is enormous. . . . In the United States, health services are among the top 10 services exports (health services exports totaled US$921 million in 1997)." In OECD countries, "the public sector is, by far, the largest financier of health services. From 1970 to 1990, public sector health spending within the OECD grew to 74.2 percent of total health spending." This has lowered very slightly in the 1990s as governments tried to rein in escalating costs. "In the European Union, 76.6 percent of all health spending was publicly financed, while the U.S. and Korea with a public share of 46.4 percent and 45.5 percent respectively were clear outliers among OECD countries." These statistics show the potential gains to be made by private entities in this sector if it is liberalized.

There is ample evidence that American investors would like to see European and Canadian health care systems opened up to competition. The United States is something of an exception among OECD countries because its health care system has such a large private, for-profit component. American health care entities are already quite active around the world, perhaps most recently in Latin America. For example, in 2001, Quorum Health Resources of Brentwood, Tennessee, working with a local partner, began construction of three hospitals in Brazil. Quorum will manage the facilities once they open. Quorum's senior vice president of marketing is quoted as saying about his company's foreign undertakings, "We are very optimistic at the growth prospects and consider it an organization that would be a significant contributing business unit for our company going forward. . . . We would see the U.S. business remaining robust, but the Brazilian business would be a very strong growth platform" (Kirchheimer 2001, 31).

Among the obstacles to further expansion of U.S. and other health care industries into foreign markets are, indeed, the extensive public funding arrangements in most of the Western world outside of the United States. In testimony before the U.S. Trade Deficit Review Commission in March of 2000, Steven J. Thompson, vice-dean of the School of Medicine at Johns Hopkins University, asserted that "the expansion of American health care services into international markets is challenged by a host of complex barriers. Among the most challenging is the method and availability of health care financing in other regions of the world" (Thompson 2000, 1). Thompson goes on to note that "it can be shown the [*sic*] when governments, such as Brazil, allow private insurance, the climate for private investment in the private health care sector opens and grows as well. For this reason, it would be particularly advantageous to encourage the liberalization of insurance markets around the world as a necessary precursor to the entrance of American health care into a given country" (Thompson 2000, 2). Thompson's comment provides a stark illustration of the difficulty involved in preserving favored domestic regulatory approaches when they are viewed as trade impediments.

One area where there is strong support for expansion of the private component of the system is in the realm of telehealth. Remote communities in Canada are especially keen on development of this service, which uses information technology to link them to physicians and specialists in urban centers. In addition, suppliers of telehealth technology see a promising export market. Sanger (2001) argues that the pursuit of telehealth possibilities may resemble those associated with Alberta's proposed reforms. Thus, even in areas where the introduction of privately funded activities may bring great benefit, perhaps even enhancing the principles of the Canada Health Act, the inadvertent consequences may be serious. Governments may find it difficult to circumscribe the terrain where private activity would be deemed beneficial and welcome. Many oppose this not for economic reasons, but for cultural ones. Indeed, introducing private components into the Canadian health care system would likely lower the tax burden of the average citizen and it may even save lives. Nonetheless, such a move cuts across identity issues. Those opposed to privatizing public health services articulate their resistance in terms of a desire to avoid American-style healthcare and to preserve a powerful symbol of national identity.

Meeting Evolving Needs—Expanding the Public Component

Perhaps, given the foregoing, the solution for reform may be to expand the public elements of the system. Outside of the United States, there is still great support for publicly funded health care systems. Inherent in the arguments of those opposing further privatization of the health care provision sector is the fear that diminished public participation will jeopardize achievement of the sociocultural goals associated with the sector.

In the Canadian context, public funding of the system remains quite popular and, indeed, the Romanow Commission and the Chrétien government discussed expanding the public elements of the system to encompass a wider range of services. In talks with provincial premiers, Jean Chrétien raised the issue of introducing (in some cases) and expanding (in other cases) publicly funded services to include things like a home care program. Such a move could be controversial, however, given Canadian NAFTA and GATS commitments. If private insurers lose out as a result of such a reform, they have recourse under NAFTA chapters 11 and 12. Expansion of the public component that has the effect of excluding private actors counts as "expropriation" under NAFTA and may be actionable. While the prospect of a dispute need not prevent expansion of the list of publicly insured services, it may require costly compensation of private actors forced to exit the sector (Johnson 2002, 16). As the Romanow Commission argued, "rather than conclude, then, that Canada is hemmed in to the current system and cannot change, the more reasonable conclusion is that if we want to expand the range of services in the public system, it is better to do it now while there is still very little foreign presence in health care in Canada and the potential costs of compensation are low" (Romanow 2002, 238).

Ultimately, we must assume that national governments want to find economical ways to provide the highest quality health care. As the population ages, among other developments, it seems reasonable to explore new combinations of public and private actors. Nonetheless, as the joint WHO/WTO report points out:

> The need to regulate the private sector typically increases as competing suppliers enter the market. Governments need to act to prevent any adverse effects and channel any gains to benefit health. Greater, not less, regulation has accompanied more open markets in financial services and telecommunications, and this will be essential for health services as well. (WHO/WTO 2002, 121)

The report further notes that regulatory strategies could be used to reduce risks associated with liberalization of health services, but only if governments can enforce an effective regulatory framework (WHO/WTO 2002, 113). In other words, private actors can operate within the sector, but a strong government regulatory framework must exist to ensure that these private entities conform to the sociocultural principles underpinning the system. Paradoxically, though, GATS commitments may constrain governments in the implementation of such a regulatory framework at the same time it encourages greater participation by private entities.

The preceding analysis of the agricultural and health services cases points to the same sorts of conclusions that I drew from the culture industry trade disputes. Indeed, the controversies in these unrelated sectors signal a new category of trade debate that is clearly not confined to the cultural sector. They further suggest that there are limits beyond which governments are unwilling to promote further liberalization. These limits become salient when liberalization has perhaps unintended, but certainly undesired, consequences for the domestic social arrangements, practices, and values that underpin collective identity. The resistance to liberalization in these cases has very little to do with conventional protectionism. Instead, it is motivated by a desire to offset the new costs of liberalization. These costs are unlike those encountered in earlier periods of liberalization in that they are increasingly cultural in nature. They are, however, just like previous dislocations in that citizens still expect their national governments to use domestic regulatory frameworks to temper them.

Conclusion

Globalization has been hailed as the source of great benefit. However, even among those who are propelling it, there is ambivalence about its implications for local cultures. This book has explored one area where this tension is prominent—trade in culture industry products.

Signatories concluded the two largest multilateral trading agreements on record in the early 1990s. Both the North American Free Trade Agreement (NAFTA) and the General Agreement on Tariffs and Trade (GATT) devote hundreds of pages to regulations governing thousands of commodities worth billions of dollars in trade revenue. In both cases, disagreement over the regulation of culture industries seriously threatened the successful completion of negotiations. The preceding chapters have sought to solve the puzzle of these trade disputes by bringing the cultural dimension of culture industries to the fore and attributing to them their proper weight in the process.

Culture industries do not exhibit the traits of industries that typically garner protection. Cultural policies are not motivated by the same considerations that typically inspire conventional protectionist policies. Cultural products clearly have economic value. Nevertheless, an understanding of their regulation based strictly on economics overlooks the importance that Canadian and European governments attribute to them as vectors of culture and identity. Emphasizing the ways in which cultural policies sometimes resemble discriminatory trade practices ignores the fact that these same policies provide national governments with important tools for offsetting the cultural costs of economic liberalization.

What is at stake in the challenge posed to governments by economic liberalization? Why did Canadian and European officials insist so adamantly that culture industries be excluded from NAFTA and GATT? The homogenizing forces of the global economy trigger a psychological or a nostalgic reaction to the loss of meaning that accompanies the dilution of a unique "national idiom." However, politicians are rarely motivated by nostalgia in making multilateral trade policy, therefore something much more important must be at stake: the ability of a society to represent itself as it chooses and "to be different within a multilateral framework" (Wolfe and Mendelsohn 2004, 262). Canada has been called a " 'statistical outlier' amongst Western democracies in its degree of ethnic, linguistic and religious diversity" (Kymlicka 2003, 368). Domestic culture industries can provide a site for expression of these various perspectives, promoting in the process Canadian identity and national social cohesion. Similarly, at a time when the European Union seeks to move European integration forward, culture industries can provide the vehicle through which member-state populations come to know each other, potentially easing the transition toward full political union.

Canada and the members of the European Union have all been strong proponents of open trade. Indeed, their continued participation in multilateral trade talks attests to the degree to which they construe their interests to be consistent with a norm of open trade. However, developments in the current international context—especially the expansion of the trading regime beyond goods to services and beyond tariff reduction to the harmonization of domestic regulatory frameworks—threaten their cultural distinctiveness and their domestic policy autonomy. Governments welcome the commercial benefits of liberalization, yet find themselves limited in their ability to help their societies absorb its costs. Governments transfer authority over regulation of certain industries to the trading regime only to find that the assumptions and principles that underpin the trade framework restrict their capacity to pursue certain domestic sociocultural goals, including the promotion of collective particularity and cultural diversity.

The controversy over culture industry regulation is not an isolated incident. Debates over the regulation of genetically modified organisms and health care services exhibit the same dynamic. As services and intellectual property are more fully integrated into the international trading regime, and as calls for protections for labor and the environment in multilateral agreements get louder, nonmaterial concerns that go beyond those considered here will emerge.

Already we see groups clamoring to ensure that liberalization of education services at the GATS will not mean a loss of control over domestic education systems (Sauvé 2002; Knight 2002). In addition, there is a growing movement against the consequences that the agreement on Trade-related Aspects of Intellectual Property Rights (TRIPs) may have for traditional knowledge. In the developing world, indigenous groups argue against companies that seek patents on goods and practices that their communities consider central to the perpetuation of their respective cultures. For some, at issue is the misappropriation of funds that should return to the indigenous communities rather than to developed world corporations. For others, the more crucial issue is the commodification of goods and practices that underpin local cultural communities. Efforts by American, European, and Japanese companies to obtain patents on such products as turmeric, for its medicinal qualities, and basmati rice, have spurred this debate.

These concerns are not restricted to the developing world. The European Union is in ongoing discussions on geographical indications that seek to reserve use of specific product names, such as Feta or Stilton, for authentic producers. Producers that are not recognized as authentic producers of these goods must market their products under another name. In the EU, there are various requirements for this status. For example, the region or soil must contribute to the character or quality of the product and proof of this must be offered as part of the registration process; specific raw materials required in the production of the product must be available in the specific region only, a region that is clearly delimited; the product is produced according to a special manufacturing technique; and the production of the product is based on the knowledge of manufacturers, built up over generations. To be sure, there are economic stakes in these debates. However, there is also a genuine desire to recognize local goods and practices in an effort to promote distinct cultural entities (Goff 2005).

All of these debates are fueled by legitimate sociocultural concerns. They stem, in large part, from a desire of policymakers and stakeholders to shield collective identities and distinctive state practices from the potentially homogenizing forces of economic liberalization. Yet many analysts persist in discussing them using the language of trade and protectionism. In other words, commentators often explain the desire to shield these sectors from liberalization as yet another variation on protectionism. This is surprising, in large part because policies toward these sectors are quite different from traditional protectionist policies. It is all the more surprising because we have an alternative vocabulary for discussing these issues, which more accurately captures the stakes in these debates. That is the vocabulary of embedded liberalism (Ruggie 1982). Approaching these issues from the perspective of embedded liberalism allows us to reconcile the *simultaneous* pursuit of economic and sociocultural goals, rather than positing an opposition between them.

The postwar embedded liberalism compromise that emerged in the 1940s embraced economic openness. However, it also provided national governments with room to implement domestic policies to offset the dislocation that accompanies it. A commitment to liberalization was coupled with a shared recognition of social purpose in the service of which domestic policies would be deployed (Ruggie 1982). Discussions of culture industry policy, or GMO and health service regulation, that proceed in terms of the binary opposition between trade and protectionism only capture one side of the compromise. This perspective typically concludes that such policies signify a crumbling commitment on the part of national governments to the goals of openness and liberalization. What such an interpretation misses, however, is the ongoing commitment on the part of these governments to domestic interventionism in the service of shared social purpose that is the other side of the embedded liberalism equation. The language of protectionism assumes that policies like those considered in the preceding chapters are in opposition to open trade. It denies the historical relationship between the reduction in trade barriers and the continuation of domestic policy strategies designed to manage its effects.

There is a temptation to assume that the United States is immune to the sorts of challenges that Canada, the European Union, and others have faced in navigating the sociocultural consequences of globalization. This is not true. The United States encounters these challenges in a different guise, largely because how countries define their identities determines what constitutes a threat to it. The aspect of globalization that is most immediately and significantly thought to threaten American identity is not the movement of goods and services. It is the movement of people. A growing literature on immigration and American identity grapples with this issue (see Huntington 2004; Walzer 2004).

It is important to note that the United States is not immune in the cultural realm either. The increasing popularity of Japanese popular culture, especially among children, has not gone unnoted. Margaret Talbot raises the possibility that Pokémon, Manga, and Hello Kitty products may represent

> a form of what the Harvard political scientist Joseph Nye calls "soft power"—the nonmilitary, nonpolitical means by which a country can influence another country's values or its citizens' wants. And though, so far, Japan's media exports don't convey an obvious or coherent set of values—akin to the capitalist individualism that American pop culture tends to package, for example—they might, if Japan's culture-makers wake up to the consequences of their global reach. (Talbot 2002)

As far as trade in cultural products is concerned, I have argued elsewhere that identity concerns are in play for the United States as much as they are for the Canadians and Europeans (Goff 2002). The difference is that developments pertaining to the liberalization of services at the World Trade Organization *serve to reinforce* American identity rather than to weaken it. The American stance with regard to culture industries is not strictly based on commercial considerations. It is also broadly consistent with beliefs, practices, traditions, and values that underpin the American approach to regulation of these industries. Indeed, it would be strange to assume that the Canadian and European approaches are driven by a combination of economic and cultural goals while the Americans are propelled strictly by economic goals.

For example, unlike Canada and Europe, the United States has not had a tradition of public service broadcasting for decades. Instead, American broadcasting settled into a commercial pattern in the early 1900s (McChesney 1993; Schwoch 1990). Early on, American commercial broadcasters argued that it would be *unpatriotic* to embrace something other than for-profit, advertiser-supported broadcasting. As McChesney puts it, by 1935 "there was little opposition to the widely disseminated claims of the commercial broadcasters that their control of the ether was innately democratic and American; indeed, that no other system could even be conceivable to a freedom-loving people" (McChesney 1993, 226). This sort of analysis suggests that the American stance on culture industries is also linked to identity considerations.

In anticipation of the WTO panel decision in the GMO dispute, some commentators have predicted an outcome similar to the beef hormones case. It may be politically impossible for the EU to comply with an unfavorable ruling in an area where fundamental sociocultural values are at stake. At a minimum, it would seem that broader discussion and real efforts to accommodate such sociocultural concerns are necessary, if only to ensure that citizens of these countries do not remove their support for expanded trade.

> The cost of choosing to ignore one's WTO commitments is accepting retaliation from trade partners. This is the route chosen by the EU in its dispute with Canada and the US over beef produced using growth hormones. Accepting retaliation, however, signals that the political consensus that underlies the WTO has broken down and that renegotiation is required. (Isaac and Kerr 2003, 35)

One useful entry point into such a renegotiation is to inquire what our multiple goals are in the current moment. What are the most valued economic, political, social, and cultural goals we expect our domestic and global institutions to achieve? Liberalization is not an end in itself. It is, rather, a means to achieving more fundamental purposes. At best, it is a means to sociopolitical ends like stability and fairness. At worst, it works at cross purposes to our efforts to promote an egalitarian or culturally diverse or environmentally friendly notion of prosperity. There does not appear to be consensus on what belongs on this list of more fundamental goals, and in what order. The weakening of this consensus is, in no small part, due to the changing context in which we seek to regulate our economies and societies.

What, Then, Can We Do?

A variety of possibilities present themselves, some more innovative than others. On the more conventional end of the spectrum lie efforts to make domestic policy strategies relatively more compatible with trading regime principles. For example, Bhagwati (1999) asks, "Does it make sense to have audio-visual restrictions on the fraction of time allotted to showing foreign films rather than subsidies to make local ones? Surely, it makes more sense to have free imports of films from Hollywood but to use subsidies to aid the production of French films." Bhagwati (1999) continues:

> The other example I might use to drive this point home against protectionism to shore up domestic culture relates to hormone-fed beef. Given the cultural dissonance between the EU and the US, it is surely a good idea to see if, instead of simply banning the availability of such beef in the EU, we could persuade the EU to accept a labeling solution.

While this seems like a reasonable approach, for many it is problematic. Indeed, the GMO trade dispute between the United States and the EU is, in part, about the discriminatory effects of EU labeling requirements and the fact that such laws may not conform with commitments under the Technical Barriers to Trade Agreement (TBT). It would seem that Bhagwati's solution can prevail only if it is preceded by a normative shift, wherein there is a general acceptance that there may be limits to liberalization. As one EU official observed, "Why would we want to eliminate all barriers at any cost? Just to do it? There are great gains to be made in some areas. Let's concentrate on these. But there are also things we must never touch. We must know how to recognize the limits."[1] We must be willing to acknowledge and identify acceptable domestic support measures, even if they smack of protectionism for those who have forgotten that the trading regime has never been about free trade in its purest definition.

---

1. Interview with Edouard Bourcieu, economist in the research unit, office of the EU Trade Commissioner, Brussels, July 2003.

Former EU trade commissioner (and current director general of the WTO) Pascal Lamy and others have suggested that we follow the lead of the EU in devising contemporary global governance strategies. The EU has found effective ways to reconcile competing goals. However, its success may be due to the fact that it is evolving toward a genuine regional community, complete with regional institutions and a long-term political and cultural vision (Baer 2003, 6).

Of course, the Biosafety Protocol and the Convention on Cultural Diversity represent an alternative global strategy, albeit untested. This approach springs from the idea that, to be effective, global level policymaking may require an expanded range of institutions, charged with overseeing different issue areas. A single, strong institution like the WTO, overseeing one issue area, can overshadow the range of other issues societies hope to promote. As I discuss in chapter 4, establishing competing organizations and institutions is not problem-free. Nonetheless, there does seem to be some necessity to expand the capacities of institutions at the global level and to experiment with new institutional forms.

In addition, many are hopeful that we can reconcile the competing claims on signatory loyalties that overlapping institutions create. For example, drawing again on the experience of the EU, Baer (2003, 25) recommends establishing a cultural policy observatory that would be charged with making recommendations about how to measure cultural diversity. There is a danger that legitimate strategies to offset the costs of economic liberalization and to promote domestic sociocultural goals can be captured by protectionist forces. Yet there are ways of preventing this. Baer (2003, 25) notes that the EU has used the principle of proportionality as a benchmark against which to judge the desirability and viability of cultural policies. In addition, a Cultural Policy Observatory could establish a list of domestic regulations that are protected from liberalization efforts.

Officials in the office of the EU Trade Commissioner share the view that there could be an institution charged with delineating the range of policies domestic governments can employ to promote their sociocultural goals. The assumption here is that we are capable of determining whether policies have a protectionist or "mercantilist" impulse behind them or whether they spring from a genuine sociocultural aspiration shared by a population.[2]

The World Trade Organization is not the villain in this story. That is not to say that it is a perfect institution. Given the increasingly important effect it has on our daily lives, there are great strides to be made in making it more democratic and transparent. Nonetheless, the WTO is a multilateral, rules-based institution. As such, it is a framework that constrains the power of individual member states and provides a check on unilateralism. This is especially impor-

2. Ibid.

tant for smaller states that may not have influence internationally. In addition, national governments drive the trade agenda. The WTO is a forum and not an independent actor, unlike its cousins, the IMF and the World Bank. Member governments set the agenda and national parliaments ratify the agreements that are struck. This may not provide much reassurance once commitments are made because WTO rules are difficult to reverse. Nonetheless, we are still in the early stages of making rules about trade in services, intellectual property, and investment. There is ample room to make a difference, not by influencing the WTO directly, but by making sure that national governments craft trade agendas and negotiating positions with public scrutiny.

National-level policymaking must also evolve in other directions. Just as innovation is taking place in global institutions, so must national governments be open to new policy strategies that may challenge existing preferences for things like public provision of services, but that may better serve the population. In addition, the WHO-WTO joint study of trade in health care services points out that the evolving global context has made some national policymaking assumptions obsolete. In particular, they point to the traditional practice of segregating key policy areas in separate government agencies and ministries. The Ministry of Health makes health policy; the Ministry of Trade makes trade policy; the Ministry of Culture makes cultural policy. Yet health policy is increasingly trade policy and trade policy is cultural policy and so on. The report singles out Canada and Thailand as two countries that have found ways to open dialogue between ministries about policies with overlapping jurisdictions. Change, then, involves not just rethinking the content of domestic regulatory frameworks, but the structure of their implementation.

None of these strategies can succeed unless we change our language. How we talk about things matters. The language of protectionism sets up competitive oppositions. It calls into question the commitment of otherwise compliant countries, making them defend, and sometimes alter, actions with long-standing support in their domestic environments. The language of protectionism devalues the legitimate concerns of people and governments who are uneasy about the sociocultural consequences of globalization. Global politics has changed. The assumptions we make and the concepts we use must also evolve so that we do not inadvertently circumscribe the range of possible responses that will allow us to make the most of the change.

References

Adams, Paul, and Brian Laghi. 2000. "Medicare Debate Boils Over." *The Globe and Mail.* November 1.

"Alberta to Spend $1 Million on Ad Campaign." 2001. *The Globe and Mail.* December 28.

Anderson, Benedict. 1991. *Imagined Communities.* New York: Verso.

Annan, Kofi. 1999. "Secretary-General Proposes Global Compact on Human Rights, Labour, Environment, in Address to World Economic Forum in Davos." Press Release SG/SM/6881. February. http://www.un.org/News/Press/docs/1999/19990201. sgsm6881.html (accessed June 1, 2005).

Armstrong, Sarah. 2000. "Magazines, Cultural Policy, and Globalization: The Forced Retreat of the State?" *Canadian Public Policy* 26 (2): 369–85.

Atwood, Margaret. 1972. *Survival: A Thematic Guide to Canadian Literature.* Toronto: House of Anansi Press.

Audley, Paul. 1983. *Canada's Cultural Industries.* Toronto: James Lorimer.

———. 1994. "Cultural Industry Policy: Objectives, Formulation, and Evaluation." *Canadian Journal of Communication* 19: 317–52.

Baer, Jean-Michel. 2003. "L'exception culturelle: Une règle en quête de contenus." *En Temps Réel, Cahier 11* (October): 1–32. http://en.temps.reel.free.fr/activites. htm (accessed June 15, 2004).

Bail, Christoph, Robert Falkner, and Helen Marquard. 2002. *The Cartagena Protocol on Biosafety.* London: The Royal Institute of International Affairs.

Baldwin, Robert E. 1996. "The Political Economy of Trade Policy: Integrating the Perspectives of Economists and Political Scientists." In *The Political Economy of Trade Policy,* edited by Robert C. Feenstra et al. Cambridge, MA: MIT Press.

Bates, Stephen. 1999. "Tougher EU Controls Mean Moratorium on GM Crops." *The Guardian.* June 26, p. 8.

Bateson, Mary Catherine. 1990. "Beyond Sovereignty: An Emerging Global Civilization." In *Contending Sovereignties: Redefining Political Community,* edited by R. B. J. Walker and Saul H. Mendlovitz. Boulder, CO: Lynne Rienner.

Bell, David. 1996. "Recent Works on Early Modern French National Identity." *Journal of Modern History* 68: 84–113.

Berger, Emily. 2000. "The Cartagena Protocol on Biosafety: Protecting the Global Environment without Restricting National Sovereignty." May 3. http://www.american.edu/TED/class/Karin/karin2.htm (accessed May 7, 2004).

Bernier, Ivan. 2003a. "Audiovisual Services Subsidies within the Framework of the GATS." Paper prepared for the Ministry of Culture and Communications, the Government of Québec. August. http://www.mcc.gouv.qc.ca/international/diversite-culturelle/eng/update.html (accessed January 2004).

———. 2003b. "A UNESCO International Convention on Cultural Diversity." Paper prepared for the Ministry of Culture and Communications, the Government of Québec. March. http://www.mcc.gouv.qc.ca/international/diversite-culturelle/eng/update.html (accessed January 2004).

Berton, Pierre. 1974. *The National Dream: The Last Spike.* Toronto: McClelland and Stewart.

Bhagwati, Jagdish. 1995. *Protectionism.* Cambridge, MA: MIT Press.

———. 1999. "Trade and Culture: America's Blind Spot." In Jagdish Bhagwati, *The Wind of the Hundred Days: How Washington Mismanaged Globalization,* 209–13. Cambridge, MA: MIT Press.

Bourdon, Jerome. 1990. *Histoire de la Television sous de Gaulle.* Paris: Anthropos/INA.

Bové, José, and François Dufour, interviewed by Gilles Luneau. 2001. *The World Is Not for Sale.* New York: Verso.

Brown, Duncan. 1991 "Citizens or Consumers: U.S. Reactions to the European Community's Directive on Television." *Critical Studies in Mass Communication* 8: 1–12.

Cable, Vincent. 1996. "The New Trade Agenda: Universal Rules amid Cultural Diversity." *International Affairs* 72 (2): 227–46.

Cadot, Olivier, Akiko Suwa-Eisenmann, and Daniel Traça. 2001. "Trade-related Issues in the Regulation of Genetically Modified Organisms." Paper prepared for workshop on European and American Perspectives on Regulating Genetically Engineered Food. INSEAD, Paris. June 7–8.

Cahn, Sandrine, and Daniel Schimmel. 1997. "The Cultural Exception: Does It Exist in GATT and GATS Frameworks? How Does It Affect or Is It Affected by the Agreement on TRIPS?" *Cardozo Arts & Entertainment Law Journal* 15: 281–314.

Cameron, James. 2002. "The Precautionary Principle." In *Trade, Environment, and the Millennium,* 2nd ed., edited by Gary P. Sampson and W. Bradnee Chambers, 287–320. New York: United Nations University Press.

Canada. 1951. *Royal Commission on National Development in the Arts, Letters and Sciences.* Ottawa: Supply and Services.

———. 1982. *Report of the Federal Cultural Policy Review Committee.* Ottawa: Minister of Supply and Services.

———. 1991. *Citizen's Forum on Canada's Future.* Ottawa: Minister of Supply and Services.

Canada, Department of Communications. 1987. *Canadian Cultural Industries: Vital Links.* Ottawa: Supply and Services.

"Casting Hollywood North." 1986. *Maclean's,* February 17, p. 34.

Chanda, Nayan, and Robert Manning. 1984. "Washington Finesses Away Free Trade." *Far Eastern Economic Review* 26, no. 3 (October 25): 70–81.

Charland, Maurice. 1986. "Technological Nationalism." *Canadian Journal of Political and Social Theory* 10: 196–220.

Cohen, Roger. 1999. "Fearful over the Future, Europe Seizes on Food." *The New York Times.* August 29.

Collins, Richard. 1990. *Culture, Communication, and National Identity: The Case of Canadian Television.* Toronto: University of Toronto.

———. 1994. "Unity in Diversity? The European Single Market in Broadcasting and the Audiovisual, 1982–92." *Journal of Common Market Studies* 32: 89–102.

Commission of the European Communities. 1988. *The Audio-Visual Media in the Single European Market.* Luxembourg: Office for Official Publications of the European Communities.

Commission of the European Communities. 1990. "Conclusions of the Presidency: European Council." Strasbourg. December 8–9, 1989. In *The European Community Policy in the Audiovisual Field: Legal and Political Texts.* Luxembourg: Office for Official Publications of the European Communities.

Commission of the European Communities. 2004. "Making Citizenship Work: Fostering European Culture and Diversity through Programmes for Youth, Culture, Audiovisual and Civic Participation." COM (2004) 154 final, Brussels, March 9. Available at http://europa.eu.int/eur-lex/en/com/cnc/2004/com2004_0154en01.pdf. (accessed September 2004).

Commission of the European Union. 2002a. "Education and Culture at a Glance: Newsletter of the Education and Culture Directorate." Issue 7 (May). http://ec.europa.eu/dgs/education_culture/publ/news/07/newsletter_en2.htm.

Commission of the European Union. 2002b. "Questions and Answers on the Regulation of GMOs in the EU." EU Institutions Press Releases Series. MEMO/02/160, Brussels, July 1. http://europa.eu.int/comm/dgs/health_consumer/library/press/press_food_en.html (accessed July 2004).

Condron, Ann Marie. 1997. "Cinema." In *Aspects of Contemporary France,* edited by Sheila Perry, 208–25. London: Routledge.

Cook, Ian, Philip Crang, and Mark Thorpe. 1999. "Eating into Britishness: Multicultural Imaginaries and the Identity Politics of Food." In *Practising Identities: Power and Resistance,* edited by Sasha Roseneil and Julie Seymour. New York: St. Martin's Press.

Corse, Sarah M. 1997. *Nationalism and Literature: The Politics of Culture in Canada and the United States.* Cambridge: Cambridge University Press.

Cowen, Tyler. 2000. *Culture in the Global Economy.* Hans L. Zetterberg Lecture. Stockholm: City University of Stockholm.

———. 2002. *Creative Destruction.* Princeton: Princeton University Press.

Cultural Industries Sectoral Advisory Group on International Trade (SAGIT). 1999. *New Strategies for Culture and Trade.* Available at http://www.dfait-maeci.gc.ca/tna-nac/canculture-en.asp.(accessed July 2004).

de Grazia, Victoria. 1989. "Mass Culture and Sovereignty: The American Challenge to European Cinemas, 1920–1960." *Journal of Modern History* 61: 53–87.

Delanty, Gerard. 1995. *Inventing Europe: Idea, Identity, Reality.* New York: St. Martin's Press.

Department of Foreign Affairs and International Trade (DFAIT). 1996. "Canada's Health Care System Protected under the NAFTA." no. 55, April 2. http://w01.international. gc.ca/MinPub/Publication.asp?publication_id = 376523&Language = E.

de Witte, Bruno. 1990. "Cultural Linkages." In *The Dynamics of European Integration,* edited by William Wallace, 192–209. London: Pinter.

Dobbin, Frank. 1994. *Forging Industrial Policy: The United States, Britain, and France in the Railway Age.* Cambridge: Cambridge University Press.

Doern, G. Bruce, and Brian W. Tomlin. *Faith and Fear: The Free Trade Story.* Toronto: Stoddart, 1991.

Doern, G. Bruce, Leslie Pal, and Brian W. Tomlin. 1996. "The Internationalization of Canadian Public Policy." In *The Internationalization of Canadian Public Policy,* edited by Doern, Pal, and Tomlin, 1–26. Toronto: Oxford University Press.

Dorland, Michael, ed. 1996. *The Cultural Industries in Canada.* Toronto: J. Lorimer.

Dutta, Gautam. 2001. "Inequality and Health," *Two Eyes Magazine* 3 (spring). http:// home.earthlink.net/~twoeyesmagazine/issue3/health side.htm (accessed November 2003).

Dymond, William A., and Michael M. Hart. 2000. "Post-Modern Trade Policy: Reflections on the Challenges to Multilateral Trade Negotiations after Seattle." Unpublished Working Paper, Center for International Studies, University of Southern California, February.

Dyson, Kenneth, and Peter Humphreys, eds. 1990. *The Political Economy of Communications: International and European Dimensions.* London: Routledge.

Earle, Robert L., and John D. Wirth. 1995. Introduction to *Identities in North America: The Search for Community,* edited by Robert L. Earle and John D. Wirth, 1–12. Stanford: Stanford University.

Emanuel, Susan. 1992. "Culture in Space: the European Cultural Channel." *Media, Culture, and Society* 14: 281–99.

———. 1993. "Cultural Television: Western Europe and the United States." *European Journal of Communication* 8: 131–47.

Esserman, Susan, and Robert Howse. 2003. "The WTO on Trial." *Foreign Affairs* 82 (January/February): 130–40.

Falkner, Robert. 2003. "Genetically Modified Organisms and the World Trade Organization: Picking the Wrong Fight." *The World Today* 59 (8–9): 33–34.

Flynn, Gregory. 1995. "Remaking the Hexagon." In *Remaking the Hexagon: The New France in the New Europe,* edited by Gregory Flynn, 1–13. Boulder, CO: Westview.

Forbes, Jill. 1987. "Cultural Policy: The Soul of Man under Socialism." In *Mitterrand's France,* edited by Sonia Mazey and Michael Newman, 131–65. London: Croom Helm.

Ford, Peter. 2001. "Pâté, Bonhomie, and a Slap at Engineered Food." *Christian Science Monitor* 93 (August 31).

Franceschini, Laurence. 1995. *La Régulation Audiovisuelle en France.* Paris: Presses Universitaires de France.

"Free to Be European." 1999. *The Economist* 352, September 11.

Garcia, Soledad. 1993. "Europe's Fragmented Identities and the Frontiers of Citizenship." In *European Identity and the Search for Legitimacy,* edited by Soledad Garcia, 1–29. New York: Pinter.

Gathercole, Sandra. 1987. "Changing Channels: Canadian Television Needs to Switch to a New Format." In *Contemporary Canadian Politics,* edited by Robert J. Jackson, Doreen Jackson, and Nicolas Baxter-Moore, 79–86. Scarborough: Prentice-Hall Canada.

Giddens, Anthony. 1999. *The Third Way: The Renewal of Social Democracy.* Cambridge: Polity Press.

——. 2000. *The Third Way and Its Critics.* Cambridge: Polity Press.

Goff, Patricia M. 2002. "Trading Culture: Identity and Culture Industry Trade Policy in the U.S., Canada, and the EU." In *Constructivism and Comparative Politics: Theoretical Issues and Case Studies,* edited by Daniel Green. Armonk, NY: M. E. Sharpe.

——. 2005. "It's Got to Be Sheep's Milk or Nothing! Geography, Identity, and Economic Nationalism." In *Economic Nationalism in a Globalizing World,* edited by Eric Helleiner and Andreas Pickel. Ithaca, NY: Cornell University Press.

Gomes, Leonard. 2003. *The Economics and Ideology of Free Trade.* Northampton, MA: Edward Elgar.

Grant, Peter S., and Chris Wood. 2004. *Blockbusters and Trade Wars.* Toronto: Douglas and McIntyre.

Gray, H. Peter. 1985. *Free Trade or Protection?* New York: St. Martin's Press.

Guehenno, Jean-Marie. 1987. "France and the Electronic Media: The Economics of Freedom." In *The Mitterrand Experiment,* edited by George Ross, Stanley Hoffmann, and Sylvia Malzacher, 277–90. New York: Oxford University Press.

Hagelin, Theodore, and Hudson Janisch. "The Border Broadcasting Dispute in Context." In *Cultures in Collision: A Canadian-U.S. Conference on Communications Policy,* 40–99. New York: Praeger, 1984.

Hale, John. 1993. "The Renaissance Idea of Europe." In *European Identity and the Search for Legitimacy,* edited by Soledad Garcia, 46–63. New York: Pinter.

Harrington, Charlene, and Allyson M. Pollock. 1998. "Decentralisation and Privatisation of Long-term Care in UK and USA." *Lancet* 351 (June 13): 1806–7.

Hart, Jeffrey A., and Aseem Prakash. 1997. "The Decline of 'Embedded Liberalism' and the Rearticulation of the Keynesian Welfare State." *New Political Economy* 2 (1): 65–78.

Helleiner, Eric. 2003. "Economic Liberalism and Its Critics: The Past as Prologue?" *Review of International Political Economy* 10 (November): 685–96.

Hift, Fred. "Monster Movies: Blockbuster Films in Europe Made in America." *Europe* 340 (October 1994): 27.

Hornblower, Margot, and Hannah Beech. 1999. "Never Mind the Riots. The Real Threat to the WTO's Free-trade Agenda Lies in Discord among Member Nations." *Time* 154, 23 (December 13).http://www.time.com/time/asia/magazine/99/1213/index.html.

Hoskins, Colin, Adam Finn, and Stuart McFadyen. 1996. "Television and Film in a Freer International Trade Environment: US Dominance and Canadian Response." In *Mass Media and Free Trade: NAFTA and the Cultural Industries,* edited by Emile McAnany and Kenton Wilkinson. Austin: University of Texas Press.

Hoskins, Colin, and Stuart McFadyen. 1993. "Canadian Participation in International Co-Productions and Co-Ventures in Television Programming." *Canadian Journal of Communication* 18: 219–36.

Hoskins, Colin, and Rolf Mirus. 1988. "Reasons for the U.S. Dominance of the International Trade in Television Programmes." *Media, Culture and Society* 10 (4): 499–516.

Hubert-Lacombe, Patricia. 1986. "L'accueil des films américains en France pendant la guerre froide (1946–1953)." *Revue d'histoire moderne et contemporaine* 33: 301–13.

Huntington, Samuel. *Who Are We? The Challenges to America's National Identity.* New York: Simon and Schuster, 2004.

Hutchison, David. 1993. "The European Community and Audio-visual Culture." *Canadian Journal of Communication* 18: 437–50.

Irwin, Douglas A. 1996. *Against the Tide: An Intellectual History of Free Trade.* Princeton: Princeton University Press.

——. 2002. *Free Trade under Fire.* Princeton: Princeton University Press.

Isaac, Grant E., and William A. Kerr. 2003. "Genetically Modified Organisms and Trade Rules: Identifying Important Challenges for the WTO." *World Economy* 26: 29–42.

Janigan, Mary. 2000. "Stretching the Medicare Envelope." *Maclean's*, April 3, p. 46.

Jarvie, Ian. 1998. "Free Trade as Cultural Threat: American Film and TV Exports in the Post-war Period." In *Hollywood and Europe: Economics, Culture, National Identity, 1948–95*, edited by Geoffrey Nowell-Smith and Steven Ricci, 34–46. London: BFI.

Jeancolas, Jean-Pierre. 1995. *Histoire du Cinéma Français.* Paris: Editions Nathan.

Johnson, Jon R. 2002. "How Will International Trade Agreements Affect Canadian Health Care?" Discussion Paper 22, Commission on the Future of Health Care in Canada. September.

Kelsey, Jane. "Lessons from New Zealand: The Saga of the GATS and Local Content Quotas." Paper for the Conference on Cultural Diversity, Paris, 2–4 February 2003. http://www.arena.org.nz/gatspari.htm.

Kirchheimer, Barbara. "Global Ambition." 2001. *Modern Healthcare* 31 (May 7): 30–34.

Kirshner, Jonathan. 1999. "Keynes, Capital Mobility and the Crisis of Embedded Liberalism." *Review of International Political Economy* 6 (autumn): 313–37.

Knight, Jane. 2002. "Trade in Higher Education Services: The Implications of GATS." Paper prepared for the Observatory on Borderless Higher Education. March. Accessed online www.unesco.org/education/studyingabroad/highlights/global_forum/gats_he/jk_trade_he_gats_implications.pdf.

Kogan, Lawrence A. 2004. "Exporting Europe's Protection." *National Interest* (fall): 91–99.

Krauss, Melvyn B. 1978. *The New Protectionism: The Welfare State and International Trade.* New York: New York University Press.

Krenzler, Horst G., and Anne MacGregor. 2000. "GM Food: The Next Major Transatlantic Trade War?" *European Foreign Affairs Review* 5: 287–316.

Krugman, Paul, ed. *Strategic Trade Policy and the New International Economics.* Cambridge: MIT Press, 1986.

Kuhn, Raymond. *The Media in France.* London: Routledge, 1995.

Kuisel, Richard. 1993. *Seducing the French: The Dilemma of Americanization.* Berkeley: University of California.

Kymlicka, Will. 2003. "Being Canadian." *Government and Opposition* 38 (summer): 357–85.

Lamy, Pascal. 2002. *L'Europe en première ligne.* Paris: Editions du Seuil.

——. 2004. "Co-existence between Public Policy and Free Trade: Can We Achieve Good Protectionism?" Speech delivered to the Conference of the Greens/European Free Alliance at the European Parliament, Brussels, 5 March 2004. http://ec.europa.eu/archives/commission_1999_2004/lamy/speeches_articles/spla211_en.htm. Accessed July 17, 2004.

La Vina, Antonio G. M. 2002. "A Mandate for a Biosafety Protocol : The Jakarta Negotiations." In *The Cartagena Protocol on Biosafety*, edited by Christoph Bail, Robert Falkner, and Helen Marquard, 34–43. London: Royal Institute of International Affairs.

Letts, Richard. 2004. "Australia/USA Treaty and Loss for Cultural Diversity." *Choike: A Portal on Southern Civil Societies.* Third World Institute. http://www.choike.org/nuevo_eng/informes/2394.html.

Levitte, Jean-David. 1995. "La diplomatie culturelle: un atout pour la France." In *Histoires de diplomatie culturelle des origines à 1995,* edited by Francois Roche and Bernard Pigniau. Paris: Ministere des affaires etrangeres.

Lewis, Steven, Cam Donaldson, Craig Mitton, and Gillian Currie. 2001. "The Future of Health Care in Canada." *British Medical Journal* 323 (October 20): 926–29.

Liebes, Tamar, and Elihu Katz. 1990. *The Export of Meaning.* Oxford: Oxford University.

Lipset, Seymour Martin. 1986. "Historical Traditions and National Characteristics: A Comparative Analysis of Canada and the United States." *Canadian Journal of Sociology* 11: 113–55.

———. 1990. *Continental Divide: The Values and Institutions of the United States and Canada.* New York: Routledge.

List, Friedrich. 1966 [1841]. *The National System of Political Economy.* N.Y.: Augustus M. Kelley.

———. 1983 [1837]. *The Natural System of Political Economy.* Totowa, N.J.: Frank Cass.

Litvak, Isaiah, and Christopher Maule. 1974. *Cultural Sovereignty: The Time and Reader's Digest Case in Canada.* New York: Praeger.

Looseley, David. 1995. *The Politics of Fun: Cultural Policy and Debate in Contemporary France.* Washington, D.C.: Berg.

Loriaux, Michael. 1999. "The French Developmental State as Myth and Moral Ambition." In *The Developmental State,* edited by Meredith Woo-Cumings, 235–75. Ithaca: Cornell University Press.

Lorimer, Rowland. 1996. "Book Publishing." In *The Cultural Industries in Canada,* edited by Michael Dorland. Toronto: J. Lorimer.

Lorimer, Rowland, and Eleanor O'Donnell. 1992. "Globalization and Internationalization in Publishing." *Canadian Journal of Communication* 17: 493–509.

Magder, Ted. 1993. *Canada's Hollywood: The Canadian State and Feature Films.* Toronto: University of Toronto Press.

———. 1996. "Film and Video Production." In *The Cultural Industries in Canada,* edited by Michael Dorland. Toronto: J. Lorimer.

———. 1997. "Public Discourse and the Structures of Communication." In *Understanding Canada: Building on the New Canadian Political Economy,* edited by Wallace Clement, 338–58. Montreal: McGill-Queen's University.

Maggiore, Matteo. 1990. *Audiovisual Production in the Single Market.* Luxembourg: Commission of the European Communities.

Mandel, Michael J. 2001. "Health Care May Be Just What the Economy Ordered." *Business Week* 3749 (September 17): 49–50.

Marchildon, Gregory. 1995. "From Pax Brittanica to Pax Americana and Beyond." *Annals of the American Academy of Political and Social Science* 538 (March): 151–68.

Maxwell, Richard. 1996. "Technologies of National Desire." In *Challenging Boundaries,* edited by Michael J. Shapiro and Hayward R. Alker, 327–60. Minneapolis: University of Minnesota Press.:

McAnany, Emile, and Kenton Wilkinson, eds. 1996. *Mass Media and Free Trade.* Austin: University of Texas Press.

McChesney, Robert. 1993. *Telecommunications, Mass Media, and Democracy: The Battle for Control of U.S. Broadcasting, 1928–1935.* New York: Oxford University Press.

Meisel, John. "Escaping Extinction: Cultural Defence of an Undefended Border." In *Southern Exposure: Canadian Perspectives on the United States,* edited by D. H. Flaherty and W. R. McKercher. Toronto: McGraw-Hill Ryerson, 1986.

Milner, Helen. "The Political Economy of International Trade." *Annual Review of Political Science* 2 (1999): 91–114.

Minc, Alain. 1992. *The Great European Illusion.* Oxford: Blackwell.

Ming-Shao, W. 1995. "Is There No Business Like Show Business? Free Trade and Cultural Protectionism." *Yale Journal of International Law* 20 (winter): 106–50.

Moeglin, P. 1992. "Television and Europe: More Questions than Answers." *Canadian Journal of Communication* 17: 437–60.

Morley, Dave. 1980. "Texts, Readers, Subjects." In *Culture, Media and Language,* edited by Stuart Hall, Dorothy Hobson, Andrew Lowe, and Paul Willis, 163–73.. London: Hutchison.

Morley, David, and Kevin Robins. 1989. "Spaces of Identity: Communications Technologies and the Reconfiguration of Europe." *Screen* 30: 10–34.

———. 1995. *Spaces of Identity: Global Media, Electronic Landscapes, and Cultural Boundaries.* New York: Routledge.

Mullarkey, Daniel, Joseph Cooper, and David Skully. 2001. "'Multifunctionality' and Agriculture: Do Mixed Goals Distort Trade?" *Choices: The Magazine of Food, Farm, and Resource Issues* 16 (1): 31–35.

Neumann, Iver B. 2002. "Returning Practice to the Linguistic Turn: The Case of Diplomacy." *Millennium* 31, 3: 627–51.

Nevitte, Neil. 1996. *The Decline of Deference: Canadian Value Change in Cross-National Perspective.* Peterborough, Ont.: Broadview Press.

Newman, Peter C. 1994. "Canadian Magazines Like This One, Matter." *Maclean's,* April 18, p. 47.

North American Free Trade Agreement between the Government of Canada, the Government of the United States of Mexico, and the United States of America. 1992. Ottawa: Minister of Supply and Services.

Ouellet, Richard. 2002. "The Effects of International Trade Agreements on Canadian Health Measures: Options for Canada with a View to the Upcoming Trade Negotiations." Discussion Paper #32, Commission on the Future of Health Care in Canada. October.

Palmer, Michael, and Jeremy Tunstall. 1990. *Liberating Communications: Policy-Making in France and Britain.* Oxford: Basil Blackwell.

Papathanassopoulos, Stylianos. 1990. "Broadcasting and the European Community: The Commission's Audiovisual Policy." In *Political Economy of Communications,* edited by Kenneth Dyson and Peter Humphreys. London: Routledge.

Paul, Joel Richard. 2000. "Cultural Resistance to Global Governance." *Michigan Journal of International Law* (fall): 1–84.

"Peering Inward and Outward." 1999. *Maclean's,* December 20, pp. 48–49.

Peers, Frank. 1979. *The Public Eye.* Toronto: University of Toronto Press.

Pendakur, Manjunath. *Canadian Dreams and American Control: The Political Economy of the Canadian Film Industry.* Detroit: Wayne State University Press, 1990.

Perilli, Patricia. 1991. "France." In *A Level Playing Field?* edited by Patricia Perilli. London: British Film Institute.

Perry, Sheila. 1997. "Television." In *Aspects of Contemporary France,* edited by Sheila Perry, 114–33. London: Routledge.

Perry, Simon. 1991. "Introduction." In *A Level Playing Field?* edited by Patricia Perilli. London: British Film Institute.

Pickel, Andreas. 2005. "False Oppositions: Reconceptualizing Economic Nationalism in a Globalizing World." In *Economic Nationalism in a Globalizing World,* edited by Eric Helleiner and Andreas Pickel. Ithaca: Cornell University Press.

Pinto, Diana. 1987. "The Left, Intellectuals, and Culture." In *The Mitterrand Experiment,* edited by George Ross, Stanley Hoffmann, and Sylvia Malzacher, 217–28. New York: Oxford University Press.

Polanyi, Karl. 2000 [1944]. *The Great Transformation.* Boston: Beacon Press.

Pollack, Mark A., and Gregory C. Shaffer. 2000. "Biotechnology: The Next Transatlantic Trade War?" *Washington Quarterly* 23 (autumn): 41–54.

Porter, John. 1968. *The Vertical Mosaic: An Analysis of Social Class and Power in Canada.* Toronto: University of Toronto Press.

Portes, Jacques. 1986. "Les origines de la legende noire des accords Blum-Byrnes sur le cinéma." *Revue d'histoire moderne et contemporaine* 33: 314–29.

Pugel, Thomas A., and Peter H. Lindert. 2000. *International Economics.* Boston: Irwin McGraw-Hill.

Raffensperger, Carolyn. 2003. "U.S. Vs. 'Old Europe' on Biotechnology." In *The Environmental Forum.* Washington, D.C.: Environmental Law Institute, July/August: 12.

Ricardo, David. 1911 [1817]. *The Principles of Political Economy and Taxation.* London: Dent.

Richardson, Kay, and John Corner. 1992. "Reading Reception: Mediation and Transparency in Viewers' Reception of a TV Programme." In *Culture and Power,* edited by Paddy Scannell, Philip Schlesinger, and Colin Sparks, 158–81. London: Sage.

Rodrik, Dani. 1997. "Sense and Nonsense in the Globalization Debate." *Foreign Policy* 107 (summer): 19–36.

Romanow, Roy. 2002. Commission on the Future of Health Care in Canada. "Building on Values: The Future of Health Care in Canada." Available at http://www.hc-sc.gc.ca/english/care/romanow/index1.html (accessed August 2004).

Rosanvallon, Pierre. 1990. *L'état en France: de 1789 à nos jours.* Paris: Seuil.

———. 2000. *The New Social Question: Rethinking the Welfare State.* Translated by Barbara Harshav. Princeton, N.J.: Princeton University Press.

Ruggie, John Gerard. 1982. "International Regimes, Transactions, and Change: Embedded Liberalism in the Postwar Economic Order." *International Organization* 36 (spring): 379–415.

———. 1991. "Embedded Liberalism Revisited: Institutions and Progress in International Economic Relations." In *Progress in Postwar International Relations,* edited by Emanuel Adler and Beverly Crawford, 201–34. New York: Columbia University Press.

———. 1994. "Trade, Protectionism, and the Future of Welfare Capitalism." *Journal of International Affairs* 48 (summer): 1–11.

———. 1995. "At Home Abroad, Abroad at Home: International Liberalisation and Domestic Stability in the New World Economy." *Millennium: Journal of International Studies* 24 (3): 507–26.

———. 1997. "Globalization and the Embedded Liberalism Compromise: The End of an Era?" Max Planck Institute for the Study of Societies Working Paper 97/1. http://www.mpi-fg-koeln.mpg.de/pu/workpap/wp97–1/wp97–1.html (accessed July 29, 2004).

———. 2000. "Weaving the Global Compact: Sustaining the Single Global Economic Space." *UN Chronicle*, no. 37 (September).

———. 2002. "Taking Embedded Liberalism Global: The Corporate Connection." Miliband Public Lecture on Global Economic Governance, the London School of Economics and Political Science, June 6. http://www.lse.ac.uk/collections/globalDimensions/globalisation/takingEmbeddedLiberalism (accessed July 29, 2004).

Ruskin, John. 1901 [1857]. *A Joy Forever*. London: George Allen.

———. 1967 [1860]. *Unto this Last: Four Essays on the First Principles of Political Economy.* Lincoln: University of Nebraska Press,

Saltman, Richard B., and Josep Figueras. 1998. "Analyzing the Evidence on European Health Care Reforms." *Health Affairs* 17 (March/April): 85–108.

Sandblom, Lisa Oladotter. 2000. *Genetically Modified Organisms (GMOs): A Transatlantic Trade Dispute*. Masters Thesis, Monterey Institute of International Studies.

Sanger, Matthew. 2001. *Reckless Abandon*. Ottawa: Canadian Centre for Policy Alternatives.

Saul, John Ralston. 1997. *Reflections of a Siamese Twin*. Toronto: Penguin Books.

Sauvé, Pierre. 2002. "Trade, Education, and the GATS: What's In, What's Out, What's All the Fuss About?" Paper prepared for OECD Forum on Trade in Educational Services. May 23–24. Washington, D.C. http://www.oecd.org/dataoecd/50/50/2088515.pdf (accessed May 2004).

Schlesinger, Philip. 1987. "On National Identity: Some Conceptions and Misconceptions Criticized." *Social Science Information* 26: 219–64.

———. 1994. "Europe's Contradictory Communicative Space." *Daedalus* 123: 25–52.

Schott, Jeffrey. 1994. *The Uruguay Round: An Assessment*. Washington, D.C.: Institute of International Economics.

Schwoch, James. 1990. *The American Radio Industry and Its Latin American Activities, 1900–1939*. Urbana: University of Illinois Press.

Scruton, Roger. 2004. "The Cult of Precaution." *National Interest* (summer): 148–54.

Sellier, Genevieve. 1993. "Le précédent des accords Blum-Byrnes." *Le Monde Diplomatique* (November): 15.

Sewell, William. 1999. "The Concept(s) of Culture." In *Beyond the Cultural Turn: New Directions in the Study of Society and Culture*, edited by Victoria E. Bonnell and Lynn Hunt, 35–61. Berkeley: University of California Press.

Smith, Adam. 2000 [1776]. *An Inquiry into the Nature and Causes of the Wealth of Nations*. New York: Modern Library.

Spicer, Keith. 1995. "Canada: Values in Search of a Vision." In *Identities in North America: The Search for Community*, edited by Robert L. Earle and John D. Wirth, 13–28. Stanford, CA: Stanford University.

Statistics Canada. 1995. *Canada's Culture, Heritage, and Identity: A Statistical Perspective*. Ottawa: Ministry of Industry—Education, Culture and Tourism Division.

Straw, Will. 1996. "Sound Recording," In *The Cultural Industries in Canada*, edited by Michael Dorland. Toronto: J. Lorimer.

Tagliabue, John. 1996. "Local Fare Pushing U.S. Shows out of Prime Time." *International Herald Tribune*. October 15, p. 2.

Talbot, Margaret. 2002. "Pokemon Hegemon." *New York Times Magazine*. December 15.

Tanzi, Vito, and Isaias Coelho. 1993. "Restrictions to Foreign Investment: A New Form of Protectionism?" In *Protectionism and World Welfare*, edited by Dominick Salvatore, 200–218. Cambridge: Cambridge University Press.

Theiler, Tobias. 2005. *Political Symbolism and European Integration*. Manchester: Manchester University Press.

Thompson, Steven J. 2000. "Statement of Johns Hopkins University School of Medicine, Johns Hopkins International, before the U.S. Trade Deficit Review Commission." March 13. New York, N.Y., 1. http://www.ustdrc.gov/hearings/13mar00/sthompson.pdf (accessed March 1, 2002).

Trueheart, Charles. 1995. "Canadian Booksellers Dread Sheer Volume of U.S. Superstore Invasion." *Washington Post*. December 13, A33.

Van Elteren, Mel. 1996. "GATT and Beyond: World Trade, the Arts, and American Popular Culture in Western Europe." *Journal of American Culture* 19: 59–73.

Variety. 1997 "Movie Biz Enjoys Global Warming." April 7, p. 1.

Vellinga, Jake. 2001. "International Trade, Health Systems, and Services: A Health Policy Perspective." Paper prepared on behalf of the PRI-GCON Working Group on World Trade Issues. http://www.dfait-maeci.gc.ca/eet/pdf/07–eng.pdf (posted 2001; accessed August 2002).

Venturelli, Shalini S. 1993. "The Imagined Transnational Public Sphere in the European Community's Broadcast Philosophy: Implications for Democracy." *European Journal of Communication* 8: 491–518.

Vogel, Harold. 1998. *Entertainment Industry Economics*. New York: Cambridge University Press.

Vogel, Steven. 1996. *Freer Markets, More Rules: Regulatory Reform in Advanced Industrial Countries*. Ithaca: Cornell University Press.

Wachtel, David. 1987. *Cultural Policy and Socialist France*. New York: Greenwood Press.

Wall, Irwin. 1991. *The United States and the Making of Postwar France, 1945–1954*. Cambridge: Cambridge University Press.

Walzer, Michael. 2004. "What Does It Mean to Be An 'American'? *Social Research* 71 (fall): 633–54.

Wasser, Frederick. 1995. "Is Hollywood America? The Trans-Nationalization of the American Film Industry." *Critical Studies in Mass Communication* 12: 423–37.

Weber, Eugen. 1976. *Peasants into Frenchmen*. Stanford: Stanford University Press.

Wolfe, Robert. 1998. *Farm Wars*. New York: St. Martin's Press.

Wolfe, Robert, and Matthew Mendelsohn. 2001. "Probing the After-myth of Seattle: Canadian Public Opinion on International Trade, 1980–2000." *International Journal* 56(spring): 234–60.

———. 2004. "Embedded Liberalism in the Global Era: Would Citizens Support a New Grand Compromise?" *International Journal* 59 (spring): 261–80.

World Health Organization. 2000. *The World Health Report 1999: Making a Difference*. Geneva: WHO.

World Health Organization and World Trade Organization. 2002. "WTO Agreements and Public Health: A Joint Study by the WHO and the WTO Secretariat." Available at http://www.wto.org/English/news_e/pres02_e/pr310_e.htm (accessed July 2004).

WTO. Trade in Services Division. 1999. "An Introduction to the GATS." www.wto.org (accessed June 2004).

WTO. 2001. "GATS: Fact and Fiction. Misunderstandings and Scare Stories—The GATS and Domestic Regulation." Available at http://www.wto.org/english/tratop_e/serv_e/gats_factfiction9_e.htm (accessed June 2004).

WTOa (n.d.). SPS Agreement Training Module: Chapter 8—Current Issues. Section 8.1: Genetically Modified Organisms. http://www.wto.org/english/tratop_e/sps_e/sps_agreement_cbt_e/c8s1p1_e.htm.

Zedan, Hamdallah. 2002. "The Road to the Biosafety Protocol." In *The Cartagena Protocol on Biosafety,* edited by Christoph Bail, Robert Falkner, and Helen Marquard, 23–33. London: Royal Institute of International Affairs.

Index

Advertising, 66–67, 77, 81
Agence pour le développement régional du
  cinéma (France), 118
Agreement on the Application of Sanitary and
  Phytosanitary Measures (SPS), 156–57
Agriculture:
  European public opinion on, 149–51
  geographical names issue, 171
  and Uruguay Round GATT talks, 136
  See also Genetically modified organisms
Alternative strategies, 174–76
Anderson, Benedict, 8
Annan, Kofi, 138
Antiglobalization activism, 11, 14–15
ARTE (television station), 114
Audiovisual Communications
  Act (France), 112
Audiovisual industries. *See* European
  audiovisual policies; French audiovisual
  policies
Audley, Paul, 57
Australia, 134
Auto Pact of 1965, 28, 54

BABEL (Broadcasting Across the Barrier of
  European Languages), 105
Baer, Jean-Michel, 132
Balance of trade protectionism rationale, 29–30
Baldwin, Robert E., 25, 33

Bateson, Mary Catherine, 8
Battle in Seattle (1999), 14–15
BBG (Board of Broadcast Governors)
  (Canada), 76, 77–78
BCNI (Business Council on National Issues)
  (Canada), 57–58
Bennett, R. B., 74–75
Berger, Emily, 157, 158
Bernier, Ivan, 134, 135, 142
Bhagwati, Jagdish, 24, 26, 34–35, 174
Bill C-58. *See* Income Tax Act (Canada)
Biodiversity, 149. *See also* Genetically modified
  organisms
Biosafety Protocol (2003), 153–58, 173, 175
Blum-Byrnes Accord, 118–22
Blum, Leon, 119
Board of Broadcast Governors (BBG)
  (Canada), 76, 77–78
Borders (company), 69–70
Borins, Ed, 70
Bourcieu, Edouard, 174
Bové, José, 149–50
Broadcasting Act (Canada), 73, 75, 76, 79
Broadcasting industries:
  Canada, 27, 49, 61–62, 73–81
  Europe, 98, 99, 102–5
  France, 27, 85, 86, 111–12
Business Council on National Issues (BCNI)
  (Canada), 57–58

Cable, Vincent, 26
Cadot, Olivier, 149
CAFTA (Central American Free Trade
    Agreement), 134
Cahn, Sandrine, 129, 130
Cameron, James, 154
Canada:
    automobile industry, 28, 54
    radio industry, 27, 73–81
    sound recording industry, 51, 70–73
    See also Canadian collective identity;
        Canadian culture industry challenges;
        Canadian culture industry policies;
        Canadian film industry; Canadian health
        care services; Canadian publishing
        industry; Canadian television industry
Canada Council, 66–67, 69
Canada Health Act (1984), 159–60
Canada Magazine Fund, 68
Canada Music Fund, 72
Canada–U.S. Free Trade Agreement
    (CUSFTA), 73, 126–27. *See also*
    CUSFTA negotiations
Canada–U.S. similarities, 39–40, 48
Canadian aboriginal rights, 41n
Canadian Alliance, 161
Canadian Audio-Visual Certification Office
    (CAVCO), 63
Canadian Book Publishing Development
    Program (CBPDP), 69
Canadian Broadcasting Corporation (CBC),
    74, 75, 76
Canadian Broadcast Program Development
    Fund (CBPDF), 62
Canadian collective identity:
    and Canada–U.S. distinctions, 39–40
    and colonial history, 38–39
    culture industry importance to,
        37, 43–47, 55
    and health care services, 10, 159, 161, 166
    overview, 38–42
    and space-binding technology, 46–47
    See also Canadian collective identity goals
Canadian collective identity goals, 37, 81–82
    and broadcasting industry policy,
        73–75, 76, 79
    and CUSFTA negotiations,
        40, 43–44, 45–46
    and European collective identity goals, 89
    and heterogeneity, 6, 7, 41–42, 170
    and Quebec nationalism, 41–42, 48, 61
    and sound recording industry, 71, 72

Canadian culture industry challenges, 47–56
    Canada–U.S. similarities, 48
    distribution, 50–52, 64
    export markets, 52–54
    financing, 49–50, 58, 63, 64
    market size, 47–49
Canadian culture industry policies:
    broadcasting industries, 61–62, 73–81
    and Convention on Cultural Diversity, 140
    and embedded liberalism, 37
    film industry, 60–66
    and heterogeneity, 6, 7, 36, 41–42
    limited success of, 45–46
    overview, 2, 56–60
    and protectionism rationales, 27, 28–30
    public opinion on, 30, 47, 56, 58
    publishing industry, 66–70
    sound recording industry, 70–73
Canadian Feature Film Policy, 65–66
Canadian Film Development Corporation
    (CFDC). *See* Telefilm Canada
Canadian film industry:
    distribution, 51–52, 64
    employment in, 29, 55–56
    and financing, 49, 63, 64, 65
    government policies, 60–66
    weakness of, 27, 60
Canadian Film or Video Production Tax Credit
    (CPTC), 63
Canadian health care services, 158–68
    Alberta reform proposals, 163–66
    and collective identity, 10, 159, 161, 166
    and General Agreement on Trade in
        Services, 159, 162–63, 164, 165
    and North American Free Trade Agreement,
        159, 162, 164
    public expansion, 166–67
    system of, 159–61
Canadian publishing industry:
    and corporate mergers, 49–50
    distribution, 50–51
    government policies, 66–70
    longevity of, 27
    and market size, 48
    WTO periodicals case, 66, 68,
        70, 125, 129, 139–40
Canadian Radio-Television and
    Telecommunications Commission
    (CRTC), 2
    and broadcasting industries, 76, 78, 79
    country music channel case, 127–28
    and sound recording industry, 71, 72

Canadian television industry:
  and financing, 49
  government policies, 61–62, 73–81
  longevity of, 27
Capital Cost Allowance (CCA) (Canada), 63
Carney, Patricia, 43
Cartagena Biosafety Protocol (2003),
  153–58, 173, 175
Carter, Jimmy, 81
CAVCO (Canadian Audio-Visual Certification
  Office), 63
CBC (Canadian Broadcasting Corporation),
  74, 75, 76
CBD (Convention on Biological
  Diversity), 155
CBPDF (Canadian Broadcast Program
  Development Fund), 62
CBPDP (Canadian Book Publishing
  Development Program), 69
CCA (Capital Cost Allowance) (Canada), 63
Central American Free Trade Agreement
  (CAFTA), 134
Centre National de la Cinématographie (CNC)
  (France), 117
CFDC (Canadian Film Development
  Corporation). *See* Telefilm Canada
Chanda, Nayan, 31
Chapters (company), 69–70
Chile, 134–35
Chrétien, Jean, 10, 161, 167
Clark, Helen, 133
Classical economic theory, 21–22, 33–34, 54
CNC (Centre National de la Cinématographie)
  (France), 117
CNCL (Commission Nationale de la
  Communication et des Libertés)
  (France), 113
Codex Alimentarius Commission, 156, 157
Coelho, Isaias, 19
Collective identity goals, 5–8
  and agriculture/GMOs, 149, 150
  and dynamic nature of collective identity,
    5, 7, 86
  and embedded liberalism, 14
  and GMO policies, 152–53
  and heterogeneity, 5–7
  importance of culture industries to, 4, 7, 37,
    43–47, 55, 89–90, 93–97
  and national security protectionism
    rationale, 33
  U.S. goals, 173
  See also Canadian collective identity goals

Collins, Richard, 106
Colonial history, 38–39
Commission Nationale de la Communication
  et des Libertés (CNCL) (France), 113
Comparative advantage, 21–22, 25
Conseil Superieur d l'Audiovisuel (CSA)
  (France), 113–14
Constructive engagement policies, 24
Consumer choice, 22–23
Content restrictions:
  and Canadian broadcasting industries,
    77–80
  and Canadian film industry policies, 62–63
  and Canadian sound recording industry
    policies, 71
  and economic value assumptions, 33
  and European audiovisual policies, 2–3,
    102–4
  and French audiovisual policies, 113–14
Convention on Biological Diversity (CBD), 155
Convention on Cultural Diversity, 125–26,
  139–45, 175
Convention on the Protection and Promotion
  of the Diversity of Cultural Expressions.
  See Convention on Cultural Diversity
Cook, Ian, 149
Copps, Sheila, 62, 80, 140
Coproductions, 101, 104, 106, 107
Copyright law, 72–73
Corporate mergers, 49–50
Cowen, Tyler, 142–43
CPTC (Canadian Film or Video Production
  Tax Credit), 63
Crang, Philip, 149
CRTC. *See* Canadian Radio-Television and
  Telecommunications Commission
CSA (Conseil Superieur d l'Audiovisuel)
  (France), 113–14
Cultural discount, 53
Cultural diversity. *See* Heterogeneity
Cultural Industries Development Fund
  (Canada), 58
Cultural Policy Observatory proposals, 175
Cultural protection institution. *See* Convention
  on Cultural Diversity
Culture industries:
  definitions of, 59n, 126–27, 128–29, 133–34
  value of, 4, 7, 37, 43–47, 55, 89–90, 93–97
Currie, Gillian, 161
CUSFTA negotiations, 2, 17, 36
  and Business Council on National Issues,
    57–58

CUSFTA negotiations *(continued)*
  and Canadian collective identity goals, 40,
    43–44, 45–46
  and Canadian culture industry policies
    overview, 59
  and Canadian film industry policies, 64
CUSFTA. *See* Canada–U.S. Free Trade
  Agreement; CUSFTA negotiations

Dawkins, Kristin, 152
The Declaration on European Identity, 88
Declining industry protectionism
  rationale, 30
De Gaulle, Charles, 111
Delors, Jacques, 90, 91
Democracy, 6, 7–8
Developing countries, 132, 142, 170–71
Digital technologies, 68, 72, 129
Dingwall, David, 159
Distribution:
  and Canadian culture industries, 50–52, 64
  and European audiovisual industries,
    99–100, 106, 118
Diversity. *See* Heterogeneity
Dobbin, Frank, 9, 10, 153
Doern, G. Bruce, 57
Doha Development Round GATT talks,
  122, 144
Donaldson, Cam, 161
Dubbing/subtitling, 29–30, 52n
Dufour, François, 150
Dymond, William A., 20, 137

Earle, Robert L., 39
EAVE (European Audiovisual
  Entrepreneurs), 105
Economic value assumptions:
  and European collective identity goals,
    90–91
  and free trade/protectionism argument
    limitations, 20, 26, 29, 31, 33–34
  and free trade/protectionism traditional
    theory, 20, 24, 26
  and genetically modified organisms, 148–49
ECSC (European Coal and Steel
  Community), 87
Education, 170
Eggleton, Art, 159
Emanuel, Susan, 114
Embedded liberalism:
  and Canadian culture industry policies, 37
  and Convention on Cultural Diversity, 145

  and criticisms of free trade ideology,
    11–12, 13–15
  desirability of, 35, 171–72
  and European audiovisual policies, 122–24
  and Global Compact, 138–39
  and GMO policies, 151, 152, 154
  and trade agreement inadequacy for cultural
    protection, 125–26, 135–39
  and Uruguay Round GATT talks, 136
Employment protectionism rationale, 28–29
Environmental issues, 147, 149, 155
Equity Investment Program (Canada), 62
ERASMUS program (EU), 89
EUREKA program (EU), 106
European audiovisual policies, 85, 101–8
  British positions on, 106–7
  and content restrictions, 2–3, 102–4
  and embedded liberalism, 122–24
  and EU accession rules, 124
  Hahn Report, 101–2
  and industry challenges, 97–101
  MEDIA program, 104–6, 145
  and protectionism rationales, 29–30, 31
  successes of, 107–8
  Television without Frontiers, 3,
    102–4, 113, 130
  and Uruguay Round GATT talks,
    92–93, 107
European Coal and Steel Community
  (ECSC), 87
European collective identity goals,
    84, 86, 87–97, 170
  audiovisual industries importance to,
    89–90, 93–97
  and economic value assumptions, 90–91
  and heterogeneity, 6–7, 88–89, 96, 106
  and Uruguay Round GATT talks, 92–93
European Commission, 93, 94–95, 96–97
European Community, 87
European Council, 93–94
European Film and Television Year (1988), 106
European Film Distribution Office, 105
European Union (EU):
  GMO policies, 147–49, 151–52
  heterogeneity in, 6–7, 96
  new members of, 96, 124
  origins of, 87–88
  Polygram case, 64
  See also European audiovisual policies;
    European collective identity goals;
    Uruguay Round GATT talks
EU. *See* European Union

FACTOR (Foundation to Assist Canadian
    Talent on Record), 72
Fair trade, 34
Falkner, Robert, 151
Feature Film Fund (Canada), 62
Film festivals, 106
Film or Video Production Services Tax
    (Canada), 64
Financing:
    and Canadian culture industries,
        49–50, 58, 63, 64, 65, 68, 69
    and European audiovisual industries, 2–3,
        100–101, 105, 117–18
Finn, Adam, 44–45
Flynn, Gregory, 109, 110
Food safety issues, 147, 149
Foundation to Assist Canadian Talent on
    Record (FACTOR), 72
Free trade/protectionism argument
    limitations, 3, 4–5, 18–20
    and balance of trade protectionism
        rationale, 29–30
    and Canadian culture industry policies, 37
    and declining industry protectionism
        rationale, 30
    and economic value assumptions,
        20, 26, 29, 31, 33–34
    and employment protectionism
        rationale, 28–29
    and infant industry protectionism
        rationale, 27
    and interest group protectionism
        rationale, 30–31
    and national security protectionism
        rationale, 31–33
    and optimal tariff protectionism
        rationale, 28
    and strategic trade policy protectionism
        rationale, 30
Free trade/protectionism traditional theory,
    21–26
    criticisms of, 10–15
    and economic value assumptions, 20, 24, 26
    on free trade benefits, 21–24, 34
    and GMO policies, 151, 153
    on political gains, 23–24
    See also Free trade/protectionism argument
        limitations; Protectionism rationales
French audiovisual policies, 108–22
    and Blum-Byrnes Accord, 118–22
    and content restrictions, 113–14
    and definitions of culture, 115–16

film industry, 3, 117–18
    longevity of, 85, 110, 117–18, 119
    and protectionism rationales, 27
    and state role, 85, 109–13, 118
    and U.S. culture as threat, 85, 86, 108–9,
        111, 115–16, 120n
    and Uruguay Round GATT talks, 3n, 84,
        108, 109, 118–19, 121–22
French collective identity goals, 85, 86
    and heterogeneity, 109
    longevity of, 6, 110
French film industry:
    challenges to, 97
    government policies, 3, 117–18
    intrinsic importance of, 85–86, 108–9
    longevity of, 27
French television industry:
    longevity of, 27
    and state role, 111–12
    and U.S. television industry, 85, 86
    See also French audiovisual policies
From Creators to Audience (Canada), 72

Gathercole, Sandra, 45
GATS. *See* General Agreement on Trade in
    Services
GATT. *See* General Agreement on Tariffs and
    Trade; Uruguay Round GATT talks
General Agreement on Tariffs and Trade
    (GATT):
    and Convention on Cultural Diversity, 144
    Doha Development Round, 122, 144
    inadequacy for cultural protection, 129–30
    See also Uruguay Round GATT talks
General Agreement on Trade in Services
    (GATS), 17, 83, 130–35
    and education, 170
    and health care services, 159, 162–63,
        164–65
    and Uruguay Round GATT talks, 3
Genetically modified organisms (GMOs),
    147–58
    Cartagena Biosafety Protocol, 153–58, 173,
        175
    and collective identity goals, 152–53
    and economic value assumptions, 148–49
    European policies, 147–49, 151–52
    European public opinion on, 149–51
    U.S. policies, 148, 150, 151–52
Giddens, Anthony, 163
Giscard d'Estaing, Valéry, 113
Global Compact, 138–39

GMOs. *See* Genetically modified organisms
Gomes, Leonard, 21, 24
Grant, Peter S., 46, 127–28, 132, 133
Green Box, 136
Grierson, John, 60–61
Gulf War, 87

Hahn Report (1983), 101–2
Hart, Michael M., 20, 137
Haute Autorité de la Communication
    Audiovisuelle (France), 113
Hayes, Carol-Anne, 50n
Health care services. *See* Canadian health care
    services
Heckscher, 21–22
Helleiner, Eric, 11
Herriot Decree (1928) (France), 117
Heterogeneity:
    and Canadian collective identity goals,
        6, 7, 41–42, 170
    and Canadian culture industry policies,
        6, 7, 36, 41–42
    and collective identity goals, 5–7
    and Convention on Cultural Diversity,
        142–43
    and corporate mergers, 49–50
    and European audiovisual industries,
        99–100, 105
    and European collective identity goals,
        6–7, 88–89, 96, 106
    and French collective identity goals, 109
High Level Group on Audiovisual Policy
    (EU), 96
"Hollywood North", 29, 55–56
Hoskins, Colin, 44–45, 49, 52n, 53
Hubert-Lacombe, Patricia, 120–21
Hutchison, David, 89

Immigration, 172. *See also* Heterogeneity
INCD (International Network on Cultural
    Diversity), 142, 143, 144
Income Tax Act (Canada), 66–67, 81
INCP (International Network on Cultural
    Policy), 140, 141, 142
Indigenous knowledge, 170–71
Infant industry protectionism rationale, 27
Intellectual property, 158, 170–71
Interest group protectionism rationale,
    25–26, 30–31
International Monetary Fund (IMF), 13, 14
International Network on Cultural Diversity
    (INCD), 142, 143, 144

International Network on Cultural Policy
    (INCP), 140, 141, 142
Internet. *See* Digital technologies
Intraindustry trade, 22–23
Investment Canada Act, 58, 70
Investment. *See* Financing
Irwin, Douglas A., 22, 23, 24–25, 28, 31

Japanese popular culture, 172
Jarvie, Ian, 129–30
Jeanneney, Jean-Noel, 110
Johnson, Jon R., 164

Kirchheimer, Barbara, 165
Kissinger, Henry, 81
Klein, Ralph, 164
Kogan, Lawrence A., 152–53
Krauss, Melvyn B., 19
Krugman, Paul, 25, 30n
Kuhn, Raymond, 27, 111, 112
Kuisel, Richard, 108
Kymlicka, Will, 40

Labor issues. *See* Workers' rights
La Cinq (French television station), 114
Lamy, Pascal, 122–24, 136, 139, 150–51, 175
Lang, Jack, 115–16, 118
Language:
    Canada, 47–48, 71
    Europe, 6–7, 86
La Sept (French television station), 114
Laskin, Bora, 79
La Vina, Antonio G., 156
Levitte, Jean-David, 116
Lewis, Steven, 161
Lindert, Peter H., 22–23
Lipset, Seymour Martin, 39–40
List, Friedrich, 12. *See also* Listian economic
    nationalism
Listian economic nationalism, 11, 12–13
Litvak, Isaiah, 45
Loosely, David, 111, 112, 115
Loriaux, Michael, 9, 110, 111
Lorimer, Rowland, 50

Maastricht Treaty (1992), 87–88, 92
MacDonald, Flora, 40, 43
Mad cow disease, 147, 149
Malbouffe, 150
Malraux, André, 111, 115
Manning, Robert, 31
MAPL system (Canada), 71

Market size, 47–49, 99
Marshall Plan, 24
Marxism, 11–12
Marx, Karl, 11
Massey Commission Report (1951), 45
Maule, Christopher, 45
McChesney, Robert, 173
McDonald's, 149–50
McFayden, Stuart, 44–45
MEDIA program (Measures to Encourage the
    Development of the Audiovisual Industry)
    (EU), 104–6, 145
Meech Lake Accord, 41
Meisel, John, 36, 81
Mendelsohn, Matthew, 14, 124, 154, 170
Mercantilism, 21
MFN (most-favored nation) principle, 131
Miami Group, 155–56
Mill, John Stuart, 23
Milner, Helen, 25, 26
Ming-Shao, W., 133
Mirus, Rolf, 49, 52n, 53
Mitterand, François, 109, 112, 113, 114, 115
Mitton, Craig, 161
Monnet, Jean, 83
Most-favored nation (MFN) principle, 131
Mulroney, Brian, 41, 54–55

NAFTA. *See* North American Free Trade
    Agreement
National Film Board of Canada (NFB),
    60–61
National identity. *See* Collective identity
National security protectionism rationale,
    31–33
National treatment principle, 131
New International Instrument on Cultural
    Diversity (NIICD). *See* Convention on
    Cultural Diversity
New Zealand, 133
NFB (National Film Board of Canada),
    60–61
NIICD (New International Instrument on
    Cultural Diversity). *See* Convention on
    Cultural Diversity
Nora, Pierre, 110
North American Free Trade Agreement
    (NAFTA):
    and health care services, 159, 162, 164
    inadequacy for cultural protection, 126–29
    national security provisions, 32
    negotiations, 2, 17, 36, 45–46, 169

O'Donnell, Eleanor, 50
Ohlin, 21–22
Oil industry, 31
Optimal tariff protectionism rationale, 28
Oreja, Marcelino, 95
Ouellet, Richard, 162
Ownership/control requirements, 2, 58–59, 69

Paul, Joel Richard, 26
Peers, Frank, 73n
Perry, Sheila, 114
Perry, Simon, 106–7
Pickersgill, Jack, 57
Polanyi, Karl, 13. *See also* Embedded liberalism
Pollack, Mark A., 158
Polygram case, 64
Pompidou, George, 111–12
Post–World War II period:
    Blum-Byrnes Accord, 118–22
    embedded liberalism compromise, 13–14,
        123–24
Product differentiation, 22–23
Production Services Tax Credit (Canada), 29
Propaganda, 32
Protectionism as negative, 1, 5, 19, 20, 23,
        34. *See also* Free trade/protectionism
        argument limitations; Free trade/
        protectionism traditional theory
Protectionism (Bhagwati), 34
Protectionism rationales, 24–33
    balance of trade, 29–30
    declining industry, 30
    employment protectionism, 28–29
    infant industry, 27
    interest groups, 25–26, 30–31
    national security, 31–33
    optimal tariff, 28
    strategic trade policy, 25, 30
Public opinion:
    on Canadian culture industry policies, 30,
        47, 56, 58
    on Canadian health care services, 161
    on genetically modified organisms, 149–51
Pugel, Thomas A., 22–23

Quebec nationalism, 41–42, 48, 61
Quiet Revolution (Quebec) (1960), 41, 61

Radiodiffusion de France, 112
Radiodiffusion-Télévision de France
    (RTF), 112
Radio industry. *See* Broadcasting industries

Radiotelegraph Act (1913) (Canada), 73, 74–75
Raffensperger, Carolyn, 158
Regional diversity. *See* Heterogeneity
Regulation on Novel Foods and Novel Food Ingredients (EU), 148
Reisman, Heather, 70
Rents, 25
Ricardo, David, 21
Rice, Condoleezza, 144
Rio Earth Summit (1992), 155
Ritchie, Gordon, 45
Romanow, Roy, 161, 167
RTF (Radiodiffusion-Télévision de France), 112
Ruggie, John Gerard, 11, 13, 14, 15, 138
Ruskin, John, 11

SAGIT (Sectoral Advisory Group on International Trade) (Canada), 140–41, 142
Sanger, Matthew, 166
Saul, John Ralston, 42
Scale economies, 23
Schimmel, Daniel, 129, 130
Scruton, Roger, 153
Sectoral Advisory Group on International Trade (SAGIT) (Canada), 140–41, 142
Sewell, William, 7–8, 10
Shaffer, Gregory C., 158
Signal carriage regulations, 76–77
Singapore, 134–35
Smith, Adam, 12, 21, 26
Socialist Party (France), 112, 113, 115–16
Social Sciences and Humanities Research Council (SSHRC) (Canada), 66–67
Sociocultural policies:
    and culture as practice, 7–8
    expansion of, 170–71
    and heterogeneity, 36
    longevity of, 4
    and national uniqueness, 8–10
    U.S. sociocultural concerns, 172–73
    See also Canadian culture industry policies; European audiovisual policies
Sociocultural policies as protectionism, 1–2, 15–16, 35
    and GMO policies, 152–53
    and international trade negotiations, 17–18
    and protectionism as negative, 19, 20
    and U.S. popular discourse, 5

See also Free trade/protectionism argument limitations
SOFICAs (Société de financement de l'industrie cinématographique et de l'audiovisuel) (France), 118
Sound Recording Development Program (SRDP), 71–72
Sound recording industry (Canada), 51, 70–73
Space-binding technology, 46–47
Spicer, Keith, 41
Spillover effects, 25, 30
Split-run magazines, 67–68, 70
SPS Agreement (Agreement on the Application of Sanitary and Phytosanitary Measures), 156–57
SRDP (Sound Recording Development Program), 71–72
SSHRC (Social Sciences and Humanities Research Council) (Canada), 66–67
State roles:
    and former Soviet bloc countries, 142
    and French audiovisual policies, 85, 109–13, 118
    and national uniqueness, 9
    See also Canadian culture industry policies
Strategic trade policy protectionism rationale, 25, 30
Suwa-Eisenmann, Akiko, 149

Tagliabue, John, 107–8
Tanzi, Vito, 19
TBT (Technical Barriers to Trade Agreement), 157, 174
Technical Barriers to Trade Agreement (TBT), 157, 174
Telecommunications, 135
Telefilm Canada, 61–63
Telehealth, 166
Television industries. *See* Broadcasting industries; European audiovisual policies; French audiovisual policies
Television without Frontiers (EU), 3, 102–4, 113, 130
Theiler, Tobias, 31, 89, 91, 95
Thompson, Stephen J., 165–66
Thorpe, Mark, 149
Tomlin, Brian W., 57
Trade agreement inadequacy for cultural protection, 125–26
    and Convention on Cultural Diversity, 125–26, 139–45
    and embedded liberalism, 125–26, 135–39

General Agreement on Tariffs and Trade, 129–30
General Agreement on Trade in Services, 130–35
North American Free Trade Agreement, 126–29
and paradigm shift, 20, 137
Trade-related Aspects of Intellectual Property Rights (TRIPS) agreement, 158, 170–71
Treaty on European Union. *See* Maastricht Treaty
TRIPS (Trade-related Aspects of Intellectual Property Rights) agreement, 158, 170–71

UNESCO, 141, 144
United Nations, 138, 141
United States:
  biotech industry, 151–52
  film industry, 29, 55–56, 61, 85, 97
  health care services industry, 165–66
  television industry, 53, 85, 97
  See also U.S. policies
U.S. policies, 3
  bilateral trade agreements, 134–35
  and Blum-Byrnes Accord, 118–22
  and Canadian broadcasting industries, 81
  and Convention on Cultural Diversity, 143, 144
  and European collective identity goals, 90
  and GMO policies, 148, 150, 151–52, 158
  and NAFTA grievance mechanisms, 127n
  noneconomic motivations, 81, 120–21
  and popular discourse, 5
  sociocultural concerns, 172–73
  See also North American Free Trade Agreement; Sociocultural policies as protectionism; Uruguay Round GATT talks
Uruguay Round GATT talks, 2–3, 17, 83
  and Blum-Byrnes Accord, 118–19, 121–22
  British positions, 107

double-layered nature of, 84–85, 87
and embedded liberalism, 136
and European audiovisual policies, 92–93, 107
and European collective identity goals, 92–93
French role in, 3n, 84, 108, 109, 118–19, 121–22
and health care services, 159
and trade agreement inadequacy for cultural protection, 130

Vellinga, Jake, 160–61, 165
"Virtual good" term, 133–34

Wall, Irwin, 120n
Wealth of Nations (Smith), 21
Weber, Eugen, 6
Wirth, John D., 39
Wolfe, Robert, 14, 124, 136, 154, 170
Wood, Chris, 46, 127–28, 132, 133
Workers' rights, 34
World Trade Organization (WTO):
  and alternative strategies, 175–76
  and Canadian film industry, 64
  Canadian periodicals case, 66, 68, 70, 125, 129, 139–40
  and Convention on Cultural Diversity, 143
  establishment of, 130–31
  and GMO policies, 148, 151, 156–57, 158, 173
  and health care services, 162, 163, 164–65, 167
  and paradigm shift, 20, 137
  and trade agreement inadequacy for cultural protection, 126, 129
  See also General Agreement on Trade in Services
WTO. *See* World Trade Organization

Zedan, Hamdallah, 155